Mac
Manual

Published by: Haynes Publishing
Sparkford, Yeovil, Somerset BA22 7JJ
Tel: 01963 442030 Fax: 01963 440001
Int. tel: +44 1963 442030 Fax: +44 1963 440001
E-mail: sales@haynes.co.uk
Web site: www.haynes.co.uk

British Library Cataloguing in Publication Data:
A catalogue record for this book is available from the British Library

ISBN 1 85960 805 1

Printed in Britain by J. H. Haynes & Co. Ltd., Sparkford

Mac
Manual

THE STEP-BY-STEP GUIDE TO UPGRADING AND REPAIRING

Keith Martin

Contents

Introduction

So you have a Macintosh computer. You made the right choice, but is it working as smoothly as you'd like? Does it seem confusing and complex, has it seen better days, is it too slow and does it keep crashing? Would you like to give it a new lease of life but aren't sure where to start? The answer is almost certainly 'yes' – so take heart, we're here to help.

This book is for normal people trying to get more out of their computer. In it we tackle all that really matters to everyday Mac users. We give you the confidence and provide the technical know-how for you to keep things running well, with as little fuss and expense as possible.

Computers age faster than just about any other form of technology. It isn't that they fall apart more quickly, but that development is so rapid that their capabilities are soon surpassed by later speedier models.

Don't let this get you down. A computer is for using, not an investment. Just because a model is getting on a bit doesn't mean it can't do what you want. Macintosh computers in particular tend to run and run, particularly with the right kind of help.

There are a few things we need to check before we begin:

We assume that you have at least a basic understanding of your Mac. This means knowing how to find your way around the folders, run your programs and manage your files. We also assume that you're prepared to poke inside your Mac, at least with a guide to help you find your way. (Relax, it really isn't that hard!)

And finally, we presume that your Mac dates from around 1997 or later. Older Macs can also be given a new lease of life, but many of the internal and external upgrades and add-ons are either rather expensive or are simply not available any more. With very old Macs you're generally better off picking up a more recent model before going down the upgrade path.

Why upgrade?

Before you start down the upgrade path you should ask yourself some important questions. First, do you really want or need to do this? If your Mac is ticking over perfectly well and you have no pressing need to fix something or speed it up, then don't. Whilst handling basic upgrades is well within your capacity (particularly with this book in hand), if there's no reason to perform surgery, then leave well alone.

Second, make sure the issue isn't to do with the way things are set up rather than some faulty or outdated component. In short, it may be software rather than hardware, which means tackling things in a very different, and often cheaper, way – see Troubleshooting on p.159 for details. In fact, see Troubleshooting before going anywhere with an upgrade, just in case things aren't quite as you think they are. Most specific problems tend to be software or configuration-related. Actual hardware failure is relatively rare.

If the issue is hardware, then ask yourself if an upgrade is worth it. Yes, you can extend the life of older Macs by replacing fading parts or adding extra hardware. However, at some point it will make more sense to get yourself a new machine which will inevitably be faster, more ready to deal with current technology

and come with a full warranty. Of course, you'll probably have to spend a lot more, and some of your peripherals – printer, scanner and so on – may not work with it, so we certainly don't automatically recommend buying new.

If some form of upgrade really is on the cards, then the next step is to figure out exactly what is involved. Not everything in a computer can be upgraded, particularly if you have an iMac or a laptop. You can add RAM to most Macs with ease, particularly relatively young ones, but adding or swapping hard disks is a step up with the desktops, and with laptops this can be a task for the professionals.

Of course, adding things to a Mac doesn't have to involve cracking open the case; sometimes it is better to use the right peripheral rather than go in for Mac surgery. For instance, if you need more storage space, an external hard drive may be preferable to fiddling with wires and jumper pins. Of course, everyone has different needs, so in the following pages we'll look at all the options available to you.

Old Macs can be given a new lease of life with the right upgrades, so don't give up hope.

What's in an upgrade?

Computers are made from sets of hardware components. These are, to put it extremely simply, the screen, hard disk, RAM and central processor, and the parts that make all these things work together. Add to this your keyboard and mouse, and you've got a computer. You can swap some of these parts for newer ones with ease, and others with great difficulty.

The easiest hardware upgrades of all involve adding or swapping things that live outside your Mac; keyboards and mice, screens (usually), scanners, extra hard disks and so on. Next come the simple 'invasive' upgrades. Depending on your particular Mac these can include RAM, graphics cards and the like. Going further, you can find yourself swapping internal ribbon cables and power leads and using a screwdriver a lot. Until you've done this sort of thing it will be more than a little daunting, and even then it isn't something to tackle lightly. But when taken one step at a time and with the right guidance it is within most people's reach.

Software upgrades are equally important, and can be as simple or as complex as any hardware fix. One may happen as part of the other – for example, adding a scanning program for a new scanner, or more memory when updating the operating system – or you may change some software on its own. These changes are generally much simpler, taking the form of popping a CD into the drive and double-clicking an installer, so we'll only look closely at software where it can be less clear.

Take things step-by-step and you'll be able to upgrade most things in your Mac, whether it is an iMac, an eMac, a PowerMac, an iBook or a PowerBook.

What *can't* be done

There are, of course, things which we recommend you don't try. Built-in screens should be left alone, some processors just can't be swapped for others, and soldering irons are completely verboten. We'll make it clear where the boundaries are, as well as point out alternative solutions wherever possible.

Macintosh computers don't have upgradeable logic boards, partly because there's only one source – Apple – and partly because the logic board in your Mac was specifically designed for where it is and what's connected to it. If your Mac is so fundamentally slow that the logic board is a serious bottleneck, you'd be better off seeking out a later model.

Consumer-level Macs such as the iBooks and iMacs are designed not to be highly upgradeable, at least internally. Still, most needs can be met with external devices. There are still limitations, though, as you can't upgrade the graphics hardware or add a second screen, and specialist solutions such as ISDN cards are out of the question.

Finally, Mac OS X itself forces limits on older hardware. It will only run on Macs with G3 processors or better; it won't work with every processor upgrade, and needs at least 128Mb of RAM to run reasonably. On top of this the oldest G3-based Macs, including the older iMacs, can be annoyingly slow when running Mac OS X.

Pretty soon now, development on applications will be confined to the OS X versions. Apple has already ended development of OS 9 itself. Bear this in mind if you are thinking about making upgrades – in a few short years your beloved Mac may not be capable of running the latest applications and games.

One final thing before you get started: consider what you need to do with your Mac in the coming days. Do you have a pressing deadline, perhaps an important report, CV update, term paper, presentation or design job? If this is the case, and if your Mac is functioning, wait until you have met the deadline before starting any invasive tinkering or even buying a new system. We will do our best to keep you safe, but please don't tempt fate.

PART **1**

Getting to know your Mac

When you want to order parts for your Mac, whether internal or external, a hard disk connector or a replacement monitor cable, it is important that you are clear about which computer you have. Not just the fact that you have a Mac (although if you're dealing with a PC-oriented store that's a good start), you'll need to make sure the person you speak to knows which model of Mac you have, too. Sometimes simply saying that you have, for example, an iMac is enough. But there have been a number of different iMacs produced through the years, and some of the differences are quite important.

Having all the information needed to positively identify your Mac will make life easier for you and whoever you deal with. It will help prevent mistakes – and it also puts you in a much stronger position should you still end up with unsuitable goods.

We've compiled a list of every Mac model Apple has released since the very first G3 Power Macs in 1997, and we've supplied nicknames given to the models by the general users. Obviously these are a little subjective, but where a model's nickname is in widespread use and is reasonably descriptive we've included it here.

PART ① Which Mac, which upgrade?

Model	Apple indentifier	Nickname and other identifying characteristics	Processor Type speed (MHz)	upgrade if applicable	RAM Type	slots	upgrade if applicable
Power Mac G3		Beige G3 Desktop	G3 233, 266, 300	page 51	PC66 SDRAM	3	page 44
Power Mac G3		Beige G3 Mini-Tower	G3 233, 266, 300, 333	page 51	PC66 SDRAM	3	page 44
Power Mac G3	Blue & White	Blue & white G3	G3 300, 350, 400, 450	page 51	PC100 SDRAM	4	page 44
Power Mac G4	PCI Graphics	Graphite G4	G4 350, 400	page 51	PC100 SDRAM	4	page 45
Power Mac G4	AGP Graphics	Graphite G4 First with AGP graphics slot	G4 350, 400, 450, 500	page 51	PC100 SDRAM	4	page 45
Power Mac G4	Gigabit Ethernet	Graphite G4	G4 400, Dual 450 & 500	page 51	PC100 SDRAM	4	page 45
Power Mac G4	Digital Audio	Graphite G4	G4 466, 533, 667, 733	page 51	PC133 SDRAM	3	page 45
Power Mac G4	Quicksilver	Quicksilver	G4 733, 867, Dual 800	page 51	PC133 SDRAM	3	page 45
Power Mac G4	Quicksilver 2002	Quicksilver	G4 800, 933, Dual 1GHz	page 51	PC133 SDRAM	3	page 45
Power Mac G4	Mirrored drive doors	Mirrored drive doors, wind tunnel	G4 Dual 867	page 51	PC2100 DDR SDRAM	4	page 45
Power Mac G4	Mirrored drive doors	Mirrored drive doors, wind tunnel	G4 Dual 1Ghz, Dual 1.25GHz	page 51	PC2700 DDR SDRAM	4	page 45
Power Mac G4 Cube		The Cube	G4 450, 500	page 52	PC100 SDRAM	3	page 44
PowerBook G3	M3553	Kanga, multi colour Apple logo	G3 250	page 53	PBG3	1	page 46
PowerBook G3	M4753 series	Main Street, Wall Street, white Apple logo	G3 233, 250, 292	page 53	SO-DIMM SDRAM	2	page 46
PowerBook G3	M4753 series Rev 2	PDQ	G3 233, 266, 300	page 53	SO-DIMM SDRAM	2	page 46
PowerBook G3	M5343 bronze k/b	Lombard, 101, first with USB (still has SCSI)	G3 333, 400	page 53	PC66 SO-DIMM	2	page 46
PowerBook G3	M7572 FireWire	Pismo, first with FireWire	G3 400, 500	page 53	PC100 SO-DIMM	2	page 46
Powerbook G4		Titanium, Ti-book, Titanium body shell	G4 400, 500		PC100 SO-DIMM	2	page 46
Powerbook G4	Gigabit Ethernet	Titanium, Ti-book, Gigabit Ethernet port	G4 550, 667		PC133 SO-DIMM	2	page 46
Powerbook G4	DVI	Titanium, Ti-book, DVI digital monitor port	G4 667, 800, 867, 1GHz		PC133 SO-DIMM	2	page 46
iMac	Rev A/B	Bondi blue iMac, tray loading	G3 233	page 54	PC66 SO-DIMM	2	page 47
iMac	Rev C/D	Fruit-flavoured iMacs, tray loading	G3 266, 333	page 54	PC66 SO-DIMM	2	page 47
iMac	Slot-loading	Slot-loading	G3 333		PC100 SO-DIMM	2	page 48
iMac	Summer 2000	Slot-loading	G3 350		PC100 SO-DIMM	2	page 48
iMac DV/SE		Slot-loading	G3 400		PC100 SO-DIMM	2	page 48
iMac DV+		Slot-loading	G3 450		PC100 SO-DIMM	2	page 48
iMac DV SE	Summer 2000	Slot-loading, First 'Snow' colour option	G3 500		PC100 SDRAM	2	page 48
iMac SE	Early 2001	Slot-loading, 'Dalmation' and 'Flower power'	G3 600		PC100 SDRAM	2	page 48
iMac	Summer 2001	Slot-loading	G3 500, 600, 700		PC100 SDRAM	2	page 48
iMac G4		Flat panel, angle-poise	G4 700, 800		PC133 SO-DIMM	1	page 48
iMac G4	17 inch	Widescreen	G4 800, 1GHz		PC133 SO-DIMM	1	page 48
eMac			G4 700, 800, 1GHz		PC133 SDRAM	2	page 48
iBook		The handbag iBook	G3 300		PC66 SO-DIMM	1	page 48
iBook SE		The handbag iBook	G3 366		PC66 SO-DIMM	1	page 48
iBook	FireWire	The handbag iBook, FireWire port	G3 366		PC66 SO-DIMM	1	page 48
iBook SE	FireWire	The handbag iBook, FireWire port	G3 466		PC66 SO-DIMM	1	page 48
iBook	Dual USB	White iBook	G3 500		PC100 SO-DIMM	1	page 49
iBook	Late 2001	White iBook	G3 500, 600		PC100 SO-DIMM	1	page 49
iBook	Opaque, Early 2003	White iBook	G3 700, 800, 900		PC100 SO-DIMM	1	page 49
iBook	14.1 inch	White iBook, large-screen iBook	G3 600, 700, 800, 900		PC100 SO-DIMM	1	page 49

Graphics		Hard drive		Optical drive	Ports		Network	
Slot	upgrade if applicable	BUS	upgrade if applicable	upgrade if applicable	ports	upgrade if applicable	Ethernet speed	AirPort upgrade if applicable
PCI 33MHz	page 100	IDE	page 65	page 81	1 ADB, 2 Serial, SCSI	USB, Firewire page 105	10Base-T	
PCI 33MHz	page 100	ATA or SCSI	page 66	page 81	1 ADB, 2 Serial, SCSI	USB, Firewire page 105	10Base-T	
PCI 66MHz	page 100	Ultra ATA/33 or SCSI	page 68	page 82	1 ADB, 2 USB, 2 FireWire	SCSI page 108	10/100 Base-T	page 112
PCI 66MHz	page 101	Ultra ATA/33	page 70	page 82	2 USB, 2 FireWire	SCSI page 108	10/100 Base-T	page 112
2 x AGP	page 101	Ultra ATA/66	page 70	page 82	2 USB, 3 FireWire (1 internal)	SCSI page 108	10/100 Base-T	page 112
2 x AGP	page 101	Ultra ATA/66	page 70	page 82	2 USB, 2 FireWire	SCSI page 108	10/100/1000 Base-T	page 112
4 x AGP	page 101	Ultra ATA/66	page 70	page 82	2 USB, 2 FireWire	SCSI page 108	10/100/1000 Base-T	page 112
4 x AGP	page 101	Ultra ATA/66	page 70	page 83	2 USB, 2 FireWire	SCSI page 108	10/100/1000 Base-T	page 112
4 x AGP	page 101	Ultra ATA/66	page 70	page 83	2 USB, 2 FireWire	SCSI page 108	10/100/1000 Base-T	page 112
4 x AGP	page 101	Ultra ATA/66 and ATA/100	page 71	page 84	2 USB, 2 FireWire	SCSI page 108	10/100/1000 Base-T	page 112
4 x AGP	page 101	Ultra ATA/66 and ATA/100	page 71	page 84	2 USB, 2 FireWire	SCSI page 108	10/100/1000 Base-T	page 112
4 x AGP	page 101	Ultra ATA/66	page 73	page 85	2 USB, 2 FireWire		10/100 Base-T	page 113
		ATA	page 76		1 ADB, 1 Serial, SCSI		10 Base-T	page 114
		IDE	page 76		1 ADB, 1 Serial, SCSI		10 Base-T	page 114
		IDE	page 76		1 ADB, 1 Serial, SCSI		10 Base-T	page 114
		ATA	page 76		2 USB, SCSI		10/100 Base-T	page 114
		ATA	page 76		2 USB, 2 Firewire		10/100 Base-T	page 114
		ATA	page 77		2 USB, 1 Firewire		10/100 Base-T	page 114
		ATA	page 77		2 USB, 1 Firewire		10/100/1000 Base-T	page 114
		ATA	page 77		2 USB, 1 Firewire		10/100/1000 Base-T	page 114
		ATA	page 74	page 86	2 USB		10/100 Base-T	
		ATA	page 74	page 86	2 USB		10/100 Base-T	
		ATA	page 75	page 87	2 USB		10/100 Base-T	page 115
		ATA	page 75	page 87	2 USB		10/100 Base-T	page 115
		ATA	page 75	page 87	2 USB, 2 FireWire		10/100 Base-T	page 115
		ATA	page 75	page 87	2 USB		10/100 Base-T	page 115
		ATA	page 75	page 87	2 USB, 2 FireWire		10/100 Base-T	page 115
		ATA	page 75	page 87	2 USB, 2 FireWire		10/100 Base-T	page 115
		ATA	page 75	page 87	2 USB, 2 FireWire		10/100 Base-T	page 115
		ATA/66			3 USB, 2 FireWire		10/100 Base-T	page 116
		ATA/66			3 USB, 2 FireWire		10/100 Base-T	page 116
		ATA/66			3 USB, 2 FireWire		10/100 Base-T	page 116
		ATA			1 USB		10/100 Base-T	page 117
		ATA			1 USB		10/100 Base-T	page 117
		ATA			1 USB, 1 FireWire		10/100 Base-T	page 117
		ATA			1 USB, 1 FireWire		10/100 Base-T	page 117
		ATA			2 USB, 1 FireWire		10/100 Base-T	page 117
		ATA			2 USB, 1 FireWire		10/100 Base-T	page 117
		ATA			2 USB, 1 FireWire		10/100 Base-T	page 117
		ATA			2 USB, 1 FireWire		10/100 Base-T	page 117

PART ① Taking stock

Before you install anything you need to know the type and capacity of your system. When you have the details, check them against the requirements listed on the box of the product you plan to buy. If you're buying online or over the phone, check system requirements from magazine reviews, the manufacturer's Website and from the reseller. In most cases the requirements listed will be the minimum, but sometimes they also mean exactly that and no different; for example, 'requires Mac OS 8.6' doesn't always mean 'works with Mac OS 9 and X'. Do some research before you buy.

It may seem obvious, but make sure you know exactly which Mac model you're using. There are many iMacs, most of which look pretty much the same apart from, perhaps, the colour. You'll also need to know how much RAM you have (see Memory spotter on p.43), what version of the Macintosh operating system (Mac OS for short) you're using, and so on. The Inventory on the next page should help you keep track of all this information, but you'll need to get it in the first place.

Final check

Before starting any kind of computer upgrade there are a few things you should always check first. It is unlikely that things will go wrong, but you should still be prepared in case something does go awry.

First, know where your system installer CD is. Don't just glance at the packet or CD case, check that the CD is actually there. This is a useful emergency restart CD; you should rarely, if ever, need it, but don't ignore it. Bear in mind also that if your Mac is running say, MacOS 9.1, and your Installer CD is for 9.0.2 (check the small print on the front of the installer CD), you will also need to have the 9.1 updater utility to hand if you need to restore your System to the current level. It's easy to forget the incremental updates.

Next, see if you can remember when you last made a backup. If you looked sheepish or blank at that question you're in good company; most people don't do this. However that won't help at all if you lose part or all of the contents of your hard disk. A backup is a 'safety net' copy of the important things on your Mac, and should be kept up to date. It is something you can turn to if you accidentally trash important files in any way. You've almost certainly never made any proper backups, so read all about it on p.152.

Finally, make sure you have room to work and have all the right tools handy. We'll cover this in detail in the next chapter.

1 The first place to look is the Apple menu, at the top-left of your screen. The very first item in there, assuming you're not in the middle of running a program, will be called 'About This Mac' (or About This Macintosh or About This Computer, depending on the system version).

2 Pick this, and a small window opens to show you some very basic information: which system version you're running and how much installed memory (RAM) you have. In Mac OS 8 and 9 the amount of installed memory will be reported in KB (kilobytes) rather than MB (megabytes). To convert, divide the KB figure by 1024, or 1000 for an easier rough calculation.

3 The next step is to run the Apple System Profiler. This is a small software program, called a 'utility', found on any Mac running Mac OS 8.1 or newer. If you're running anything up to Mac OS 9, look in the Apple menu at the top-left of your screen. You should see 'Apple System Profiler' near the top. If you're using Mac OS X this lives in the Utilities folder, inside the Applications folder on your hard disk.

The model name, processor info and 'machine' labels tell you which Mac you have and its speed, and the Built-in Memory shows you the installed RAM. Click the triangle (known in the trade as a 'disclosure arrow') next to the Built-in Memory label, and you'll see how much memory is installed, the number of cards, and their individual sizes.

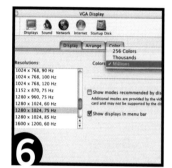

4 At the top of the window the second tab, *Devices and Volumes*, shows details about all the drives it can see, from CD to Zip.

5 Some external hard drives, such as ones connected through FireWire or USB, only show obscure information. The solution is to quit Apple System Profiler, click once on the hard drive icon on the desktop, then choose Get Info or Show Info from the File menu. The resulting window tells you all about the drive, including the all-important Available info.

6 For your screen's resolution (the number of dots, or pixels, it is showing) and colour depth, see the Monitor control panel (in Mac OS 8 or 9's Control Panels, found in the Apple menu), or the Displays pane in Mac OS X's System Preferences, again found in the Apple menu.

7 If you're using Mac OS 8 or 9 you can use the Extensions Manager control panel – look in the Apple menu, in Control Panels – to see all the extra components that go to make your Mac more functional. You can open up the bottom of this to see snippets of information about selected items, and you can disable or enable items with a click. But don't do this here, wait until you get to the right stage.

Inventory

Component	For instance...	Your system
Macintosh model	iMac	
Serial number	CK9471D4HNZ	
Mac OS version	Mac OS 8.6	
Processor type and speed	233MHz G3	
Installed RAM	64Mb	
RAM type	SO-DIMM	
Hard disk size	5Gb	
Hard disk type	IDE	
Optical drive type	CD-ROM	
Other built-in drive?	None	
Monitor size and type	15 inch CRT	
Modem type and speed	Built-in Apple 56K V.90	
Graphics card	ATI Rage Pro	
Any additional cards	None	
Printer	Epson 760	
Scanner	Canon CanoScan D670U	
Other peripherals		

PART Outside explained

Some Macs have built-in screens and some don't. Those with screens are aimed at consumers, while most of those without are aimed at professionals. But this is just marketing; many professionals love the consumer-oriented iMacs, and some home users prefer the pro-level 'Power Mac' range.

The ports are grouped together on the back or side of most Macs.

Power switch button Press to turn your Mac on. Pressing this briefly while your Mac is on will put it into its low-power sleep mode; wake it up by pressing keys on the keyboard. To shut the Mac down, choose Shut Down from the Apple or Special menu.

Reset button For emergencies only! If your Mac has frozen or become so stuck that it won't respond, this is the 'kick in the head' restart solution. Unsaved work will be lost, but stuff saved on your disk will be fine. Definitely a last resort, so if you have to do this often please see Troubleshooting on p.159. Note: This is on the side on older iMacs. The eMacs and the new flat-panel iMacs have no reset button. If you are forced to shut down these Macs without using the onscreen menu, hold down the power button for five seconds.

Programmer's button As the name implies, only for programmers. This interrupts what the Mac is doing, but won't actually help most people, so don't bother using it. This is slightly recessed to make it harder to press by mistake. The eMacs and flat-panel iMacs don't have this button. Note: This is on the side/back on older iMacs.

Security connectors Tower Macs are extremely easy to get into, which is why the side door can be padlocked. The small doors at the back of many iMacs can also be padlocked. The small Kensington Lock slot is the industry-standard method for tying computers down; slide the lock into the slot and loop the other end around something secure.

Headphone socket A stereo minijack audio socket, ready for regular walkman-style headphones. When used these automatically mute the Mac's built-in speakers. Note: This is on the back on Power Macs.

 Microphone socket Virtually every Mac has a headphone-style audio-out socket. Some Macs also have microphone sockets for sound input, but a few rely entirely on USB (and you'll have to buy an audio adaptor) to record external sound. More on Mac audio is on p.136.

 Serial ports Only found on mature Macs, serial ports were used to connect personal printers, modems and similar devices. Now superseded by USB, so finding Mac-compatible serial devices is hard.

 **ADB port** Short for Apple Desktop Bus, this was how keyboards, mice, joysticks and the like connected to beige G3 Macs and early powerbooks. ADB is long gone, replaced by USB. For ADB help, see p.123.

 USB ports The standard for connecting peripherals such as consumer-level scanners, personal printers, digital cameras, MP3 players, external modems and so on. Also used with certain broadband Internet hardware. See USB on p.104 for more.

FireWire ports Much faster than any form of USB, these are ideal for external hard drives, high-quality scanners and, of course, digital video (DV) cameras. Simpler than SCSI, and faster than many SCSI varieties. For FireWire details see p.104.

 **SCSI port** SCSI (pronounced 'scuzzy') is built into older Macs, optional on newer Power Macs, and not available for iMacs (other than by way of an external USB adaptor). Used for older hard drives and scanners. Specialist forms can provide very fast connections for tasks such as high-end video editing. SCSI formats (and their various connector types) can get confusing – see more information on pages 106-108.

Monitor ports Connections for monitors are the VGA format (small trapezoid shape), the older Apple monitor format (like VGA but wider), or newer digital formats. Digital sockets will be DVI or ADC, and need digital monitors with the right plugs. Details are on p.96.

 Modem port If the Mac has a built-in modem this is where the phone cable goes. This socket, called an RJ-11, matches the American telephone socket format. Not to be confused with the larger Ethernet port. See p.134 for Internet connection methods.

 Ethernet port Used for linking computers in networks for sharing files and using network printers, and for some forms of broadband Internet connection. See p.110 for more information on networking.

PART 1 Inside explained

Opening up a computer for the first time takes a bit of nerve. Don't worry though, it is all very logical stuff. You don't need a degree in electronics, just a bit of commonsense. Most of the things you can tackle on your own won't even affect your warranty, unless you do something daft like spilling coffee all over the innards. Before you start, make sure you have plenty of space and good lighting. Don't work with your head under a desk!

Make sure you know what's in your Mac before attempting to add or replace anything. The Apple System Profiler utility (see p.14 for where to find this and how to use it) will tell you almost everything you need to know about your Mac's innards. Write down all details about the area you're upgrading, for example the names of the locations of installed memory as well as the sizes.

The tools

Before you start work on your Mac's innards make sure you have everything you'll need at hand.

Screwdrivers *Most things clip on and off, but even with the latest Macs you'll eventually have some screws to deal with. Have a small Phillips cross-head screwdriver handy, and if possible a regular flat head one as well.*

Torch *Modern Macs don't generally have deep, dark nooks and crannies, but older ones do. Anyway, more light is always a good thing when performing technical surgery. Make the torch (or flashlight) a small one that you can hold in your mouth, just in case you need two hands for fiddling.*

Anti-static precautions

Anti-static wrist strap *First of all the thing that most people forget. You may not know it, but small static charges build up around us all the time. They're so small you rarely ever notice it, but even a tiny static shock can spell damage and even instant death to delicate electronics. Wear this whenever you poke into your Mac.*

The right procedure *Unplug all cables except the power cord. Yes, unless you're working with an iMac leave this one in, as it provides the earth (ground) connection which, with your wrist-strap, helps protect the Mac's inner bits from static discharges. Connect the end of the anti-static strap to the power supply box inside the Mac or another convenient grounded metal part.*

However, make sure the power socket's switch really is turned off. This ensures there are no dangerous currents anywhere in your Mac. If you can't find a switched power socket, leave the Mac unplugged but attach the anti-static strap to a suitable earth point, for example a metal electrical point cover or a radiator.

Logic board The bedrock of your Mac's components where everything connects together. Everything that your Mac does passes through the logic board. It is designed to fit your Mac model and isn't itself upgradeable.

Processor The CPU (short for Central Processor Unit) is the brain of your Mac. All the processing that is involved in everything from checking your spelling to editing video is worked out here. Some Mac models have processors which can't be upgraded, some use chunky 'daughtercard'-based CPUs, while others use compact ZIF (Zero Insertion Force) processor designs. To see whether your Mac can be upgraded and which kind of CPU it has, see p.12.

Hard disk This is where all of your programs, games, music, e-mails and work are stored. Think of the disk as simple storage space, just like a filing cabinet. Whenever you save something in your word processor, it is written to the disk. You can add a second and even third hard drive into many Macs. For more on hard disks see p.57.

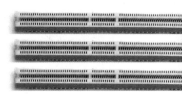

Optical drive Traditionally a CD-ROM drive capable of reading music and data CDs, but nowadays as likely to be a CD-RW (for writing your own CDs), DVD (for reading DVD data and video discs), a CD-RW/DVD reader 'combo' drive, or even a SuperDrive for reading and writing both CDs and DVDs. Some are slot-loading, while others use trays. See p.78 for more.

Floppy drive Found on older Macs (including the beige G3 models) the traditional floppy drive was abandoned on the iMac and all subsequent models. All you need to know is on p.90.

Zip drive found as options on some G3 and G4 desktop machines, Zip drives offer much more useful storage capacity than the humble floppy drive. More information is on p.88.

PCI slots PCI stands for Personal Computer Interconnect, but just think of it as the way to add all sorts of extra hardware features to your machine. This is where extra monitor cards, super-fast SCSI cards, USB and FireWire cards (with older Macs), ISDN and more are fitted. In-depth information starts on p.94.

Memory slots RAM, or Random Access Memory, is your Mac's thinking space – not to be confused with the hard disk, which is simple storage. 'Not enough memory' messages mean you don't have enough RAM, not that your hard disk is full. The more RAM you have the more your Mac can deal with at once. Depending on which Mac model you have, upgrading the RAM can be simple, or very complex. For instructions on how see p.42.

AirPort slot AirPort is Apple's form of the wireless networking standards known by the rest of the computer industry as 802.11b and 802.11g. Technically they are the same. To use AirPort you'll need to add an AirPort card and set up the software. See more on the various forms of networking on p.110.

PRAM battery This keeps a small part of your Mac's memory alive while shut down. This is how the Mac remembers the correct time and date and basic details for starting up correctly. It will wear out eventually which can cause mysterious problems. See Troubleshooting on p.160 for details.

Inside the desktop 'Beige' G3 Power Mac

1 Depress the two rounded latch buttons under the front edge of the casing. Grab the sides of the casing and slide it forward, clear of the chassis. If it sticks as it slides off, don't force it – check where the casing has caught and ease it off.

2 Flip up the grey cover; this clips into place and can just be pulled up and swung open. At this stage you can access the floppy and CD drives, the two additional drive bays, the power supply and, with a bit of a squeeze, the PCI slots.

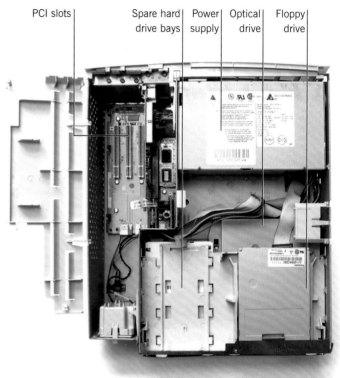

PCI slots | Spare hard drive bays | Power supply | Optical drive | Floppy drive

3 Next you need to release the two catches which lock the chassis into place.

4 Pivot the chassis upwards through 90°. Note that the chassis is quite heavy, and is supported while open by a plastic 'foot' on the outside and a black plastic prop on the inside. Check that these engage correctly or there is a risk of damage or injury if the chassis drops while you're working. With the chassis lifted up, access to the main board and hard disk are unrestricted.

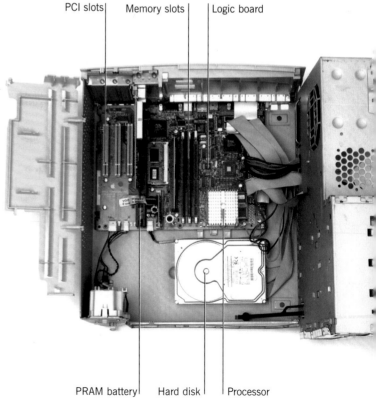

PCI slots | Memory slots | Logic board

PRAM battery | Hard disk | Processor

Inside the tower 'Beige' G3 Power Mac

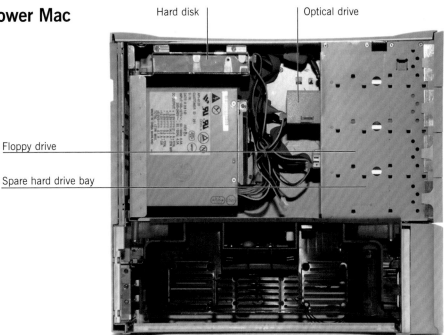

Hard disk   Optical drive

Floppy drive

Spare hard drive bay

1

Open the side cover by pressing the green button on the top and lifting the cover away. Unhook the cover and remove it. You can now access the hard drive, optical and floppy drives and the spare drive bays.

2

Place the machine on its side, then lift up the two green levers which lock the chassis in place.

3

Disconnect all cables then grab the black plastic handle and pivot the chassis upwards. As it swings clear, the main board components become accessible. The drive(s) and power supply are contained in the chassis assembly. Reconnect the power cable to provide an earth connection. (See Anti-static precautions on p.18.)

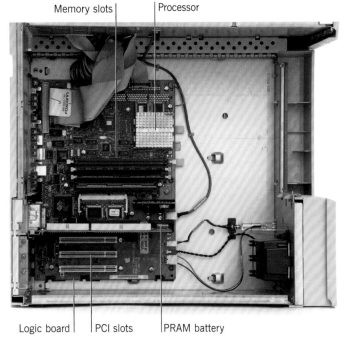

Memory slots   Processor

Logic board   PCI slots   PRAM battery

Inside the Blue and White G3 and G4 Power Macs

If you have a modern mini-tower Power Mac – (a two-tone Blue and White, Graphite or Quicksilver model) open the door on the side by lifting the handle and pulling out. Virtually everything you need is presented right there in the open, but before you do anything observe ant-static precautions (see page 18).

It is possible to open up the case while your Mac is running, though this is not really advisable. There is a small LED on the logic board designed to remind you that you have not shut down your Mac!

This case design was first seen in the Blue and White G3. It proved to be so good that it was used all the way through to the mirror door – the only differences are in the internal layout.

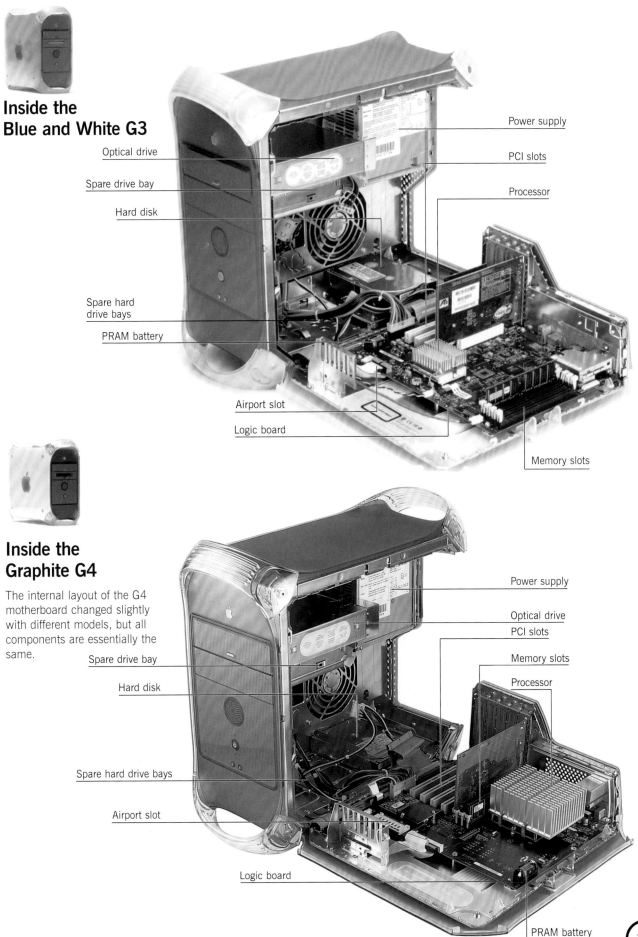

Inside the
Blue and White G3

Optical drive

Spare drive bay

Hard disk

Spare hard
drive bays

PRAM battery

Airport slot

Logic board

Power supply

PCI slots

Processor

Memory slots

Inside the
Graphite G4

The internal layout of the G4
motherboard changed slightly
with different models, but all
components are essentially the
same.

Spare drive bay

Hard disk

Spare hard drive bays

Airport slot

Logic board

Power supply

Optical drive

PCI slots

Memory slots

Processor

PRAM battery

Inside the Quicksilver G4

The internal layout of the G4 motherboard changed slightly with different models, but all components are essentially the same.

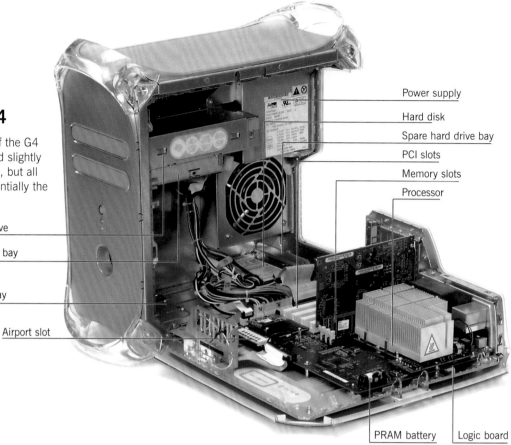

Power supply

Hard disk

Spare hard drive bay

PCI slots

Memory slots

Processor

Optical drive

Removable drive bay

Spare hard drive bay

Airport slot

PRAM battery

Logic board

Inside the Mirror door G4

The internal layout of the G4 motherboard changed slightly with different models, but all components are essentially the same.

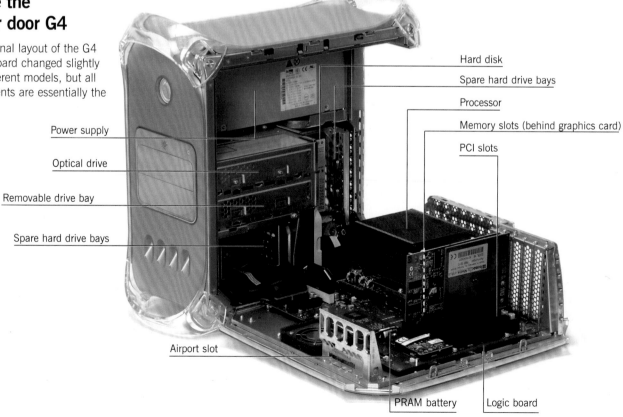

Hard disk

Spare hard drive bays

Processor

Memory slots (behind graphics card)

PCI slots

Power supply

Optical drive

Removable drive bay

Spare hard drive bays

Airport slot

PRAM battery

Logic board

Inside the G4 Cube

Access to the Cube requires the core of the machine to be removed from the outer enclosure. Before you start work, check that the Cube is shut down (and not just sleeping!), and then leave it for at least five minutes to cool down. (The Cube uses convection cooling, and the internal heatsinks can get very hot.) Take the usual anti-static precautions when working on the Cube – touch the bare metal near the video port to discharge any residual static charge before you start.

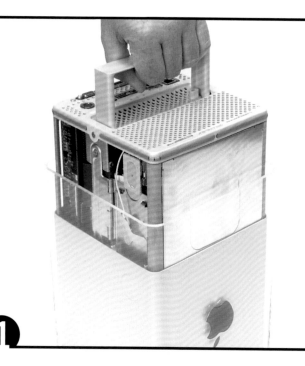

1

Place the cube upside down on a towel or some soft cloth. From the underside of the enclosure, press the latch handle and allow it to extend fully. Grab the handle, and pull the core out of the enclosure. Place the enclosure safely to one side. Many of the internal components are now visible from three of the four sides as shown below. Further dismantling will be required to access some of them, and this will be described in the relevant sections of this book.

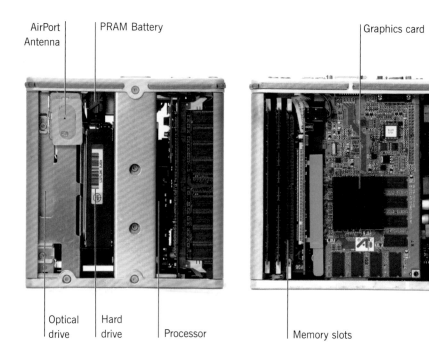

AirPort Antenna | PRAM Battery | Graphics card

Optical drive | Hard drive | Processor

Memory slots

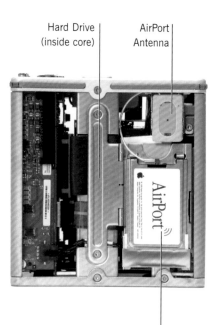

Hard Drive (inside core) | AirPort Antenna

AirPort card

Inside the G3 PowerBook

Portable computers can be devilishly complex because of the way everything is packed into such a small space. However, it is possible to upgrade RAM in any G3-based PowerBook without too much hassle. With further dexterity and steady nerves you can also upgrade the hard drive, and even the processor in some PowerBooks. This comes close to the kind of thing best left to paid technicians, but it can be done. It may seem obvious, but before you do anything please make certain the Mac is shut down, not just asleep; and remove the battery.

Before you do anything else, you need to figure out which model you are dealing with. OK, this is tedious, but you only need to do it once. Refer to the table on p.12.

On early (M3553 and M4753) PowerBooks eject both expansion bay modules (normally the battery and a CD-ROM drive) by flipping out the eject levers.

Just inside the expansion bays, near the edge of the keyboard, are two latches. Pull these back and the keyboard will flip up slightly.

On 'Bronze Keyboard' PowerBooks (M5343) check that the keyboard is unlocked. There is a small screw next to the lock symbol on the back panel which releases the keyboard.

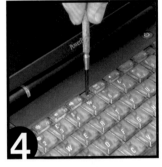

On FireWire PowerBook models (M7572) there is a small screw slot in the spacer between the F4 and F5 keys which should be positioned horizontally.

There are two small tabs located next to the F1 and F9 keys at the top of the keyboard. Press these towards you and lift the keyboard gently up from the back. It will be connected to the rest of the Mac by a thin ribbon cable – take care not to strain or break it.

Unhook the front edge of the keyboard, flip it over and rest it on the trackpad like this. The keyboard is attached to the PowerBook by a thin ribbon cable, so just lay it face-down on the trackpad.

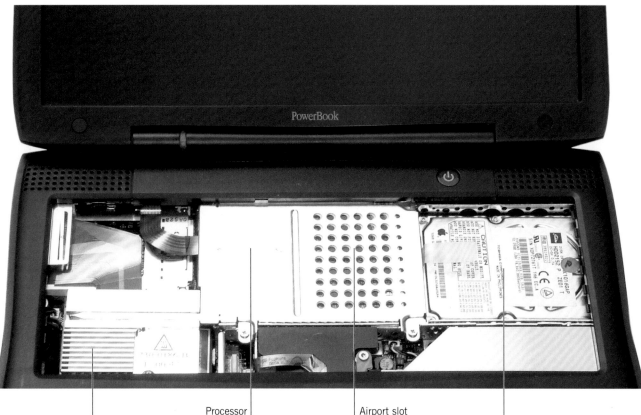

Processor heat sink | Processor (under metal shield) | Airport slot (under metal shield) | Hard disk

Identifying your G3 PowerBook

There were several basic types of G3 PowerBook, and you need to know which one you have before you attempt to work on it. You can do this by referring to the 'Family Number' which you'll find on the product label attached to the bottom of your PowerBook's casing:

● The original PowerBook G3 had a Family Number of M3553. You can recognise it by the multi-colour Apple logo on the screen housing, which also featured vent slots on each side.

● Next came a redesigned slimmer-cased model, M4753, distinguished by the white Apple logo on the outside of the screen housing.

● This was followed by M5343, which had a similar casing to its predecessor, but had a bronze-coloured keyboard, rather than the black version used previously.

● The final model, M7572, was again similar to its predecessor, but had two FireWire ports in place of the earlier machines' SCSI port.

There – that was easy, wasn't it?

Reassembly

1

Whichever model of G3 PowerBook you're working on, reassembly is similar. Hook the tabs along the edge of the keyboard into place, then pivot the keyboard into position.

2

You may need to press the keyboard down slightly until the latches click into place. Install the battery and any other Media Bay device, then check that the PowerBook starts up normally.

Inside the G4 PowerBook

Before you do anything else, shut down your PowerBook, disconnect the power lead and leave it for at least 30 minutes to cool down; the G4 processor gets pretty hot in use!

Next, prepare your work area. You'll need a clean desk or table to work on, plus a towel or soft cloth to put the PowerBook on to avoid damage to the casing or screen.

Make sure that the PowerBook is shut down, and allow it to cool for about 30 minutes before you start – it can get pretty hot in use.
Turn the closed PowerBook over and remove the battery after sliding the battery catch to the right to release it. Place the PowerBook upright and open the display.

To access the memory slots or the modem, you will need to remove the keyboard. If it is locked, release the keyboard lock screw (between the F4 and F5 keys) by turning it a half turn anticlockwise – the screw slot is horizontal when it is unlocked.

Now pull back the two keyboard catches (next to the F1 and F9 keys) to free the back edge of the keyboard.

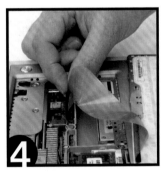

Lift the keyboard up and unhook the tabs along the front edge. Now flip the keyboard over and lay it on the trackpad area of the casing. Take care not to twist or pull on the ribbon cable. Alternatively, carefully unplug the keyboard ribbon cable connector and remove the keyboard.

To access the bottom casing components, place a towel or similar over the edge of table. Open the PowerBook a little more than 90° and lay it on the cloth with the display hanging over the edge. Remove the screws from the bottom casing using a Phillips #1 or Torx T8* screwdriver, depending on your model.

(*Although Apple specifies Torx T8, we found that T9 was a much snugger fit. Check and use whichever fits the screw heads best to avoid damage.)

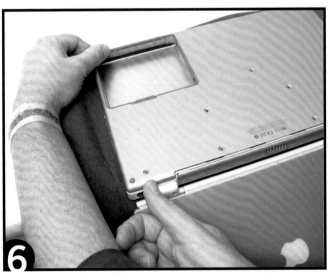

Push the bottom casing away from you, starting as shown above. Next, release the other side, pushing only on the casing – not the rubber feet. Note how far it moves before it lifts off, as this will help during reassembly. Make sure that the casing is disengaged on both sides. Carefully lift the bottom case from the hinge edge and pivot it up until it unhooks. Don't force this if it seems to stick – check to see where it is caught and free it off before continuing.

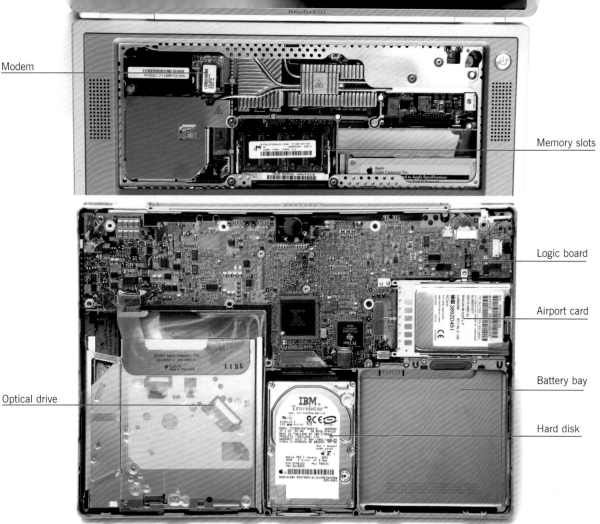

Modem

Memory slots

Logic board

Airport card

Battery bay

Optical drive

Hard disk

Reassembly

1 Once the internal upgrade or repair has been done you'll have to replace the casing. As you offer up the bottom casing, check first that the tabs along the front edge engage correctly as it is positioned.

2 Carefully close the casing, checking all round to make sure it is aligned properly. It should click into position easily – if not it is a sure sign that something is misaligned. Check carefully to make sure it is located correctly before you fit the casing screws. The casing screws should be tightened down evenly – take care not to overtighten them.

3 When you re-install the keyboard, make sure that the five tabs engage correctly along the front edge (nearest to the trackpad). Pull the catches back, then pivot the keyboard into place, pressing it down and easing the catches into place. Lock the keyboard screw by turning it a half turn clockwise.

Inside the tray-loading iMac

1 If you are working on any iMac other than the flat-screen models, start by turning it face-down. Use a folded towel or similar to protect the screen or it may end up with nasty scratches. If your iMac has a tray-loading CD drive, start by removing the single cross-head screw from its recess in the bottom cover.

2 Holding the iMac by its main lifting handle, pull the bottom cover away – you'll need to tug on the handle quite firmly. The cover will pop off, unclipping from the top downwards.

3 Touch the metal shielding to discharge any residual static charge. Unplug with the small round multi-pin connector, unhooking it from the plastic guide clip and tucking the cable to one side.

4 Unscrew the two screws which secure the large video connector. Unplug this then unhook the two cables from under the plastic guide clip.

5 Next, you need to unplug the two rectangular black connectors. The larger connector is latched; press the centre tab down to release it, then pull the plug out.

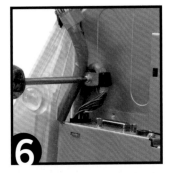

6 The lead to the smaller plug is secured by a metal clip and screw. Remove the screw, taking care not to drop it into the iMac. Unplug the connector, then tuck the four leads out of the way.

7 Remove the two screws inside the plastic handle at the top of the metal shielding. Don't drop the screws into a ventilation hole – a magnetic screwdriver will help here.

8 Finally, pull the logic board/drive assembly upwards, taking care not to snag the cables you disconnected a minute ago. The assembly contains some rather important parts of your iMac, so find somewhere safe to put it down before moving on to your chosen upgrade.

Reassembly

1

When you re-install the logic board/drive assembly, note the two small pins sticking out of the side of the metal casing; these fit behind plastic lips and guide the assembly into the correct position, making sure it slides home at just the right angle.

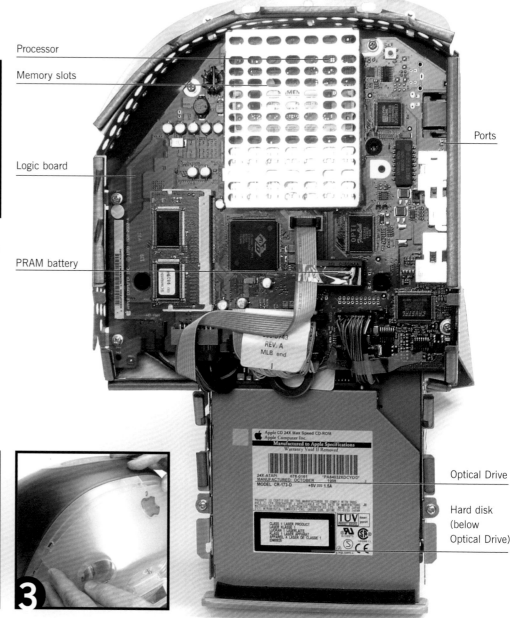

Processor

Memory slots

Logic board

PRAM battery

Ports

Optical Drive

Hard disk (below Optical Drive)

Apple CD 24X Max Speed CD-ROM
Apple Computer Inc.
Manufactured to Apple Specifications
Warranty Void If Removed

24X-ATAPI   678-0161   *PA84032XDCYD0*
MANUFACTURED OCTOBER   1998
MODEL: CR-173-D   +5V ⎓ 1.5A

2

As the assembly slides home, tip the iMac up and check that the CD door aligns correctly so that it is flush with the surrounding front panel. You can do this best by feel as shown in the picture. Once you are sure it is in the right position, refit the two retaining screws.

3

Reconnect all the plugs. Now refit the cover, working from the bottom upwards, and checking carefully to see that the various locating tabs engage correctly.

Inside the slot-loading iMac

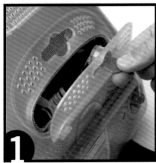

1

If you have an iMac with a slot-loading CD drive, you will see a small oval door on its rear secured by a plastic dial. Open this by turning it with a coin and you'll be staring at the memory upgrade and AirPort networking slots; you're now ready to perform either of those two easy upgrades.

If you need to perform any further upgrading, perhaps to change a drive or to install a new PRAM battery, you'll need to undertake more extensive dismantling. While not impossible, this is harder to do than it is on the tray-loading iMacs.

The bottom cover can be particularly difficult to remove on some machines, so we don't recommend this for the faint-hearted or if your iMac is still under warranty.

2

With the iMac resting screen-downwards on a folded towel, use a small screwdriver to pry off the oval vent above the memory/AirPort access hatch.

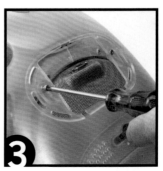

3

Once the vent is removed, you'll see two cross-head screws which secure the top half of the cover. Remove the screws and put them to one side.

4

Now locate and remove the two lower screws; these are positioned between the mounting points for the stand.

5

The cover can now be pulled off. The top should pull away easily, but you may find that the bottom edge is far harder to disengage.

6

The problem is two small plastic tabs close to the speaker grilles. In theory, the cover should pivot and allow the tabs to unhook, but in practice they feel as if they are going to break off rather than disengage. We had to pull harder than we felt comfortable with to get the cover off (but it did come off without damage). If yours seems unduly hard to remove, you might want to let an Apple-authorised technician risk the breakage instead!

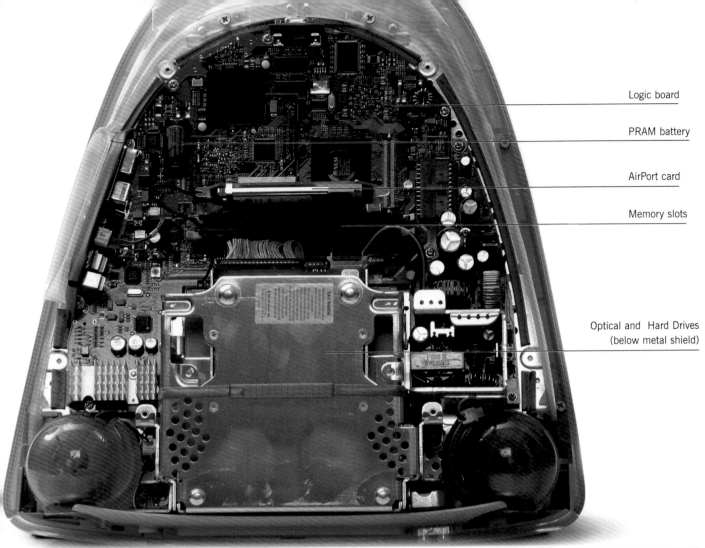

Logic board

PRAM battery

AirPort card

Memory slots

Optical and Hard Drives
(below metal shield)

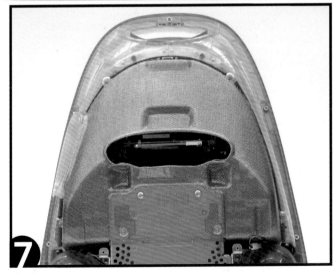

7

Once the cover is off, you need to remove the electromagnetic shielding from the bottom of the iMac. This is held on by six small cross-head screws.

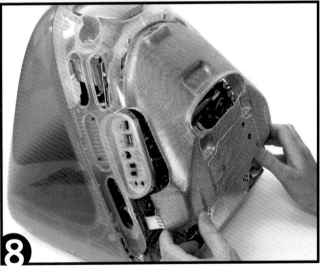

8

The screws are very easy to drop into the main casing. Take care with these, and if possible use a screwdriver with a magnetic tip to keep hold of them. Lift away the shielding and place it safely to one side.

Inside the iMac G4

Tip the iMac forward until the screen is resting on the desk. Use a soft cloth to protect the sensitive display. Use a cross-head screwdriver to undo all the screws in the base of the iMac. These are captive screws, so they won't fall out.

Once the screws are all loose, just lift the circular base plate away from the iMac. This reveals the single user-upgradeable RAM slot and the space for an AirPort networking card.

Airport slot | Memory slot

Inside the eMac

The eMac is almost as easy as a flat-screen iMac to get into (and access is just as limited). Using a soft cloth to protect the display, tip it onto its face. Remove the screws from the solid metal plate in the base of the machine.

Once the screws are out, just pull the cover off. Use the plastic foot to help remove it if necessary. The lower part with the grille opening stays in place, you're just removing the top part.

PRAm battery | Memory slot

Inside the handbag iBook

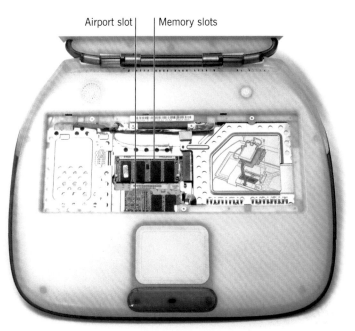

Airport slot | Memory slots

1 Check that your iBook is shut down (not just sleeping). Disconnect the power lead, then remove the battery. Use a small screwdriver to release the keyboard locking screw. You'll find this between the F4 and F5 keys as shown here.

2 Pull back the two small latches which hold the keyboard in place, lift, then flip the keyboard over and place it on the palm rest. Be careful not to strain the ribbon cable which connects the keyboard to the iBook. A handy diagram is revealed which shows how to remove the RAM shield.

Inside the dual USB iBook

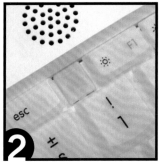

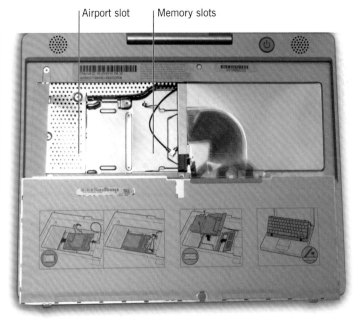

Airport slot | Memory slots

1 Check that your iBook is shut down (not just sleeping!). Next, disconnect the power lead, then remove the battery. To release the battery from the bottom of the iBook, use a coin to turn the catch next to the battery recess. Use a small screwdriver to release the keyboard locking screw. You'll find this between the F4 and F5 keys as shown here.
To open the 14 inch iBook use the same steps as the smaller iBook models.

2 Pull back the two small latches which hold the edge of the keyboard in place. Lift the keyboard, unhook the tabs along the lower edge, then flip the keyboard over and place it on the palm rest. Be careful not to strain or pull out the ribbon cable which connects the keyboard to the iBook. A diagram showing how to insert an AirPort card and remove the RAM shield is printed underneath the keyboard.

PART 1 **Peripherals explained**

Your Mac is the hub, the centre of your digital world. That means that all the things you plug into it are the peripherals. This covers everything from scanners and printers to speakers, modems, cameras and anything else that hooks up to a Mac. Technically, keyboards, mice and screens are peripherals too, although they're rather more essential than most. You can spend a lot of money getting all the tempting peripheral devices on offer, but they're not all going to be right for you. If you pick carefully you'll end up with a useful collection of kit.

Digital cameras These can range in price from under £50 to many thousands of pounds. You'll save a fortune in film and developing costs, but invest in rechargeable batteries or you'll lose it all again. Information on digital cameras is on p.142.

Scanners Consumer scanners start at around £50, while basic professional ones start at a couple of hundred and go up and up. These are great for scanning printed images, but you'll need a specialist scanner (not just an adaptor) to get good results from 35mm slides. More scanner information is on p.131.

Personal printers These are usually colour inkjets, and many can have a good stab at printing your digital camera photos. For quick business-level printing you can also get personal black and white laser printers for a couple of hundred pounds or so. Turn to Printers on p.128 for details.

Speakers There are speakers built into just about every Mac model around, but most aren't up to much. Unless you really don't care (or you use your Mac in a quiet office), get a decent set of external speakers. Some can be cheap and nasty, while others can turn your Mac into a credible hi-fi system. See Speakers on p.136 for more.

Mouse This is your pointing device. Apple's one has a single button, but you can buy models which have two or more buttons, scroll wheels, wireless links and so on. More mouse information is on p.126.

Keyboard There's not much to say about keyboards. They are essential for typing, and bigger ones will include a range of extra buttons for things like volume control. However, every one will have all the essential letters, numbers, commands and punctuation keys. Read p.123 for details.

Graphics tablet If you're into making on-screen art you'll probably enjoy a pen and graphics tablet. These make digital painting feel more like the real thing, but aren't really a good replacement for a mouse. See p.127 for details.

Modem The standard way to get onto the Internet, and can double as a virtual fax machine. Many Macs come with modems built in. However, if you're looking for fast Internet access no regular modem will satisfy you. Turn to p.134 for more.

ADSL or Cable modem Either device will give you a permanent, fast connection to the Internet, although they won't also double up as a digital fax machine. A more expensive way to get online, but good for the frequent Internet user. Turn to Modems and Broadband on p.134 for further information.

CD-RW Perfect for getting files from your Mac to someone else, making your own compilation music CDs, and archiving work, pictures, or anything else you want to keep. Newer Macs have these fitted, but with older ones you can simply plug one in.

Tape backup device Yes, these are boring – but not as boring as trying to remake lost work. At over £300 for starters, tape backup drives aren't the cheapest add-on you'll ever buy, but they could save your bacon. See p.152 for more on backups.

Monitor Make sure you're happy with your screen. After all, you'll be looking at it more than any other part of your Mac! All iMacs and laptops have built-in screens which can't be changed, but most other models can take a wide variety of displays. More information is on p.120.

USB hub Once you get more than two or three USB devices you'll need a hub to keep things under control. A powered one is generally best.

Audio mixer If you want to record and mix music with your Mac, a decent hardware audio mixer and controller can be a boon. Most modern ones connect via USB, but some now use FireWire instead. See p.140 for details.

PART 1 Software explained

Without software your Mac is just an expensive doorstop.

Software is usually installed from CD-ROMs or through Internet downloads. Commercial software is available from the regular high street and mail order resellers. Shareware and freeware software is provided on a 'try before you buy' or completely free basis, and can be as capable as expensive commercial products. Before installing software, check the system requirements to see if it will run on your system. If you need more memory, a better graphics card or a faster processor – upgrade first!

Business This means word processing, spreadsheets, presentation and database work: worthy but dull. The professional standard is Microsoft Office, specifically Word, Excel and Powerpoint, plus Filemaker for database work. AppleWorks is an easier and cheaper solution, albeit lower-powered, which can read and write most Office format files. Alternatively you could try the more basic Nisus Writer.

www.microsoft.com/mac
www.apple.com/appleworks
www.filemaker.com
www.nisus.com

Graphics The high-end of this area is dominated by Adobe Photoshop (photographic manipulation), and Adobe Illustrator and Macromedia Freehand (drawing tools). Deneba Canvas is a worthy challenger, and Adobe's Photoshop Elements is a budget-friendly version of the massive Photoshop. For shareware options try Graphic Converter or ShareDraw.

www.adobe.com
www.macromedia.com
www.deneba.com

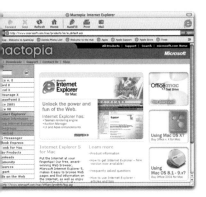

E-mail Microsoft Outlook Express or, if you're using Mac OS X, Apple's Mail will handle most e-mail needs, and comes supplied with Mac OS X. Qualcomm Eudora provides technical flexibility, while Microsoft Entourage, found in Office:mac 2001 and Office:mac v. X, is a business user's dream. Avoid the e-mail features in Web browser suites such as Netscape Communicator; these are too clunky.

www.microsoft.com/mac
www.apple.com/macosx
www.eudora.com

Web browsing Microsoft Internet Explorer is currently the most widely used Web browser, however Apple's Safari is preferred with Mac users. Netscape Navigator is an old favourite, with version 4.7 and recent releases of version 7 being worth a look. Others worth trying are Opera and OmniWeb, but some Websites may behave unpredictably with these.

www.apple.com/safari
www.microsoft.com/mac
www.netscape.com
www.omnigroup.com/applications
www.opera.com/mac

Web design If you want to make Websites, there are a number of options worth trying. Macromedia Dreamweaver, Adobe GoLive and SoftPress Freeway are the high-end market leaders, while the Website Construction Kit for Macintosh is a useful budget option. Netscape Communicator, and even Word, can be used to make Web pages at a pinch, but this approach is strictly unprofessional.

www.macromedia.com
www.adobe.com
www.softpress.com

Page layout Professionals swear by QuarkXPress, although Adobe InDesign is a serious challenger. For more general page layout work Adobe PageMaker is still favoured. AppleWorks and Word can both handle very basic layout tasks, but aren't good for anything demanding.

www.quark.com
www.adobe.com
www.apple.com/appleworks
www.microsoft.com/mac

Games Not every game is made in Mac form, but there are more than you can hope to experience. Big names such as The Sims, Tony Hawks Pro Skater, Warcraft III, Quake and Spider-Man come on CD-ROM, while countless shareware games can be found online.

www.aspyr.com
www.omnigroup.com/games
www.softline.co.uk
www.apple.com/games

Music iTunes is Apple's free MP3 player and encoder; use this to manage and play your CDs and MP3 music, and to manage an Apple iPod pocket MP3 player. iTunes is more than enough for most people, but Panic's Audion offers more flexibility if you want it. For creating your own music there's an absolute wealth of excellent software, including Pro Tools, Logic, Digital Performer and Sibelius.

www.apple.com/itunes
www.panic.com
www.protools.com
www.motu.com
www.sibelius.com

Multimedia and development If you want to make animations, multimedia, or even try making your own software, it is honestly easier than you might think. Macromedia's Director and Flash, as well as Adobe's Live Motion, are good for multimedia, animation and interactive Web work, while Solutions Etcetera's SuperCard and Runtime's Revolution make it surprisingly easy to make almost any kind of software, from custom text editing tools to games and tailored database programs.

www.supercard.us
www.runrev.com
www.macromedia.com
www.adobe.com

PART **2**

Boosting Performance

Getting more out of your Mac isn't necessarily simple, but it is generally a matter of applying some basic logic. You need to work out which parts of the device are holding things back and the best ways of fixing them. For example, if you're suffering from slowdowns and crashes when trying to run big, complex software or trying to use many programs at once, you will probably benefit from adding more RAM. If everything is generally a bit sluggish, and insufficient RAM isn't the culprit, a processor upgrade may be the best option. If games only run in low resolution and with half the visual options turned down or off, a bigger, better graphics card is a good bet.

PART 2 Upgrading RAM

RAM is essential to your Mac, and the more it has the happier it will be. RAM is essentially the thinking space for your computer's processor, where it holds everything it is working on. If you don't have enough your Mac will inevitably run too slowly, so this is often the best thing to check first.

Make sure you get the right RAM for your Mac. Check with a dealer before buying or you could end up with incompatible RAM – which can prevent your Mac from starting up.

*Mostly Harmless

RAM (Random Access Memory) is one of the simplest things to upgrade, at least on most Macs. If your Mac has a lot of RAM it can think of many things at once or concentrate on bigger tasks, like rendering alien worlds or editing movies, without slowing down.

The odds are your Mac came with just about enough memory to get by when it was new, but today's software puts more pressure on things. If you want to run a recent version of the Mac operating system such as Mac OS 9 or later, you'll need an absolute minimum of 64MB of RAM installed. If you want to run Mac OS X you'd better double that, and 256MB or more wouldn't go amiss. This all costs, of course. Exactly how much depends on the kind of RAM you need. Sadly, the older the Mac is the more expensive the RAM will be.

Very old Macs use SIMMs (Single Inline Memory Modules), but upgrading these isn't generally worth it. DIMMs (Dual Inline Memory Modules) are what anything from the last six years or so needs. But within that there's the SO-DIMM variety, Fast Paged Mode, EDO RAM, SDRAM, PC100, PC133 and so on.

All you need to know is what kind of RAM your own Mac needs so you can ask for it from your computer dealer. To find out, try the Memory Selector guide at www.crucial.com/uk/.

RAM should be supplied in anti-static protective bags. Observe anti-static procedures (see page 18) before opening the individual packs.

Memory spotter

With all these different names and codes, how can you tell what kind of memory something is when you see it? First there's the general size. Regular DIMMs are around 13cm long, SO-DIMMs are only about 7cm, while the old SIMM format is about 10cm. On top of this, SIMMs have just one central notch in the connector edge, while regular DIMMs have a second notch off to one side.

Telling how much RAM a specific memory card contains is harder. Some manufacturers put that information on a sticker somewhere on the card, but you may have to try it and see.

Before you upgrade your RAM see how much you already have. Make sure you're in the Finder (not working in any specific program), then choose About This Macintosh or About This Computer from the Apple menu. This shows how much memory your Mac has in total, listed as 'Built-in memory'. If it is listed in kilobytes (K), just divide by 1,024 (or 1,000 for an easier rough calculation) for the size in megabytes.

But before you upgrade anything, you need to know how your existing memory is divided up inside. Is it in one large memory card or a few small ones? Do you have any free memory slots, or will you have to throw something out to make room? The Apple System Profiler tool can help, so pick it from your Apple menu, or the Utilities folder in Mac OS X, and make a note of what's shown in the Memory Overview: Built-in Memory section. Different Macs have different maximum RAM capacities and you can also check this at the crucial.com/uk/ site.

Apple System Profiler can report what RAM is installed and in which slots.

Desktop and mini-tower 'Beige' G3 RAM upgrade

If you have one of the 'beige' G3 machines, upgrading the memory is fairly straightforward – once you've opened up the box. Even though the cases differ between the desktop and tower versions, the main board layout is very similar.

Before you start work, follow anti-static precautions on page 18 then see page 20 for how to get into your Mac, or you risk damaging the new memory during installation.

You'll find the memory slots near the main processor's finned aluminium heatsink. DIMM memory chips are used, held in place by a small plastic eject lever at each end – press them down to pop out any old RAM you might be replacing.

Check that the new DIMM is the right way round (the locating slot is offset to one end) and in the correct position before pressing down so that the eject levers click into place.

This picture shows the memory slots on a beige G3 desktop machine. The logic boards of these two models are almost identical. Note how similar this is to the tower-cased models in the preceding pictures.

G4 Cube RAM upgrade

Follow anti-static precautions on page 18 then see page 25 to get into your Mac. Place the new memory chip into a vacant slot, noting that the chips have a location notch which prevents them being fitted the wrong way round.

Press the chip down evenly until it seats fully. You may find that it helps to click the latches over the ends of the chip manually to help secure it.

There are three memory slots available. If you need more memory and have run out of slots, use System Profiler to identify the smallest installed chip, then replace it with a higher capacity version.

Blue and White G3 and G4 RAM upgrade

Memory Overview		
Location	Type	Size
DIMM0/J21	SDRAM	128 MB
DIMM1/J22	SDRAM	128 MB
DIMM2/J23	SDRAM	512 MB
DIMM3/J24		empty

1

Follow anti-static precautions on page 18 then see page 22 to get into your Mac. The memory slot location varies according to model, see pages 23–24. If all of the memory slots are filled, you will need to work out which of the existing DIMM need to be removed. The System Profiler utility will tell you the size and location of each DIMM fitted.

2

If you need to remove an old DIMM, press down firmly on the small eject lever at each end of its slot. This will release the DIMM, which can then be removed.

3

To fit new memory align it in the slot, noting the two notches on the DIMM's edge. The DIMM will only fit one way and will be damaged if aligned incorrectly and forced. It can take real pressure to click the DIMM into place, so be sure it is positioned correctly first. Squeezing them shut by hand as the DIMM clicks into place make this easier. If the levers don't end up vertical, pop out the DIMM and try again.

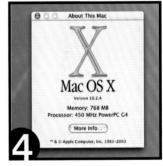

4

Once you're done, just close up the Mac and start it up. Go to the Apple menu and choose About This Macintosh to see how much RAM is now installed. If things don't seem right, check again in the Apple System Profiler for what's in each RAM slot, shut down, and investigate. And finally, if things don't go according to plan and your Mac starts to misbehave, don't panic. Read Troubleshooting on p.159 for advice on setting things right.

45

G3 PowerBook RAM upgrade

Follow anti-static precautions on page 18 then see page 26 to get into your Mac. The G3 Powerbooks have two RAM slots, one directly accessible, the other requiring the processor card to be removed for access. Upgrading is relatively simple in each case. Start by removing the screws which retain the RAM shield.

The exact design of this varies according to the casing type, but all are similar in principle; the pictures above show the RAM shield being removed from early (left) and later (right) case designs.

G4 PowerBook RAM upgrade

The first RAM slot is now accessible, sitting on the top of the PowerBook's processor card. Remove existing memory, if necessary, by pulling the small locking clips out from the RAM card's sides. Insert new memory tilted at roughly 30 degrees, then press flat until the retaining clips hold it down.

If you want to add RAM to the second slot you'll have to remove the entire processor card, along with the heatsink to the left with the connecting pipe. Unscrew the single screw holding the heatsink in place at the near-left, then carefully lever the processor card up from the right. It sits in a socket mounted flat on the logic board beneath, but you'll find you have to lever it from the right to get it moving.

Once the processor and heatsink unit is free, turn it upside down to find the second RAM slot. The memory card is inserted in just the same way as before. Then replace the processor and heatsink, being sure to align the card carefully before pressing it home.

Follow anti-static precautions on page 18 then see page 28 to get into your Mac. RAM upgrades for a G4 PowerBook are easy to perform. Once the keyboard is off, both RAM slots are directly accessible. If you need to remove existing memory to make room for a larger capacity card, pull the small locking clips out from each side. Slide the RAM card in at a 30 degree angle, then press it flat. The retaining clips will hold it down once in place.

tray-loading iMac RAM upgrade

Follow anti-static precautions on page 18 then see page 30 to get into your Mac. Adding RAM to the first generations of iMac, the ones with the tray-loading CD drives, can be pretty straightforward.

These iMacs have two upgrade slots, above and below the processor daughterboard which you'll find covered by a metal cage.

Note that Apple does not recommend that users upgrade the memory in the lower slot. However this is not too difficult to do, and since these machines are well out of warranty, what have you got to lose?

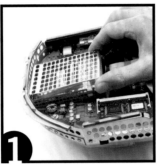

Remove the metal cage near the middle of the logic board. Beneath this is the top SO-DIMM memory slot. If there is already a memory DIMM in the slot (you will have checked this using Apple's System Profiler utility before you started on the upgrade), pull apart the two plastic clips to alow the memory card to pop up. You can now remove the old memory card and put it to one side.

Push the new memory card into the slot at about a 30° angle, then push it flat. The retaining clips should click into place to hold it down, but if not, just pull them open slightly as you press the memory card into place.

Getting to the lower slot requires the removal of the processor daughterboard. First, release the clip which holds the heatsink to the processor. Use a small screwdriver to unhook it, but watch that it does not fly off as you do this.

Lift the heatsink away, noting which way it is fitted, and place it to one side.

Using the heatsink clip as a tool, hook this just under the edge of the daughterboard as shown. Pull up carefully to unplug the daughterboard connector just below the edge of the board. DON'T pull up on the board at any other point or you could break it.

When the plug comes free, carefully lift the board away and turn it over to reveal the second memory slot.

Remove the old memory card and clip the upgrade card into place in the lower memory slot. Note the daughterboard connectors at the other end of the board.

slot-loading iMac RAM upgrade

eMac RAM upgrade

G4 iMac RAM upgrade

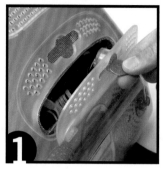

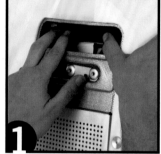

Follow anti-static precautions on page 18 then see page 32 to get into your Mac. Adding RAM to the slot-loading iMac is very easy. Once you've opened the small oval door in its base you'll see two RAM slots.

Being careful to get the memory card the right way around so the notches match the slot, push the memory upgrade into place. The clips on either end of the slot should click into place when it is properly inserted, but note that this can take an appreciable amount of force to achieve. Be sure you press straight.

Follow anti-static precautions on page 18 then see page 34 to get into your Mac. The eMac's memory is held in place with strong retaining clips. Push the memory card into a free RAM slot, making sure the clips click into place.

Follow anti-static precautions on page 18 then see page 34 to get into your Mac. The G4 iMac's single user-accessible RAM slot is an SO-DIMM. Slide the memory card into the slot at a 30 degree angle, then push it flat against the iMac's base. Make sure the retaining clips click into place. (The second RAM slot is beneath the logic board and requires serious surgery to access. Get an authorised dealer to perform this upgrade for you.)

Handbag iBook RAM upgrade

Upgrading the memory in the early iBook (Coloured casing with integral handle) is straightforward to do. The single upgradeable memory slot is positioned vertically.

You'll need to discard the existing memory card, replacing it with a larger-capacity version, rather than adding to what is already there. You should therefore always add as much memory as you can afford.

(Note: The memory card must be a 30mm height SO-DIMM; the taller SO-DIMM format that regular PowerBooks can use won't fit here.)

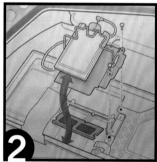

Follow anti-static precautions on page 18 then see page 35 to get into your Mac. With the keyboard removed, position it away from the working area. The ribbon cable does not allow it to rest naturally across the trackpad area, so position it to the left of the casing as shown.

If your iBook has an AirPort card fitted, you'll need to remove it from the recess on top of the RAM shield. Unplug it and place it to one side. The diagram printed under the keyboard shows exactly how the card is fitted and connected.

Remove the two screws which hold the RAM shield in position.

4 Grasp the wire handle at the top and lift the shield away, being careful not to snag the AirPort antenna wire as you go.

5 With the shield removed, and taking the correct anti-static precautions (p.18), pull apart the plastic clips to release the old memory card – it will pop up when the clips are released. Remove the old card then place the new one in position, making sure that it locates correctly.

6 When you have installed the new RAM card, fit the RAM shield, taking care to route the AirPort antenna wire correctly. Fit the retaining screws (don't overtighten). Where appropriate, refit the AirPort card, remembering to connect the antenna before sliding the card into position. The diagram printed below the keyboard shows AirPort card installation in detail.

White iBook RAM upgrade

Upgrading the memory in the newer iBook (rectangular white casing) is similar, and straightforward to do. The single upgradeable memory slot is positioned horizontally on the later models.

You'll need to discard the existing memory card, replacing it with a larger-capacity version, rather than adding to what is already there. You should therefore always add as much memory as you can afford.

(Note: The memory card must be a 30mm height SO-DIMM; the taller SO-DIMM format that regular PowerBooks can use won't fit here.)

1 Follow anti-static precautions on page 18 then see page 35 to get into your Mac. The white iBook has a single upgradeable RAM slot, accessible in much the same way as the earlier model once the keyboard is out of the way.

2 Slide the memory card in at a 30 degree angle, then push it flat until the clips at either side hold it down.

3 When you have installed the new RAM card, fit the RAM shield, taking care to route the AirPort antenna wire correctly. Fit the retaining screws (don't overtighten). Where appropriate, refit the AirPort card, remembering to connect the antenna before sliding the card into position. The diagram printed below the keyboard shows AirPort card and RAM installation in detail.

PART ② Upgrading the processor

The processor, which is also known as the CPU (Central Processor Unit), is the brain of your Mac. This is where all the processing that makes everything work takes place. The processor runs at a specific speed and, while it may be possible to push some CPUs a little faster, in general the only way to get faster processing is to get a faster processor.

This is an area where many people start to get a little nervous, and a CPU upgrade shouldn't be taken lightly. However, if you read the upgrade instructions carefully and take things one step at a time you shouldn't have problems.

Not all Macs can be given CPU upgrades, and of those that can, some are much easier to do than others. Bear in mind that Apple's intention with the consumer models is that little or no upgrading will take place, so these tend to be the most difficult models to perform upgrades on.

You can upgrade the processor on the earliest iMacs (with tray-loading CD drives), but not on the later slot-loading models, or on any of the flat-screen G4 iMacs.

In the case of the 'professional' models, the beige G3 machines are a good upgrade prospect – it is fairly easy to do, and you can

expect to see good speed gains. The later G3 and G4 models can be upgraded in some cases, though the need for an upgrade is likely to be less pressing.

Laptops are generally a different matter because of their extreme miniaturisation, but G3 model PowerBooks can be given processor upgrades. Processor upgrades on the iBooks are not really feasible; while theoretically possible in some cases, it is a frighteningly complex task and, even if successful, fraught with problems like overheating caused by the restrictions of the case design. Our advice is not to attempt it.

A faster CPU may not be the complete solution to a speed problem, as running a super-fast processor in an old Mac can be like putting a turbocharger into an old banger of a car. It may help a little, but the rest of the machine will still be as old and slow as before. The most serious limitation is the speed of the system bus, which determines how fast data can be shifted around the main board. A slow (older) system bus may mean that the new processor just spends longer waiting for data to process. Consider whether searching for a newer Mac might be a more reliable and successful way to get faster computing.

If you're thinking about upgrading to Mac OS X (and pretty soon you may *have* to), make sure the proposed upgrade supports this. Apple says it 'doesn't support' processor upgrades with OS X: this means you won't get telephone support. Many upgrades work perfectly well, but this isn't always the case. See our chart for a quick guide, and check the details of any upgrade before purchase.

Processor upgrade cards can be delicate things, so proceed carefully and follow the instructions.

If a processor upgrade does seem like the right idea, then you'll need to pick the right one. There are two main kinds of processor upgrade; daughterboard, and ZIF. The daughterboard upgrade involves plugging a moderately chunky circuit board into a special slot. This format is used by older iMac models and the G3 PowerBooks.

The ZIF upgrade is a compact unit around two inches square. ZIF stands for Zero Insertion Force, and it lives up to its name. It lies flat on the logic board, and a lever locks it into place. The ZIF format is used by the whole Power Mac G3 range.

Before trying to install a processor upgrade, read the documentation thoroughly. Some upgrades require a special software installation step, and won't work until this is done. Once you're ready to swap out the hardware, shut down and get access to the logic board. (For help with this see Getting into your Mac on p.18.)

Mac models	Processor format	Processor upgrade	OS X compatibility
iMac Rev A to D	iMac daughterboard	G3 and G4	Yes
PowerBook G3 Series	PowerBook daughterboard	G3 and G4	Yes
Power Mac G3	ZIF	G3 and G4	Yes
Power Mac G4	ZIF	Dual processor G4	Yes

'ZIF' type processor upgrade

Follow anti-static precautions on page 18 then see pages 20–24 to get into your Mac. ZIF upgrades are generally straightforward. If there is a heatsink on the processor you'll generally – but not always – have to remove this. Look for a simple flat spring clip holding it in contact with the rest of the device, and lever this off from one side. Beware of the kind that are meant to stay attached to the ZIF card as these aren't meant to be removed, but if there's a clip, it is.

Find the silver lever which runs along one side of the card and pull it upright. This releases the whole ZIF unit, allowing it to be lifted free.

Note the orientation of the pins (there's a single corner with no pin) and drop the upgrade into position. It should fit without using any appreciable force – hence 'zero insertion force'.

Finally, push the lever back down to lock the ZIF upgrade in place. If the upgrade doesn't include its own heatsink you should replace the one you removed in step one. Running a processor without adequate cooling will lead to constant crashes, so make sure it is clipped on properly. You're now ready to replace the cover and try out your upgraded Mac.

Cube processor upgrade

We fitted a Sonnet Encore processor upgrade to our Cube. This upgrade kit comes with fully detailed installation instructions. In fairness to non-Cube owners, we won't attempt to cover the same ground here – suffice to say, if you decide to fit this upgrade, the extent of dismantling necessary to fit the new processor and the addition of the necessary cooling fan can be seen here. Not for the faint-hearted, but if you follow the instructions to the letter, you can't go wrong. You even get the tools you need to perform the upgrade included in the box…

To give you some idea of what is required, here's a brief summary of the upgrade procedure:

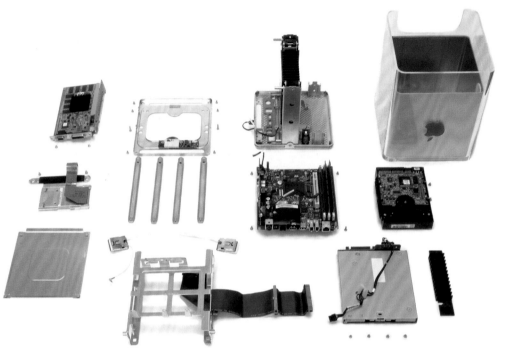

1 Follow anti-static precautions on page 18 then see page 25 to get into your Mac. The first task is to remove the top plate, making a careful note of which screws fit where. As you lift it away, disconnect the wiring from the proximity switch. The four alloy pillars at the corners of the Cube can now be pulled out – they push fit and are gripped by rubber seals.

2 Next, remove the two screws each side of the video ports, then unplug and remove the graphics card and a small connector board that it plugs into. Note the wiring connectors, unplugging them as the board is removed.

3 The logic board is secured by three spring-loaded screws. One of these (with the Torx driver in place, above) is longer than the other two, and will be coloured gold to distinguish it from the shorter two). The logic board will be stuck to the heatsink by conductive foil and must be eased away very carefully.

4 Once removed from the logic board (two screws) the heatsink plate can be unclipped from the old processor daughterboard and the new board fitted.
To cope with the extra heat from the new processor a fan needs to be added to the bottom of the core, requiring the removal of the hard drive.

G3 PowerBook processor upgrade

1

Follow anti-static precautions on page 18 then see page 26 to get into your Mac. The original G3 PowerBook processor is the rectangular circuit board which holds the first RAM slot under the main shield beneath the keyboard. Remove the two screws which hold the shield and lift it away.

2

The processor card is connected to a heatsink, in the lower-left, by a metal pipe. Unscrew the single long screw which retains the heatsink.

3

The whole unit will have to be very carefully lifted up from the right edge, and pulled out. The processor card is plugged into a small multi-pin connector immediately below the memory cards. You may need to use a flat-bladed screwdriver to ease the processor out of its socket, but be careful not to damage anything with it. A flat-bladed screwdriver with its end bent into a hook will help you to pull the connector off without twisting it.

4

When you install the processor card be very careful to ensure that the connector fits squarely into the socket. As you can see, the connector is bristling with many tiny pins which are easily damaged if not inserted absolutely in line with the socket.

5

Remove the RAM from the original processor and install it in the new one. Pull the plastic clips outwards to release the old RAM chip; it will spring up at an angle as it is released. If you're considering a RAM upgrade this is as good a time as any, as the RAM slot on the base of the processor card is not normally accessible.

6

Insert the new RAM at about 30°, then pivot it down until it can be latched in place. The RAM is fitted to each slot in the same way.

7

Finally, being very careful to line it up with the main socket (see step 4), push the processor card back squarely into place in the PowerBook. Replace the metal shield, put the keyboard back, and try things out.

Tray loading iMac processor upgrade

You should note that this procedure only applies to the original version A to D iMacs with tray-loading CD drives – later models are not upgradeable.

The iMac's processor daughterboard also contains the RAM. Remember to swap this over when upgrading the CPU.

Follow anti-static precautions on page 18 then see page 30 to get into your Mac. Unclip the metal shield which covers the processor daughtercard.

Using a screwdriver, prise up the metal clip which secures the processor heatsink. Take care that it does not fly off as you remove it.

You can now lift away the heatsink and place it to one side. Note that it can only be fitted one way.

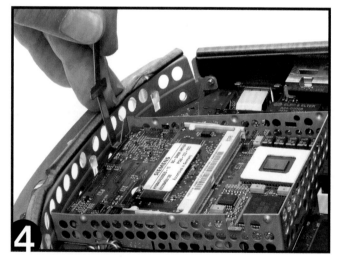

Using the clip which held the heatsink hooked under the back edge of the processor daughtercard, carefully lift the card upwards until the connector disengages.

Lift the daughtercard away and place it to one side. You now need to remove the RAM cards from either side of the daughtercard. (While you have access to the lower memory slot, it might be a good opportunity to upgrade the RAM.)

Fit the RAM cards to the new processor daughtercard. Fit the RAM cards into their slots at about 30°, then click them into place.

7 You can now fit the new daughterboard. Place the card in position and make sure that you press it down evenly to avoid damage to the connector pins.

8 Refit the processor heatsink, making sure that the surface which contacts the processor is absolutely clean. Note the offset slot which makes sure that the heatsink can only be fitted in the correct orientation.

9 Hook one end of the heatsink clip into the shielding, then click the other end into position to secure the heatsink.

10 On many processor upgrades you only need to clip the metal shielding over the processor and you're done.

12 Our featured upgrade goes a little further, however. We fitted a Sonnet Harmoni processor upgrade. This is fairly expensive, but can transform an old 233MHz iMac like this. The new processor is a 600MHz G4, and the Harmoni also adds a FireWire port to our iMac. First you need to fit a replacement side panel with an additional cutout for the new FireWire port

13 The screw which holds the metal shielding is removed and a special stand-off fitted in its place. This is used to locate and support the end of the FireWire board.

14 A wiring adaptor patches a feed for the FireWire board into the supply to the hard disk.

15 With the power lead plugged into the board, it is connected to the daughterboard through holes in the metal shielding. Fit two screws at the side panel end and one into the stand-off you fitted earlier, and you're finished. Install the main board assembly, and you should now have a very much quicker iMac and access to FireWire devices. Time to start saving up for that iPod...

3

PART **3**

Drive upgrades

Whilst the latest Macs have hard disks with acres of space, older models (when new) were sold with less bountiful storage capacity. This can be resolved with an upgrade, which may mean going inside your machine and installing a new internal hard disk or just plugging in an external drive. Either way it will give your machine a new lease of life.

PART ③ **Things you need to know**

Before you go out and buy a new hard disk drive there
are a number of things you need to know.

Connection formats

SCSI, or Small Computer System Interface (pronounced 'scuzzy'),
is a connection standard for hard disks and other devices now
only found on older Macs (except for high-speed variations for
specialist drives). The various higher-speed SCSI formats are
referred to as Ultra SCSI, SCSI-2, Fast and Wide SCSI, etc., but
the external SCSI connection built into older Macs is plain old
SCSI-1. IDE (Integrated Drive Electronics) is used for virtually all
internal drives in today's Macs and PCs. ATA (Advance
Technology Attachment) is the connection used for IDE drives.
IDE mechanisms and ATA connection buses are generally
compatible.

ATA cables connect to IDE drives,
and will be found in your Mac or
come with an ATA expansion card.

Hard disk drives operate within
staggeringly fine tolerances,
packing billions of bits of data into
a space a few inches across. As
the disks inside the drive spin at
thousands of times a minute, the
read and write heads skate back
and forth across the surfaces,
finding the strings of magnetic
codes that make up your Mac's
software and all your work.

As you might imagine, these
are sealed boxes, and should stay
that way. If something goes
seriously wrong with a hard drive
don't even consider dissecting it. If
the data is absolutely critical you
could try specialist data recovery
services. However, their charges
are high and there's no guarantee.
Make regular backups if you deal
with important data. See Backing
up on page 152 for details.

If you're going for an internal drive, which type is right for you?
G3 and G4 Power Macs come with IDE connections. (If you want
the fastest disk possible, a high-performance SCSI card and
matching disk will help – for a price.) Make sure the hard drive
vendor knows which kind you need when you buy.

For external drives things are a little different. If you have an
older (beige) Mac you'll have a standard SCSI port in the back. If
it is a newer model with translucent and coloured parts it will
have USB (Universal Serial Bus) sockets instead, and all but the
first generations of iMacs and iBooks have FireWire ports as well.

High-speed SCSI cards use
specialist cables designed to
handle the large volume of data
that is passed from device to
device. Use the right cable or the
drives will not work.

TECHIE CORNER

Hard disks are simply storage
devices, and there are other
ways of storing things than on
your internal hard disk drive. You
can use removable disk formats
such as Iomega's low-capacity
but popular 100MB or 250MB Zip
drives or the more roomy 1Gb or
2Gb Jaz drives. More usefully, CD
writers and DVD writers provide
mass storage for very little
money. Buy a bulk order of 100
CD-R discs and they can be the
price of a first class stamp each.
If you're considering buying a
drive as a dedicated backup
device, this is best done with a
tape-based backup drive,
although CD or DVD writers will
do at a pinch.

Checking your connections

To see how your drives are connected, run the Apple System Profiler (found in the Utilities folder inside the Applications folder in Mac OS X, otherwise from your Apple menu) and look in the Devices and Volumes panel. IDE became the standard for almost all Macs from the introduction of the G3 processor in 1997. Note that only two IDE devices can be connected to one ATA connector, so in this case make sure you have space before buying a new device.

Another way to find out drive details for your particular Mac is to look at www.info.apple.com/support/applespec.html. The information is quite technical, but it is presented clearly. The internal hard disk information is near the bottom of each page.

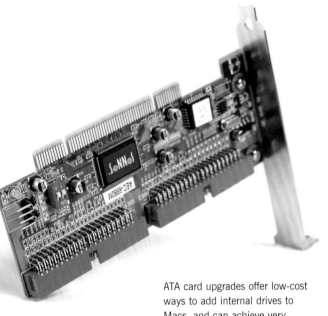

ATA card upgrades offer low-cost ways to add internal drives to Macs, and can achieve very respectable speeds.

Capacity

A disk's capacity is, naturally, how much data it can hold. It is measured these days in gigabytes: thousands of megabytes. Your existing disk may be just a few hundred megabytes, or it could be a few gigabytes or more. Today's disks generally begin at 10 or 15 gigabytes and go to 80 gigabytes and above. As with RAM, the rule of thumb is that there's no such thing as too much. Buy the biggest you can; you'll fill it eventually.

Speed

One factor which affects the cost of hard drives is their speed. The raw drive speed is measured as platter revolutions per minute (rpm) and it is a fair, although not foolproof, measure of how quick they are. Things start at 4,200 and 5,400rpm, which may sound fast but are actually the speeds of today's cheaper, relatively pedestrian drives. If you're a general user doing business work, Internet use and the odd game, this is adequate. We recommend 7,200rpm drives in general, but if you're more interested in capacity a 5,400rpm device will be fine.

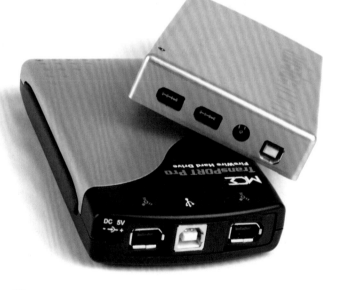

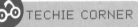

Inside or outside?

The big question is whether to put your new drive inside your Mac or plug it in from outside. If you have to replace a failed drive, then inside is the obvious answer. If you're adding an extra drive to get more storage space, outside is definitely the simpler and more flexible option. In some cases it is the only option. However, if you have the room inside and the means of connecting another drive, then inside is ultimately the neater solution, and a little cheaper. Which option you pick depends on a number of things. iMacs don't have room inside for additional drives, so the choice is made for you. Power Macs, though, generally have at least one spare drive bay.

External USB drives are relatively cheap, but this type is really too slow for serious use. FireWire drives cost more, particularly the pocket sized variety, but they are at least 20 times faster than ordinary USB devices. Pocket-sized FireWire drives can also draw their power straight from the FireWire connection.

TECHIE CORNER

If you're running a particularly old version of the Mac OS – anything before Mac OS 8 – you'll have trouble dealing with drives formatted to sizes over two gigabytes. But rather than worry about sorting the disk size issue out we'd strongly recommend you upgrade your Mac OS to version 8.6 or later. See Operating systems on p.178 for more information.

Pocket FireWire drives combine high capacity storage with portability. Models with USB ports as well can connect to Macs (and PCs if the disk is formatted correctly) without FireWire connections. Data transfer speeds are dramatically slower with USB connections.

PART ③ Configuring hard drives

Whether you are adding an extra drive or just upgrading to a larger capacity internal drive, you will need to check the drive's configuration settings. This can mean that you will need to set the positions of small links, called 'Jumpers', so that the drive will be recognised by your Mac. If the new drive is to be fitted internally it is probably going to be easier to do this before finishing the installation process; access is a lot easier while the drive is out of the case. Generally speaking, the later the machine, the easier the configuration procedure. In this section we explain how you configure a drive. Read though the instructions, and refer back to this page during the installation procedure. External drives are usually easier to configure, and much easier to put right if you get the settings wrong.

Changing the jumpers on an internal hard drive is a highly fiddly operation, but it is often the only way to configure it to work alongside other drive mechanisms. Only do this where you can find the jumpers if you drop them.

SCSI drives

SCSI devices are connected to the Mac in a daisy-chain manner, and each has a unique ID number (from zero to seven). If your internal hard drive is SCSI it will already be set to ID zero, the CPU itself lays claim to ID Seven, and the built-in CD-ROM drive will be ID Three. If you have a built-in Zip drive which uses a SCSI connection, it is customarily set to ID four or five. That of course leaves ID numbers one, two, four or five and six. But if you're replacing the original hard drive you should set the new device to ID zero, just as the original. It's just convention that the main internal SCSI drive is set to the lowest ID number, but following this helps keep things simple. Setting the SCSI ID number of an external drive, or any other peripheral for that matter, is usually just a matter of pushing a button or turning a dial. Setting the ID for an internal drive isn't quite that simple. You'll have to move tiny connection clips from one pair of metal pins to another. These clips are called jumpers, and moving these to different pins changes the ID number of the device. If you have good fingernails you may be able to do this with just your fingers, otherwise use a pair of tweezers.

The pins are in a group underneath the drive or at the back next to other sockets. You'll have to see which ones are used for the SCSI ID. Some drive manufacturers print a brief guide to the pin pairs on the drive's casing. These will be pretty technically oriented, but certainly more use than nothing. You may also have a printed reference sheet, so check the packaging.

The ID is set using three sets of pin pairs. With no connector used the ID is at zero, with a single jumper on the first pair the ID is one and with the jumper on the second pair the ID is two. For ID three, put a jumper connector on both the first and second pair of pins. Set ID four with just one jumper on the third pin pair, ID five with jumpers on pairs one and three, ID six with pairs two and three, and ID seven with all three pairs.

Termination is also something to check. This is a kind of electronic buffer used at either end of a SCSI device chain which prevents digital signals from echoing back along the cable and confusing the computer. Again, with external devices this is managed easily by a simple on-off switch or by plugging a terminator block into the last device. Internal mechanisms do this with another jumper connector on a single pair of pins. If you're replacing the main internal drive you'll need to terminate the new device – make sure the termination pin pair has a jumper connector in place. Otherwise make sure there's no termination.

If termination is set incorrectly or you use the same ID number as another device in the same chain your Mac will either not start up or just won't see one or more of the devices. Fortunately shutting down and changing the termination or ID will fix this.

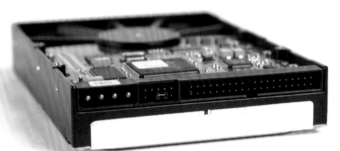

SCSI drive mechanisms use jumpers and pins for more than just SCSI ID numbers, but details should be shown on a printed label on the drive itself.

IDE drives use jumpers as well, but they have just two 'ID' settings: master and slave.

Three of the pairs of pins on a SCSI drive mechanism will be to do with setting the drive's identification number, the SCSI ID. To set the device to ID zero, leave all three pin pairs empty. ID one is set by putting a single jumper connector on the first pair of pins, ID two by using just the second pair, and ID three by fitting connectors to the first and second pin pairs. This uses basic binary counting methods, but if you're not particularly familiar with binary just follow this chart. If in doubt about your particular drive, look for diagrams or similar guides on a label on the drive itself or ask for information where you bought the mechanism.

ID 0
ID 1
ID 2
ID 3
ID 4
ID 5
ID 6
ID 7

IDE drives

IDE drives are simpler, although they also use jumpers to change settings. An IDE device connects to an ATA connection, or bus. Each ATA bus can have a maximum of two devices connected. These are given an ID of zero or one, but the terminology doesn't revolve around this. Instead each item on a bus is either a master or a slave device, and this is what's set with the jumpers. If there is one item in a bus it must be set as a master, and you can't have two masters or two slaves on the same bus.

As with SCSI ID and termination, this setting is selected using small pins and jumper connectors on the drive. See the drive casing or documentation for which pins to use to get the master or slave setting. But note that it is common for IDE drives to ship already configured as masters, so that's what the existing jumper position probably is.

Help with the pins

If you can't figure out which pin pair is which, get in touch with the drive supplier and ask them for the info. If that doesn't help, you may find help on the drive manufacturer's Website, or just try things out. Getting it wrong will prevent your Mac from working properly but it won't cause any damage. The forced power-downs you may have to perform before resetting the jumpers aren't ideal, so run your best disk checker software over your disks once you've finished, but don't get unduly worried. Do keep track of what IDs are available and which positions you try.

Preparing a hard drive for use

Disks must be formatted (prepared in a particular format) before they can be used by your Mac.

If you have your original disk still installed (and working) and it contains a working system folder, just connect up the new drive as described in 'Transferring your data' on the next page and restart. If your old hard drive has failed, you'll need to restart using a system installer CD and install a new system folder on the new drive. See Reinstalling Mac OS on p.172 for details.

When you restart you may be faced with a message telling you that a disk couldn't be dealt with and offering to format or initialise it for you. (Initialising refers to erasing data on a formatted disk.) If you're certain that this refers to the new drive (the reported size of the disk matches up) rather than any existing drive you may still have, go ahead. But note that if, for some reason, this refers to another drive, perhaps with work and software on it, initialising it will throw away everything on the drive. If you're unsure, click the Cancel button and proceed using a disk utility program once you've finished starting up.

Preparing a disk is generally done using the Drive Setup tool in Mac OS 8 and 9 or the Disk Utility in Mac OS X. If necessary you can use a third party formatting tool – LaCie Silverlining or Charismac Anubis are two good choices – but if Apple's supplied tools work with your new drive this keeps things simpler, and may also mean better compatibility with later operating system upgrades.

TECHIE CORNER

Disk formats The formatting type is usually either HFS (Mac OS Standard) or HFS+ (Mac OS Extended). Plain HFS should generally not be chosen. It isn't compatible with Mac OS X, and it is relatively inefficient with large disks. HFS+ is the best choice for virtually everyone.

If you're running Mac OS X you can choose the UNIX File System (UFS), but this is a format designed for highly specialist use and isn't compatible with most current Mac software. You may also be able to pick MS-DOS, a format compatible with Windows-based PCs. However, this is also not advisable except for removable disks used to transfer files between Macs and PCs.

Disk formatting, Mac OS 8 & 9

Disk formatting, Mac OS X

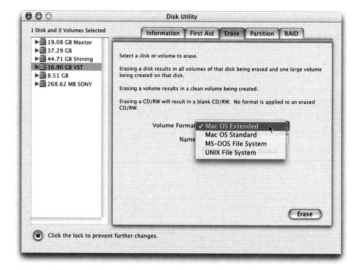

Launch the Drive Setup program, found in the Utilities folder on the system installer CD. In its window it will list all drives it can see. Your newly installed disk should show up here, even if it hasn't mounted on the desktop. Select it – be sure you pick it rather than any other drive – and click the Initialize button. You'll be warned that this will destroy any data on the disk. Confirm the action, then a few seconds later your disk will mount on the desktop.

Formatting a disk can be done as part of installing Mac OS X, or using the Disk Utility program found in the Utilities folder within the Applications folder. It will list all drives it can see in the left of its window; select your new drive (make sure you pick the right one) and click the Erase tab at the top. Pick your preferred format then click Erase. Confirm the action, and a few seconds later your disk will be ready.

Transferring your data

If you are fitting a replacement drive it is highly likely that you will want to copy some or all of the data from your old drive to the new one. How you go about this will depend on a number of factors, but you will need to carry out the transfer as precursor of the drive installation procedure. (Obviously, if the reason for fitting the new drive is to replace a failed mechanism, you may not have the option of doing this.)

The best plan is to connect the new drive while leaving the old unit in place. That way, you can simply copy your files straight onto the new drive before you perform the final installation. See below for details.

In the case of operating systems up to OS9.x you can simply drag the contents of your old drive onto the new one, and everything will copy across quite happily.

Things are not so simple with OSX, however, because of the large number of essential, but hidden, system files. You have two options here. It is probably best to install a fresh operating system on the new drive, and then copy across the 'Users' folder from your old drive (which should then mean that your custom user settings are retained). Alternatively, you will need to use a 3rd-party utility to help you make a functional copy of your existing disk or just its 'System' folder. At the time of writing, Mike Bombich's donationware utility 'Carbon Copy Cloner' does a great job. (Check www.versiontracker.com for a download link to the latest version). Just remember that if there were problems with the operating system, these will get copied too…

IDE drives

Each ATA bus can support just 2 devices (one Master and one Slave). One option is to set the jumpers on the new drive to configure it as a Slave unit, after which it can be connected to the same ATA bus as the old drive, the Mac restarted, and the files copied over to the new drive. Once you have copied the data across, shut down, remove the old drive, set the new drive's jumpers to 'Master' and carry on with the installation.

In practice, you may find that you don't have the spare data and power connectors to do this, or that your particular machine is one which does not support 'Slave' drives. If so, you'll need to cheat a little. Leave the jumpers on the new drive set to 'Master', and connect it to the data and power cables normally used for the CD-ROM mechanism, which is on a separate ATA bus. You will need to make sure that the drive is placed on an insulating layer to avoid having it short out on the chassis (use a piece of card or a mouse mat). Now you can start your Mac and copy the data across. (Note that you may have to initialise the new drive before it is recognised by your Mac. See 'Preparing a hard drive for use' on the previous page.)

SCSI drives

The procedure here is pretty much the same as for IDE mechanisms, except you will need to set the drive jumpers to an unused SCSI address before you connect the drive and start up the Mac. Details of SCSI addresses can be found in Configuring Hard Drives on p.60. Once the address is set, connect the drive to the SCSI data and power cables, then start the Mac up and check that you can see the new drive mounted on the desktop. If the drive does not mount, check that it is recognised by the Mac using the System Profiler utility. If the drive does not show up here, shut down the Mac and check that you have set the SCSI address correctly. Once System Profiler can see the drive, you will need to initialise it before it appears on the desktop. See 'Preparing a hard drive for use' on the previous page.

Once the new drive mounts you can copy over the data from the old unit. Once this is done, you should set the SCSI address to that of the old drive, then substitute the new drive for the old unit.

PART ③ Upgrading internal hard drives

Upgrading a hard disk in a desktop Mac is just a matter of following the right procedure. Make sure you have a good backup of your work, be certain you've bought the right kind of drive for your Mac, then work through the relevant steps that follow.

Not all Macs are designed for users to upgrade beyond the basics such as RAM, so be sure to follow our steps very carefully. Bear in mind that you will need to check that the drive is configured correctly as part of the installation procedure. Refer to page 60 for more information.

TECHIE CORNER

If you are fitting a replacement drive because the original one has simply run out of space, you may be able to retain the old unit as additional storage space. (If the old drive is dead, this is obviously not such a good option.)

Do note, however, that some early beige G3 models do not support 'slave' drives. You can determine this by looking at the main logic board. Find the graphics chip (a large, square device marked with the ATI logo). If this is marked 'ATI Rage Pro II', your G3 is a Revision A model and cannot support slave drives. The later Revision B machines have graphics chips marked 'ATI Rage Pro Turbo' and do support slave units.

If your chip looks like this then it is OK to re-use your old drive. Remove it from the main drive bay, then set the jumper to configure it as a 'Slave' drive and install it in an expansion bay. Note that you may need to obtain additional cables to reach the drive in its new location.

After the new drive has been fitted and configured, you can copy over data from the old drive if required. The old drive could be a great place to keep your MP3 collection or your digital photos.

'Beige' G3s: Things you need to know

The beige G3 models have an empty drive bay as standard. To add a drive to these models you will first need to decide whether to use a SCSI drive (fast, but expensive) or to opt for a much cheaper IDE drive.

If you choose IDE you will need to add an IDE card to one of the PCI slots in your Mac. You will also need the necessary cables. Check that these are supplied with the drive or card, or order them at the same time.

The beige G3 models had SCSI as standard, so the SCSI option is easier in some ways. Do check that you have a spare power and data cable available, though – you may need to obtain adaptors and splitters if all yours are in use.

Check this before ordering, and take advice from the drive supplier. You would be wise to choose a Mac-savvy supplier; we suggest that you talk to an Apple Centre or other specialist Mac parts supplier when sourcing these parts – a general PC parts supplier will not be much help with the cables or other minor parts you may need.

Remember that the beige G3s are getting pretty old now, so you may need to hunt around a little to find minor items for upgrades like this.

The beige G3 models come from an era where a 2GB drive was considered very big indeed – nobody at the time anticipated the exponential growth of disk size and the correponding decline in price. Consequently, they are amongst a number of Mac models where drives of a capacity above 8GB must be partitioned before use – see 'The 8GB partition trap' on page 63 for details.

Fitting a replacement hard drive to a 'Beige' Desktop G3

Follow anti-static precautions on page 18 then see page 20 to get into your Mac. The factory-fitted hard drive in the beige desktop G3 models is fixed to the bottom of the main chassis, next to the logic board. Press down the plastic latch which holds the bracket to the chassis and slide the drive until it can be lifted away. Before fitting a drive see pages 60–63 for information on configuring.

Unplug the data and power cable connectors from the old drive – this is much easier to do after the drive is clear of the chassis.

Release the four screws which secure the drive to the plastic mounting plate. Lift away the old drive, then fit the new unit in its place. Fit the mounting screws loosely at first, tightening down when all four have been connected. Don't overtighten or you may damage the bracket.

Check that the jumpers are set in the correct positions to configure the drive as the Master drive, referring to the documentation which came with the new drive (or check with the manufacturer's Website) for details. Install the new drive unit, then start the machine from the Mac OS installer disk. If you are starting with a new drive, you'll need to format the drive before you can install an operating system on it. See page 62 for details.

Fitting an additional hard drive to a 'Beige' Desktop G3

Follow anti-static precautions on page 18 then see page 20 to get into your Mac. If your machine is suitable, there is a spare drive bay next to the CD-ROM drive, accessible after the cover is removed. Before fitting a drive see pages 60–63 for information on configuring.

First, unlatch the plastic 'sled' from the empty drive bay. You now need to fit the bare drive to the plastic sled; it is held in place by four screws. Check the jumper settings (see 'Configuring hard drives' on page 60 for full details). Remember that the new drive needs to be configured as a secondary 'Slave' drive, not as the main, or 'Master' drive.

Plug in the power cable connector before you fit the drive in the bay – the connector is quite stiff and it is easier to insert it this way. Now you can slide the drive into place. The sled will click into position in the drive bay.

Plug in the data connector, noting that it is keyed to ensure it fits correctly. Refit the top cover and check that the drive works as expected.

Fitting a replacement hard drive to a 'Beige' Tower G3

1

Follow anti-static precautions on page 18 then see page 21 to get into your Mac. Access is easier if the machine is placed on its side. Before fitting a drive see pages 60–63 for information on configuring.

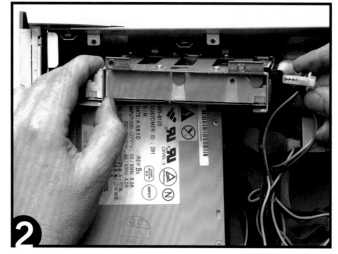

2

The two screws which secure the drive mounting bracket are easily accessed. Remove the screws, then manoeuvre the drive back and out of the case. You now have access to unplug the data and power connectors.

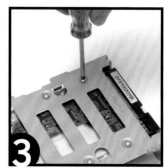

3

The drive mechanism is held in the mounting bracket by four screws. Remove the old drive, then fit the new unit. Leave the screws finger-tight until all are in place, then tighten them evenly. The data and power cables can now be connected, and the drive assembly installed in the case.
If you transferred the data from your old drive you should now be able to boot the machine normally and resume use. Alternatively, see page 174 to install the operating system.

Fitting an additional hard drive to a 'Beige' Tower G3

1

Follow anti-static precautions on page 18 then see page 21 to get into your Mac. Pull off the blanking bezel immediately above the Apple logo on the front panel. This unclips at the left edge and then pivots round until the right edge can be unhooked. Before fitting a drive see pages 60–63 for information on configuring.

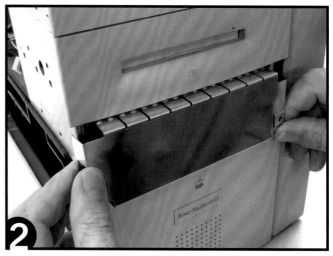

2

Behind the bezel you'll find a metal shield which can be pulled away to reveal the empty drive bay. At the bottom of the drive bay you'll find a metal drive carrier. This is also held in place by the two screws which secured the shield, and it can be slid out of the bay.

Place the drive carrier over the inverted drive and align the mounting holes...

...noting that the holes are marked to show the correct screw positions for fitting a hard drive (HD) or a floppy drive (FD).

Loosely fit the four mounting screws, then tighten them down evenly. If you find that the screws get tight before they have secured the drive to the plate, check that you have the right ones; there are different thread types in common use in computers, and if the screws don't fit easily it means you have the wrong ones!

Now you can slide the assembled drive and mounting plate into the drive bay.

Moving to the back of the drive, connect the ribbon and power cable connectors. Space is a bit tight, so let the drive move forward a little if you can't quite get the connectors plugged in.

Refit the metal shielding and secure with the two screws. Finally, hook the end of the outer bezel in place and clip it onto the main casing. Install the side cover on the main case and you're done.

Fitting hard drives to a Blue and White G3

Follow anti-static precautions on page 18 then see page 22 to get into your Mac. Adding additional drives to your Blue and White G3 is fairly easy, but you do need to establish the existing configuration before you order the new mechanism. Hard drive(s) are installed in a carrier fitted to the bottom of the casing. There are three drive mounting positions number 1 (near the front), 2 (centre) and 3 (near the back).

If your particular machine was supplied with an Ultra ATA drive this will be fitted in position 3, while models originally fitted with SCSI drives will have them fitted in position 1. Before fitting a drive see pages 60–63 for information on configuring.

If your G3 has a SCSI drive you will need to unplug the SCSI connector from the PCI SCSI card as shown here.
If your particular machine has more than one SCSI drive these will probably be 'daisy-chained' from the drive in position 1, and so can be left interconnected for now.

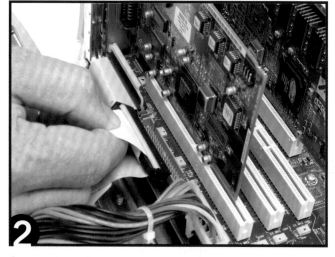

On machines with an ATA drive in position 3, trace the ribbon cable from the drive and unplug it from the main logic board. Note: DO NOT unplug the adjacent connector from the main board.

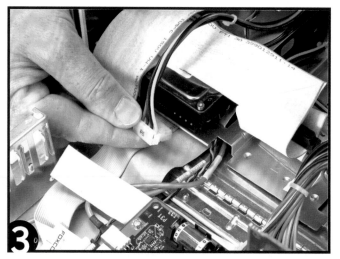

Disconnect the power connector(s) from the drive(s) fitted to the carrier. These are unlatched connectors, but can be quite hard to remove. Use a screwdriver to dislodge the connector(s) if you need to.
Check that you have removed all connectors which would impede removal of the carrier before moving to the next step.

SCSI drives

If you machine does not have SCSI and you wish to fit a SCSI drive, you will need to buy a PCI SCSI card as well as the drive mechanism. The card will come with detailed instructions about its configuration and how it should be connected to the drive. Check that the proposed SCSI card is supported by OS X, even if you don't use OS X yet. With the drive carrier removed as detailed in the preceding pages, install the additional drive mechanism in a spare position (normally position 2 in the centre of the carrier).

If the additional drive is an Ultra 2 SCSI device to supplement an existing factory-fitted unit, you will need to set the jumpers to ID 1. (IF you already have two SCSI drives, set the extra drive to ID 2 and install it in position 3). Note that the factory-fitted ribbon cable is terminated, and no additional termination of the SCSI chain is required.

Whichever position your drive is fitted in, check that the SCSI ribbon cable is routed correctly. You may need to experiment a little with the routing of the cable, and it may help to tape the cable in place once you have worked out the best route for it.

4 At the back of the carrier is a metal retainer plate held by a single screw. Remove the screw and retainer and place them to one side.

5 Slide the carrier assembly towards the back of the case so that the locating tabs clear the slots in the chassis. Now carefully remove it, making sure that none of the cables get caught as you do so. You can now move the assembled carrier to a convenient work surface to replace or add drives.

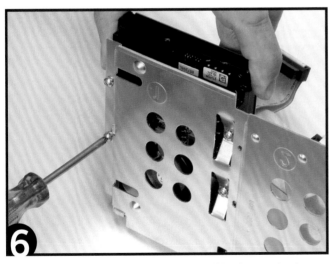

6 If you are replacing the existing SCSI or ATA drive mechanism, you'll need to remove the old unit from the carrier and then fit the replacement drive in its place. Before you do so, check that the jumpers are set correctly.

With factory-installed Wide Ultra2 SCSI drives, the Master drive is set to ID 0 (with 2nd and 3rd drives set to ID 1 and ID 2 respectively), so you will need to set the jumpers on any replacement drive accordingly.

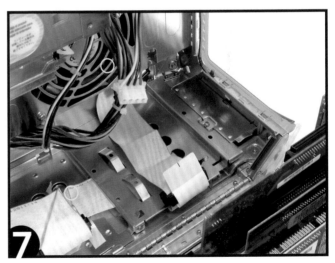

7 If your G3 is fitted with an Ultra ATA drive that you want to replace, check that the jumpers are set to configure the drive as 'Master' – refer to 'Configuring hard drives' on page 60 for more information.

Install the carrier with the drives in place, making sure that the locating pin and tab (circled yellow) engage correctly. Fit the retainer plate and its screw. Reconnect the data and power cable connectors in their original locations.

Fitting a replacement hard drive to a 'Graphite' or 'Quicksilver' G4

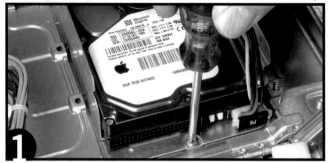  

Follow anti-static precautions on page 18 then see page 22 to get into your Mac. The Graphite and Quicksilver G4 models are fitted with an ATA drive carried in a carrier bracket towards the back of the case. Whether you're replacing an existing drive or fitting an extra drive, you'll need to remove this carrier. It is held by a single screw at the outer edge. Before fitting a drive see pages 60–63 for information on configuring.

Remove the screw, then unhook the back edge of the carrier. This will allow better access to unplug the power cable and ribbon cable connectors.

Remove the four screws from the underside of the carrier to release the old drive from the carrier.
The new drive can now be attached to the carrier using the same screws. Check the jumper settings are correct (see p.60) then connect the power and data cable connectors. Hook the back edge of the carrier into place and fit the single carrier mounting screw to complete.

Fitting an additional hard drive to a 'Graphite' or 'Quicksilver' G4

 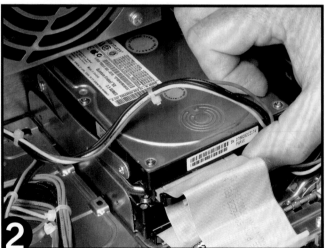

Follow anti-static precautions on page 18 then see page 22 to get into your Mac. If you want to fit an extra drive, the carrier comes with mounting holes to allow a second mechanism to be 'piggybacked' above the original unit. The screws are fitted from each side of the bracket – don't overtighten them! Check the drive is configured as a 'slave' unit following the manufacturer's settings, see pages 60–63 for information on configuring.

Fit the drive carrier with the two drives attached. Hook the carrier in position and connect the power and data cable connectors to both drives. (You should find spare power and data connectors ready to fit to the new drive.)
Both connectors are shaped so that they can only be inserted the right way up. Finally, restart to make sure everything is working. See Preparing a hard drive on p.62 for details.

Fitting a replacement hard drive to a 'Mirror door' G4

Follow anti-static precautions on page 18 then see page 22 to get into your Mac. Before fitting a drive see pages 60–63 for information on configuring. The 'Mirror Door' G4s have two drive bays as standard, each of which can hold two drives. The factory-fitted drive can normally be found in the rear bay. Release the drive carrier by pulling the grey lever forward. The carrier can now slide upwards and be disengaged. Note that some

machines may also have a locking screw fitted above the drive carrier – most don't. Once the carrier is released, you have access to the data and power cable connectors. Unplug the connector and remove the drive carrier. Note that the power cable connector can be very tight – use pliers to grip the connector to help in unplugging it, but don't twist the connector.

The drive mechanism is held by four screws to the drive carrier; remove the screws and lift out the old mechanism. When you fit the new drive, fit all four screws finger-tight, then tighten them down evenly. Remember to connect the data and power cables before you install the drive carrier in the chassis.

When you fit the carrier you'll need to hook the three mounting pegs (right) into the slots in the chassis (left). Slide the carrier down until the grey lever clicks into place.

Fitting an additional hard drive to a 'Mirror door' G4

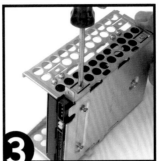

Follow anti-static precautions on page 18 then see page 22 to get into your Mac. Before fitting a drive see pages 60–63 for information on configuring. The drive carrier has provision for a second drive mechanism. Remove the carrier as described above, then slide the new mechanism into the carrier.

Secure the new mechanism to the carrier using the four mounting screws. Check that you have configured the drive correctly by setting it to the appropriate 'Master' or 'Slave' configuration using the jumpers as described on page 61.

As mentioned previously, extra expansion is provided by way of another drive bay at the front of the casing. Data and power cables are already in place. Note the two ribbon cable connectors in the foreground. These allow the drives to be connected to either a 33MHz or 66MHz ATA bus according to the drive used. The drive supplier should be able to advise on this selection.

Fit the new drive in the carrier and slide it into position before you connect the data and power cables. Locate the centre peg on the carrier in its slot – this supports and guides the carrier into the correct position as it slides home in the chassis.

Adding a high-speed SCSI hard drive to G3 and G4 Powermacs

Adding a specialist SCSI drive isn't hard, although it is vital to use the right PCI-based SCSI card for the type of drive you plan to use. It is normal to use this in addition to your existing hard drive rather than as a replacement. This is largely because you'll be using a separate connector regardless, and because this makes it easier to dedicate the new fast drive to the tasks that really need the best disk performance. Once the SCSI card has been installed (see p.108 for detailed steps) you're ready to install the hard drive itself.

Note that on early 'beige' G3 models, additional IDE drives are not supported, so fitting a SCSI card and drive may be your best option if you need another drive.

Follow anti-static precautions on page 18 then see pages 20–24 to get into your Mac. Before fitting a drive see pages 60–63 for information on configuring. Remove the empty hard drive plate from the inside of the Power Mac. Just take out the single screw and lift the whole thing out of the Mac.

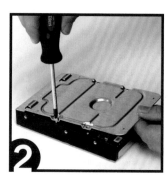

Using the screws that should be included with the new drive, fasten the plate to the base of the hard drive. Make sure to connect it with the upper part of the plate towards the drive and the drive's connectors towards the end of the drive plate with the screw hole.

Slide the plate back in the way it came out, slipping the rear metal tabs into the slots at the back on the drive area. Now replace the screw at the front to hold the whole thing in place.

Using the ribbon cable that came with the SCSI card, plug a connector into the appropriate socket in the back of the drive. The other end of the cable should be connected to a similar socket on the SCSI card.

Plug in a power connector from the ones available inside your Mac. (If there isn't one free, you can use a Y-shaped splitter cable. But there will be a spare power plug for every drive bay in your Mac, so this isn't something you should ever need to use.)

G4 Cube Hard Disk replacement

1

Follow anti-static precautions on page 18 then see page 25 to get into your Mac. Before fitting a drive see pages 60–63 for information on configuring. If your Cube has an AirPort card, disconnect and remove it. Depress the latch to release the AirPort shield door.

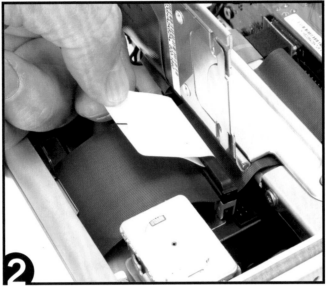

2

With the shield door open, pull on the tab to release the ribbon cable connector, then unplug the power connector. This is rather hard to reach – you may need to use a small screwdriver to release it.

3

Click the core latch back into place, then turn the core over so that the heatsink is uppermost. Slacken (don't remove) the three captive screws which retain the heatsink.

4

Lift the heatsink slightly, then slide the hard disk out of the core.

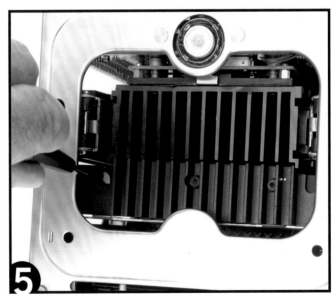

5

When installing the new drive, lift the heatsink slightly then slide the drive into position. Align the fins on the heatsink with the adjacent fixed fins and tighten the heatsink screws.

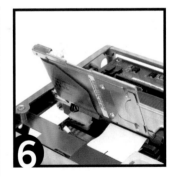

6

Reconnect the power and ribbon cable connectors, then close and latch the AirPort shield door. Install the AirPort card (if fitted originally), then slide the core into the enclosure to finish.

Upgrading the hard drive on a tray-loading iMac

Note: On 233, 266 and 333MHz iMacs, drives of over 8GB must be partitioned – see 'The 8GB partition trap' on page 63. Follow anti-static precautions on page 18 then see page 30 to get into your Mac. Before fitting a drive see pages 60–63 for information on configuring. Remove the CD drive assembly to get to the hard disk. This procedure is described on Replacing or upgrading the CD drive in a tray-loading iMac on p.86.

Now that you can actually see the drive you will be able to get to work. Take a look at the wire spring which sits on top of the drive. This will probably drop off while you're working, and it has to go in the right position, or you'll never get the CD drive back in place. This is how it should look.

Remove the two screws which secure the drive bracket to the chassis. You now need to push the drive a few millimetres into its housing then lift up the back edge. This allows two hooks on the drive bracket to come free of the chassis. If the drive won't lift up easily, the hooks are still engaged and you'll need to push the drive in a little further.

It is easier to unhook the drive if you turn the whole main board assembly over. That way you can see the hooks, and gravity works in your favour. Once you can get the bracket unhooked it will lift out quite easily. As soon as you can get access, disconnect the power leads and the ribbon cable from the drive.

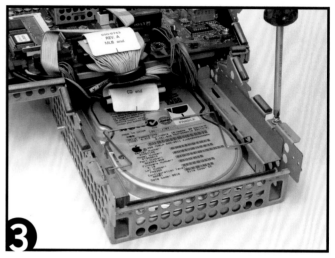

Having noted how the wire spring on top of the drive fits onto the drive bracket (see above) you can remove it and place it to one side.

6 The drive unit is held by four screws in the mounting bracket. All you need to do is remove the screws, lift out the old drive unit, and then install the new one.

7 Install the new drive assembly, remembering to fit the power lead and ribbon cable connectors before you slide the drive into its recess. Push the drive into the recess and check that the two hooks are engaged before you fit the two securing screws.

8 Place the wire spring back in position, making sure it is fitted correctly onto the bracket as shown above. If you get this wrong you won't be able to install the CD-ROM drive correctly.
Refit the CD-ROM drive, referring to p.86 for details.

Upgrading the hard drive on a slot-loading iMac

Follow anti-static precautions on page 18 then see page 32 to get into your Mac. Changing the drives on a slot-loading iMac is easy – it's getting access to them that can be a little tricky! The degree of difficulty experienced will vary from one machine to another. If you have any misgivings, get the new drive installed by an Apple authorised repairer.

Before fitting a drive see pages 60–63 for information on configuring.

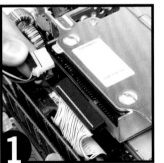

1 The drive sits inside a large aluminium bracket which also holds the optical (CD or DVD) drive. The hard drive is the easiest of the two to get at, and you can just about do this with the bracket in place (though if you need to do anything involving the optical drive, removing the whole assembly). You can start by unplugging the ribbon cable and the power lead connector from the back of the drive.

2 The drive is held in place by four screws. As you remove these, be aware that the drive will drop down slightly and should be supported.

3 Withdraw the drive from the bracket. Check that the jumper settings on the new drive are set correctly. (They usually come set up as master drives, which is how you want it to be.) Slide the new drive into the bracket, holding it in position while you fit the screws. Reconnect the ribbon and power cables, and you're done. Reverse the sequence on pp.32–33 to refit the shielding and bottom cover.

Replacing the hard drive in a PowerBook G3

Follow anti-static precautions on page 18 then see page 26 to get into your Mac. Start by making sure that the PowerBook is shut down (not sleeping) and eject the battery from its bay. Release the keyboard and lay it on the palm rest area. See page 26 for details.

Before fitting a drive see pages 60–63 for information on configuring. You now need to remove the metal shield and the processor assembly as described on page 26.

Note: On PowerBook G3 Series models drives of a capacity above 8GB must be partitioned before use. See 'The 8GB partition trap' on page 63 for details.

Very carefully unplug the hard drive ribbon cable connector from the logic board as shown.

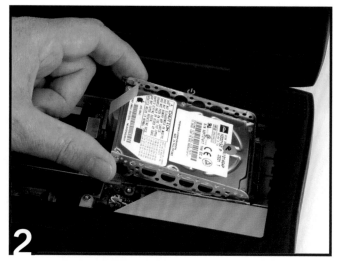

Pull on the translucent tab to lift the back edge of the drive upwards. Some resistance will be felt; the drive bracket screws pass through rubber grommets which form a resilient mounting in the chassis and help to minimise noise transmission from the drive mechanism as well as external vibration to the drive. Lift the drive assembly out of its recess and place it to one side. The old drive mechanism can be removed after releasing the four Torx T8 screws which secure it to the bracket.

Transfer the ribbon cable onto the edge connector on the new drive mechanism.

Fit the new mechanism into the mounting bracket, noting how the ribbon cable is routed through the oval slot in the bracket.

Fit the four Torx screws, tightening them evenly (avoid overtightening).

Install the drive assembly, easing the grommets into position in the chassis. Fit the ribbon cable connector, pressing it down squarely. Install the processor board, metal shield and keyboard to complete the operation.

Replacing the hard drive in a PowerBook G4

Follow anti-static precautions on page 18 then see page 28 to get into your Mac. This takes a steady hand, but it is certainly not impossible. Make sure that you're going to replace the hard drive with a unit designed to fit into such a small space. Laptop hard drives are physically smaller and a bit more expensive than their desktop counterparts.

You will also want to be sure that the replacement drive is of a type which doesn't generate too much heat; G4 PowerBooks get hot enough as standard, and extra heat could lead to problems. For this reason, only buy a replacement drive from an Apple Authorised reseller or other Mac specialist. Before fitting a drive see pages 60–63 for information on configuring.

The drive is held in place by four rubber washers that fit into holes in the drive bay sides. Using a small flat blade screwdriver, carefully lever the nearest end up. The rubber washers will come free from the holes. Don't worry if they fall off entirely, that's quite normal.

Remove the stiff protective plastic sheet from the base of the drive and set it to one side. This protects the electronics in the base of the drive from being touched. If any rubber washers are still on the drive's sides, pull them off and put them somewhere safe.

Working carefully, pull the ribbon cable connector out of the socket on the back of the drive. Be careful not to yank it, as this kind of ribbon cable can be damaged fairly easily. Once this is done, simply plug it into the connector on the new drive, and you're ready to put it all back together.

Put the protective plastic sheet back in place, push the rubber washers into the sides of the drive, and lower it into place. Put the farthest end in first, and pull the right-hand side of the drive bay open a little to help get it all in. Keep pushing it into place until the back washers pop into the holes in the drive bay sides.

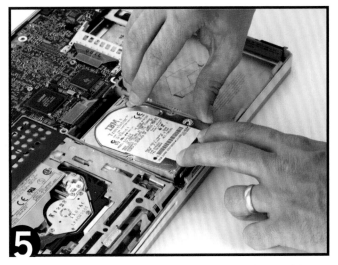

Now push the front of the drive down into place. Be careful not to put any pressure on the top of the drive, as this may flex it or put pressure on delicate components inside. The edges of the drive are safe territory, however. Once the front two rubber washers are in their holes, you've finished. You'll have to get the PowerBook's baseplate back on (as shown on p.29), and probably format the new drive, but the hard part is over.

PART **3** # Upgrading CD or DVD drives

CD-ROM drives

CD-ROM drives are vital in modern computers; virtually all software installers are supplied on CD-ROM discs, and of course they can be used to play audio CDs.

If you'd like a faster drive or one which can write CDs as well as read them, or if you'd like to move up to using DVDs as well as CDs, replacing your old drive with a newer, better one is relatively simple. Keep in mind, though, that a Mac with an Apple CD drive can be started up from a bootable CD by holding down the 'C' key immediately after power-on, which can be very useful in an emergency situation with a troubled machine. Not all non-Apple CD drives respond to this keystroke, although they are functionally identical in other respects.

Internal optical drive upgrades take less space and don't need a spare power socket.

External optical drives can be moved around from Mac to Mac whenever necessary.

Internal or external?

Before seeking out the right internal CD or DVD drive you should, as with other drive upgrades, consider whether an external drive might suit your needs better. If your existing drive is misbehaving, then by all means replace it. But if it still works, you may find it more convenient to add an external device. For one thing, you could then read data directly from a CD in the old drive to a recordable disc in the new drive. This can be a real boon when building a customised emergency CD, as well as making backup copies of existing discs.

An external CD or DVD drive will connect via SCSI, USB or FireWire. If you have both USB and FireWire available, pick FireWire every time. This is a much faster connection format than ordinary USB and can support very fast CD recording speeds. USB on the other hand, at least the format available in all but the very newest Macs, is inherently slow, and not really suitable for recording CDs faster than a very pedestrian 4x speed.

Speeds

CD drive speeds are measured as factors of the speed used for playing audio CDs, the baseline '1x' speed, or 150rpm. Today's drives reach speeds of 24x to 40x when reading data CDs. Writing to CD-R discs, the record-once format, is generally done at speeds of between 12x to 24x or so, although you should pick CD-R media rated for the speeds you choose to use when writing. CD-RW, the rewritable format, records significantly more slowly than CD-R discs, usually with a maximum speed of 6x to 12x, depending on the drive. These speeds are written as a three-figure set, so a drive rated as being '32x16x10x', will read CDs at up to 32x speed, record CD-R at up to 16x, and record to CD-RW at a maximum of 10x. In real-world terms, writing a 650MB CD at 1x speed would take roughly 74 minutes, writing it at 4x speed would take 16 minutes, and writing it at 16x speed would take just 4 minutes.

DVD drives

DVD stands for Digital Versatile Disc, although it is sometimes also referred to as Digital Video Disc. It is a high-capacity storage medium, capable of holding anywhere from 4.7Gb to around 17Gb per CD-sized disc depending on the exact type being used. It is best known as the successor to VHS video tapes, but it is also a useful medium for storing data. It is gradually displacing CD-R and CD-RW, but this isn't likely to happen for at least a couple of years.

Adding a DVD drive to your Mac is physically no more difficult than adding a CD drive. In fact the process is pretty much identical, as these devices double as CD drives as well. Where it gets more complicated is choosing which type of drive to go for. In this section we look at the options. Be warned – it is not a simple choice, and the dust is yet to settle in the battle between the various formats!

You'll also have to decide whether to go for the internal or external upgrade, something which will be partly decided by whether you have a failed drive to replace or just want to extend your Mac's abilities. See the previous page for the pros and cons of internal and external CD and DVD drives, and the following pages for step-by-step fitting instructions.

There are many forms of DVD available, from DVD-RAM to DVD-R, DVD+R, and of course the -RW and +RW forms.

TECHIE CORNER

CD-R or CD-RW?

All CD-RW drives double as CD-R devices. CD-R stands for CD-recordable, a record-once format, while CD-RW is for CD-rewritable. The idea of CD-RW discs seems great; a CD that you can use again and again seems much better than a format that can only be written once. However, there are some serious downsides which you should know before splashing out on a box of CD-RWs. First of all, rewritable doesn't mean you can use them like hard disks, editing files and putting things on and off at will. To reuse a CD-RW you have to erase it first, and this takes as long as writing it. Not all audio or older CD-ROM drives can read CD-RW discs, and on top of this, ordinary CD-R discs generally cost less than half the price of CD-RW media. CD-RW can be useful, but you may find it simpler to get a stack of CD-Rs and be done with it.

DVD speeds and formats

A DVD read speed of 8x is usually teamed with a CD read speed of around 32x, so be aware that the numbers aren't directly equivalent. Unlike CD drives, there are still a number of different DVD formats to worry about. They all read CDs, so which you choose depends on why you feel you need DVD in the first place.

DVD-ROM A read-only format used specifically for data.

DVD-RAM The writable relation of the DVD-ROM. DVD-RAM is supported by certain older Apple and third party DVD drives but not the more recent models. Discs appear on the desktop just like hard disks. Unless you need compatibility with this format, say for reading existing DVD-RAM discs, don't pick it.

DVD-R Recordable DVD format. DVD-R is the format used by Apple's CD and DVD writing SuperDrive (itself based on a mechanism made by Pioneer). Some manufacturers now offer DVD-R/RW drives.

DVD-RW Rewriteable DVD format.

DVD+RW Rewriteable DVD format. DVD+RW disks should play back in about 99% of all consumer DVD players ever built. DVD-RW disks will play back in 'many' consumer DVD players. There are lists of compatible models available, but it is a limited subset of the total range of players produced. If you plan to produce DVD-RW disks for use in a domestic player and aren't getting an Apple SuperDrive, you should consider getting a DVD+RW drive. More info available at http://www.dvdplusrw.org/.

There are other formats as well, but while the format battle isn't over it seems likely that DVD-R and the rewritable RW will remain a widely used format. If you like to keep your options wide open, drives which write to both DVD-RAM and DVD-R (although not CDs as well) can be found. A Combo drive is one which teams CD-RW features with DVD playback; a good compromise if a full CD-RW/DVD-R SuperDrive isn't an option.

Making videos

If you want to make your own DVD Videos you'll either need an Apple-supplied SuperDrive (only available by buying a Mac with one fitted) or an external third party drive based on the same CD-RW/DVD-R mechanism. With an Apple drive you can use Apple's free iDVD software for authoring DVD Video. But with a third party drive – generally the only option for upgraders – you'll need to pay for the expensive (but powerful) Apple DVD Studio Pro, as iDVD doesn't work with these.

Apple's free iDVD software makes DVD video production extremely easy, although DVD Studio Pro provides more flexibility.
(Image courtesy of Apple)

TECHIE CORNER

Slow DVD writing

With any kind of recordable DVD, whether it is DVD-RAM, DVD-R or DVD-RW, you'll have to accept that the speed of writing data to the disks isn't exactly fast. Although it may operate at speeds which are reasonable in a CD writer, if you're putting a few gigabytes (thousands of megabytes) of data onto a DVD-RAM or DVD-R, it will take a very long time to complete.

If you're burning your own DVD video using iDVD or a commercial package it can take even longer because of the process of converting footage to the correct MPEG format for DVD playback. There's no way to speed this up, so be patient and plan ahead.

Watching videos

What most people want a DVD drive for isn't data or video creation, it is for watching DVD Videos. Unfortunately this is actually the hardest thing to achieve with an upgrade.

First of all, Macs with G3 processors of around 500MHz and slower need a dedicated decoder card to be able to handle decoding and drawing the video data to the screen fast enough. This decoder is only found in Macs of that speed which originally came with DVD drives, so unless you're replacing a DVD drive in a 'Blue and White' G3 Power Mac, iMac DV or similar model, this isn't an option.

To play DVD without a specialist decoder your Mac really needs to be fitted with a G4 processor. With this it can work fast enough to handle the DVD decoding purely with the processor and regular graphics card. Unfortunately the Apple DVD Player program won't work with any old DVD drive mechanism. In fact, the only ones it is meant to work with are ones from Apple itself. See shareware search sites such as **www.versiontracker.com** for alternative DVD video players.

The real-world bottom line is simple. Unless you're replacing an existing DVD drive and are using a replacement drive from an Apple reseller, you're unlikely to get DVD video playback to work. If that is all you want from DVD this will be a bit of a blow. But look on the bright side: watching videos on a computer screen, probably from the dubious comfort of your desk chair, isn't that much fun in the long run. If you really want to watch DVDs get a budget DVD player and plug it into your TV.

Replacing a CD drive in the Beige G3 Desktop models

Follow anti-static precautions on page 18 then see page 20 to get into your Mac. With the cover removed, carefully unclip the two pieces of metal shielding which cover the fronts of the various drives, noting how the shielding clips into position. Take care not to bend the thin metal of the shielding – it will be hard to refit if it gets distorted.

Unclip the data cable connector from the back of the CD drive, but leave the power connector for now. Depress the plastic tab at the front of the drive bracket, which can now be slid out of the chassis.

As is comes away, unplug the power cable connector, which will now be more accessible.

The drive mechanism is held in the bracket by four small screws. Remove the screws, then fit the new mechanism to the bracket.
Install the drive and bracket assembly, remembering to fit the power connector before the bracket is slid back into position.

Replacing a CD drive in the Beige G3 Tower models

  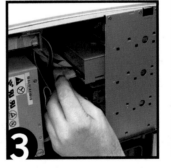 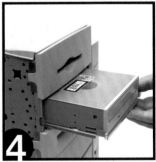

Follow anti-static precautions on page 18 then see page 21 to get into your Mac. With the side cover removed, unclip the fascia as shown. Swing it through about 90° and unhook it from the case. Behind the fascia, the metal shielding and the drive assembly is held in place by two screws.

Unclip and remove the shielding, then slide the drive forward a little, pushing it from the back of the drive to guide it along its mounting slots.

Moving the drive forward gives better access to the power and data cable connectors. With these unplugged, slide out the drive assembly and remove the drive mechanism from the mounting bracket on its underside – it is held in place by four screws.

Fit the new drive to the mounting bracket, tightening the screws evenly. Slide the assembly back into the case, plugging in the cables before you fit the shielding and the two securing screws. Finally, refit the fascia panel and close the side cover.

Replacing a CD or DVD drive in Blue and White and Graphite Power Macs

Replacing an optical drive in a Blue and White Power Mac G3 or a Graphite Power Mac G4 is pretty simple, once you work out how to get the drive out of the Mac and its metal box.

Make sure the replacement drive has its jumper pins correctly configured. See the old device for clues once you have it out of the Mac. Remember that SCSI CD or DVD drives should be set to ID 3 and unterminated, while IDE drives should be set as slaves if they share the same ATA connection with a hard drive, and masters if they're the only item on that ribbon cable.

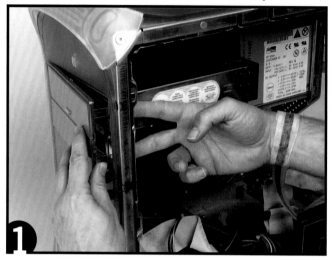

Follow anti-static precautions on page 18 then see page 22 to get into your Mac. The CD or DVD drive in your Mac will be a standard mechanism hidden behind a fascia, either with a hinged door covering the tray or with a simple slot aligned with a slot-loading mechanism. To replace a CD drive you'll need to remove the fascia as well as get at the insides of the Mac. In most Macs this will be fastened with a simple plastic clip, accessible once the Mac has been opened up.

You may need to unscrew the drive chassis from the Mac to get at the cables. In Power Macs from the Blue & White G3 onwards, the whole unit is held to the front of the Mac with a couple of screws.

Slide the drive case part of the way out of the Mac to give yourself room to manoeuvre inside. The drive will still be connected by the data and power cables, so we'll deal with that in the next step.

Like a hard drive, this drive has a power cable and ribbon cable to unplug. Older drives also have another smaller cable and plug to disconnect. This takes CD audio from the drive to the logic board. Disconnect these and slide the whole thing out.

Turn it upside down and unscrew the drive from the metal chassis. Replace with your new one, and go through these steps in reverse order. Once the new drive is in, slide the drive bay back into the Mac and plug in the ribbon cable, power and audio leads. Fasten securely using the screws you removed then replace the fascia. Start up the Mac and try the drive. Check with the Apple System Profiler to ensure it is recognised correctly.

Replacing a CD or DVD drive in a QuickSilver Power Mac

Replacing an optical drive in a QuickSilver Power Mac G4 isn't quite the same as with earlier models, even though the internal structure looks the same at first glance. Instead of having to remove part of the Mac's front fascia and pull the drive chassis through there, it is simply unscrewed from the case and removed through the open side access.

1 Follow anti-static precautions on page 18 then see page 22 to get into your Mac. Remove the four screws (Circled in yellow in the picture) holding the entire drive chassis box to the Mac's internal walls. One screw holds the lower part to the front, two more are found at the upper back, and the last is hidden underneath, near the back of the unit.

2 Before you can get much further you will probably need to displace the plastic tab on the vacant Zip drive bay bezel (see picture) to get enough clearance to rotate the drive and manoeuvre it out – the drive is a very tight fit, and the plastic tab prevents part of the drive bracket from moving.

3 Once the screws have been removed, rotate the whole unit clockwise then pull the front part out. It will now be held on only by the ribbon and power cables.

4 Using the white cable tape label if necessary, remove the ribbon cable from the drive. If a Zip drive is fitted remove the ribbon cable from this as well. Remove the power cable from the drive, and from the Zip drive if applicable. Now you can take the drive case completely out of the Mac.

5 Turn the whole unit upside down, then remove the four screws that hold the optical drive in place. The drive is a pretty tight fit in the bracket, but should push out. Now you can replace this drive with your new one, then go through these steps in reverse order to put everything back.

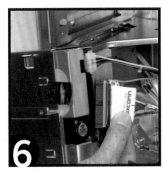

6 Slide the drive bay back into the Mac and plug in the ribbon cable and power leads. Fasten it securely using whatever screws you removed when taking the old mechanism out. Start up the Mac and try the drive. Check with the Apple System Profiler to ensure it is recognised correctly.

Replacing or adding an Optical drive in a 'Mirror Door' G4

2 Using the two dimples in the back panel of the carrier, slide the panel off the carrier and remove it to reveal the back of the drive(s) and the cable connectors.

3 Unplug the data and power cable connectors. It is easier to do this after the drive carrier has been slid part-way out of the chassis. Use pliers to help release the power cable plug, which can be very tight in its socket.

1 Follow anti-static precautions on page 18 then see page 22 to get into your Mac. The 'Mirror Door' G4s normally ship with a single optical drive (Combo or Superdrive) plus space for a second mechanism within the carrier. This allows another drive to be used for more efficient disc-to-disc copies.
To gain access to the drive(s), start by removing the two screws (circled) which hold the carrier to the chassis.

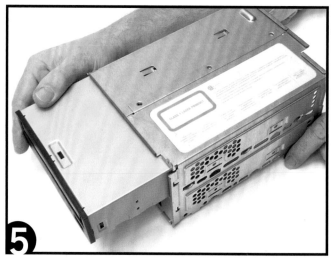

4 The carrier assembly is now free to be removed from the chassis for access to the drive mechanism(s).

5 Remove the four securing screws from the sides of the carrier. The drive mechanism slides into the carrier, which has sprung tabs to grip the drive casing.
If you are adding a second drive to the carrier, slide it into position and secure it with the four mounting screws which should come with the drive kit.

6 When installing the drive carrier assembly, note how the power cable bundle and data ribbon cables are routed in a specially formed channel in the metalwork. Make sure that the cables are positioned correctly so that they do not get trapped or damaged by the carrier when it is slid back into place.

7 As you slide the carrier forward, note how this tab on the carrier (circled) engages in the chassis to lock the carrier in position. Fit the two mounting screws and slide the back panel into position – it hooks into a channel along the top edge and won't fit correctly unless this is engaged.

Replacing an Optical drive in a G4 Cube

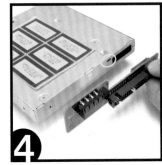

1 Access to the Cube's optical drive requires the removal of the core from the enclosure. You then need to remove the top plate assembly. This is secured by a screw at each corner (circled red), *plus two addition screws on each side. Note that these differ in length - those nearest the power switch are longer (circled yellow).*

2 Remove the AirPort card, if fitted (see page 113). Unlatch the AirPort Card door and swing it open.
Lift away the metal side panel. This is located by four tabs on the back - you need to slide it up until these clear, then remove it. (We've removed one of the support pillars for clarity - you don't need to do this)

3 The drive mechanism can be removed after releasing the Torx T10 mounting screws (two each side, circled). *Lift the drive clear of the core, unplugging the power and data connectors from the connector board on the bottom of the drive. Take care not to accidentally squeeze the drive mechanism - you could damage the laser lens if you do.*

4 You'll need to swap the connector board onto the new drive mechanism. While doing this, check the the small selector switch (circled) is set to the 'Slave' position (move it towards the connector port). When installing the drive, make sure you route the cables correctly, and that the side panel hooks in place without trapping any of them. Refit the top plate noting the location of the longer side screws.

Replacing or upgrading the CD drive in a tray-loading iMac

The original iMacs used a tray-loading CD-ROM mechanism similar to that used in many laptop computers. Though more robust than they appear, many are now wearing out or breaking.

Instead of just replacing like with like, we chose to fit a 3rd-party upgrade in the form of this MCE CD-RW. Not only does this function as a replacement for the old drive, but it means that you can burn your own CDs using iTunes, the Finder, or Toast for maximum control.

Follow anti-static precautions on page 18 then see page 30 to get into your Mac.

The old drive is removed by pushing it back against light spring pressure as shown, until you can unhook the front edge. DO NOT remove the two screws next to the drive – they don't need to be disturbed. As you pull the drive away, study the way the hook on the base of the drive engages on the wire spring below the unit. This has to be refitted correctly or the main board assembly won't fit back correctly.

Unhook the old drive, lift it clear of its recess in the main board assembly, then pull off the ribbon cable from the back of the drive.

You may now need to remove this small adaptor board from the back of your old drive so that it can be transferred to the new one (unless your replacement drive came with the adaptor board installed). The board is held on by a small screw at each end.

Next, remove the metal mounting plate from your old drive. You can now transfer this and the adaptor board to your new drive ready for installation.

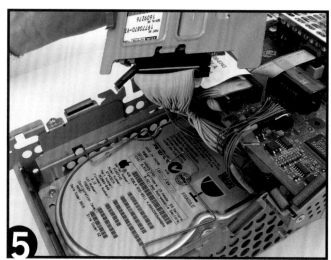

Reconnect the ribbon cable, then offer up the new drive. Note carefully the small hooked tag on the underside of the drive bracket. This MUST engage the wire spring as the drive is repositioned.
The best way of doing this is to slide the drive into its recess while peering underneath to make sure it hooks in correctly. You should need to push against spring pressure to latch the drive in place – if it feels loose, you've missed the spring.

Here we have one Bondi blue iMac complete with brand new CD-RW drive. It even came with stick-on buttons in a range of iMac colours.

Replacing or upgrading the optical drive in a slot-loading iMac

Like the hard drive, replacing the optical (CD or DVD) drive on slot-loading iMacs is pretty easy – its just getting into the thing in the first place that can be a problem. Follow the anti-static precautions shown on page 18 then see page 32 to get into your Mac.

This procedure is not always easy to do, and the degree of difficulty experienced will vary from one machine to another.

If you have any misgivings, get the new drive installed by an Apple authorised repairer.

You will need to remove the drive bracket assembly complete with the hard and optical drives. This is retained by four screws (circled, above). Take care not to drop these – a screwdriver with a magnetic tip will help, especially during installation.

With the screws removed, lift out the drive bracket assembly, disconnecting the data and power leads as they become accessible.

Remove the screws which retain the CD drive carrier to the bracket, and slide the drive out.

Remove the carrier from the old drive and transfer to the new one.

Install the assembled drive bracket, remembering to connect the power and data leads while you still have good access...

...then fit and tighten the mounting screws.

TIP If you don't have a screwdriver with a magnetic tip, try putting a small blob of Blu-Tack on the screw head to help hold it in place.

PART ③ **Alternatives**

If you need more disk space the answer isn't always to buy another hard disk, either internal or external. You may find it more convenient to buy a removable disk drive of some kind, so you can simply swap disk cartridges to get more storage space. The drives themselves aren't generally very cheap compared with many hard disk prices, but once a few extra cartridges have been bought the relative price per megabyte can drop dramatically.

So what are the options available to someone interested in greater or more flexible storage? There are some interesting choices, but each format has drawbacks as well as benefits.

The Zip disk is still used by many people, but the capacity isn't great. Other forms of removable disk are around for those that need them.

Iomega's Zip disk format was very popular through the late 1990s, but the 100MB size is just too small these days and the 250MB Zip variety didn't really catch on. Zip disks can be useful for moving documents between home and work or college, but their reliability record isn't the greatest. Consider this only if you must share files with people that already own Zip drives, or work with computers with Zip drives already installed.

Zip drives come in internal and external formats. An internal drive requires an appropriate drive bay as well as a new fascia with the appropriate Zip-sized slot. The only modern compatible external model is the USB Zip drive, which runs a little more slowly than an internal model.

The Iomega Peerless drive reads 10Gb and 20Gb Peerless disks, and comes with either USB or FireWire connection 'Base Stations'. Claimed data transfer speeds are close to hard disk levels, but don't approach this in practice. This is the logical successor to Iomega's discontinued Jaz drive, but the cartridge prices are the same as the equivalent pocket-size FireWire/USB hard drives.

If you're in need of something to read those quaint old floppy disks, an Imation SuperDisk drive can do the trick as well as offer its own 120MB variation on the floppy disk format. They are available as internal and USB-based external drives. But this is an extremely slow medium indeed, only suitable for very occasional use. See p.90 for more information.

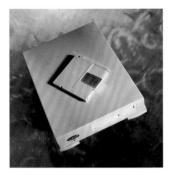

Magneto-optical drives, or MO drives for short, never managed to sort out the problems of format compatibility. They can still be founds in a number of sizes and types, but they are all fairly slow and really shouldn't be considered if you ever hope to share disks with others. These are rarely found in anything but SCSI form.

CDs are the cheapest convenient mass-storage medium and can be useful for taking the strain off an overflowing hard disk, but aren't a solution for actually expanding disk space.

DVD-RAM discs, unlike other writable DVD formats, act like regular hard drives by mounting directly on the desktop. You can move things around, rename them, and even work directly on files stored on these discs. However, these are dreadfully slow compared with hard disk speeds. Moreover, DVD-RAM disks aren't generally compatible with many DVD-ROM drives even when removed from their casing. The drives can be found in SCSI and FireWire varieties.

Pocket flash memory cards are a different kind of removable storage format. They offer convenient ways of getting files from A to B, but that's all. Almost all connect via slow USB, the sizes are generally a few hundred megabytes at most, and they don't stand up well at all in the price-per-megabyte stakes. But they can occasionally be very useful, and generally fit onto a keychain for instant access wherever you are.

Pocket-sized FireWire hard drives pack a huge amount of storage into a small box, and can draw all the power they need from the single FireWire cable.

We've tried to paint as clear a picture as possible of the main removable disk formats available to you. If the good points of one type aren't outweighed by the bad points, then it could well be the solution you need. But if you've just read through to here without feeling inspired then you probably do need to get a regular hard disk of some type.

An excellent solution for anyone who regularly needs to move around large amounts of data (if you sometimes work from home, for example) it to use a portable FireWire hard drive like LaCie's Pocketdrive. These units are rugged, connect via FireWire or USB formats 1.1 and 2.0, and have high storage capacities.

TIP

If you were considering a second drive as somewhere to keep backup copies of your work, don't. In reality you'll just end up using it as extra room rather than real backup space, and you'll be back where you started. The same thing is also generally true of removable disks, although a very disciplined user can resist this more easily. For backup strategies and solutions see Backing up on p.152. In the meantime record CD copies of critical documents if you can.

PART ③ What about floppy disks?

Floppy disks? What, those old, slow, fragile things that never have enough room and fail at the worst possible moment? Okay, most people have switched to other disk formats and to e-mailing small files, but some PC users still seem to think floppies are a good idea. Because of this you may still need to use a floppy disk every once in a while. The trouble is that floppy disk drives in older Macs are likely to be a little unreliable by now because of dust, fluff and old age, and of course modern Macs simply don't have such things any more.

As with hard disk upgrades, the first choice is whether to get an internal or external drive. External models are definitely more flexible, and can be plugged into whichever Mac happens to need it. However, you'll need to get one which connects using USB, so your Mac must either have USB as standard or through an add-in PCI card. An internal drive will be neater, and can be fitted in place of the original floppy drive. Newer Macs simply can't take these, as there's no readily available space or connector for such units. Anyway, it is almost certainly not worth

the hassle of fitting an internal floppy drive unless you plan on dealing with large numbers of floppy disks.

If you'd like to get more out of a floppy drive upgrade you could consider getting an Imation SuperDisk drive, otherwise known as an LS-120, instead. This device can read and write to special 120MB floppy-like disks, as well as handling the standard high density 1.4MB floppy disk format. It can't handle the older 800Kb floppy disk size and it isn't really any faster at writing data, but the option of larger capacity disks could be a bonus. However, never rely on something like this for backups as the medium isn't proven to be secure enough for that use.

If you have a floppy disk drive and see messages about disks being in a foreign format, this isn't a fault of the floppy drive, it is because your File Exchange control panel (or PC Exchange control panel in older versions of the Mac operating system) is set not to read PC disks, is disabled, or has been removed. See Troubleshooting on p.159 for further information. If you're told that the disk is unreadable this could mean the drive is faulty, but it could be that the disk is damaged. Try it in another computer if possible, and see if the documents could be delivered in some other way.

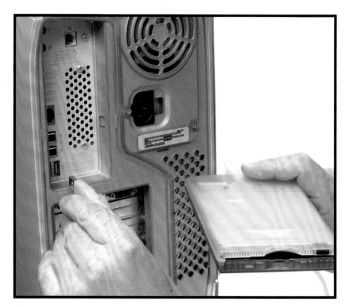

👓 TECHIE CORNER

Unreliability

The floppy disk is highly unreliable compared with most other formats. The circular disk inside the square plastic shell is made of much the same material as audio cassette tape; magnetic oxide on a thin plastic substrate. Most people are happy to slip a floppy disk containing vital data into a shirt pocket or loose into a bag, but this is a particularly bad move. The slightest speck of grit or even fluff can damage the floppy beyond recovery. It is also a bad habit to flick the metal shutter on the floppy disk open and closed. This exposes a section of the disk to the elements – as if they weren't fragile enough already. If you need to store a floppy disk and you don't have an appropriate plastic case or sleeve, find an envelope or something similar to keep it out of harm's way.

If you can arrange to have a USB socket available, then an external USB floppy drive is much simpler to deal with. Just plug it into a free USB socket and you're done. Even if you have a dead floppy drive in your Mac, it is generally best to go for an external one as a replacement. These can easily be used with other Macs as the need arises, and it will be ready for use with your next Mac when you decide to upgrade your entire system.

Replacing the floppy drive on a Beige G3 desktop

Follow anti-static precautions on page 18 then see page 20 to get into your Mac. With the cover removed, carefully unclip the two pieces of metal shielding from the front of the machine. Look at how these overlap and clip into place before you remove them, and take care to avoid damaging them as they are removed.

Pull apart the two plastic 'ears' to allow the drive mechanism to be pivoted up. This unusual mounting method may make sourcing a replacement drive more difficult than normal – try Apple dealers rather than general computer stores.

Lift the drive away and unplug the wiring connector, then substitute the new drive. Note that if you can't obtain the correct type of drive, a little ingenuity may be required to fit an industry-standard mechanism – you may want to get professional help with this.

Replacing the floppy drive on a Beige G3 tower

Follow anti-static precautions on page 18 then see page 20 to get into your Mac. With the side cover removed, unclip the left edge of the floppy drive bezel, swinging it around until it can be unhooked and removed.

Remove the two screws which retain the metal shielding, noting that these also hold the drive mounting bracket to the front of the chassis.

Unplug the wiring connector from the back of the drive, taking care to avoid sharp metal edges.
The drive and its mounting bracket can now be slid out of the chassis. Remove the four screws which secure the drive to the bracket, noting that the screw positions for various types of drive are marked on the bracket.

Position the new drive on the bracket, fitting the screws loosely until all are in place, then tightening them evenly. When you install the drive and bracket, you may find it easier to plug in the wiring connector before you fit the metal shield and the mounting screws.

4

PART **4**

Expansion cards

Your Mac will do whatever it was designed to do when it first came off the assembly line. But as new technologies appear, what once seemed fast and cutting-edge will start to seem outmoded. However, you don't necessarily have to get a new Mac to catch up with the pack. One relatively easy way to upgrade a computer is to add expansion cards. These bring newer and often better technologies and extend the usefulness of a Mac in many ways.

PART **4** **The different technologies**

Not every Mac can take expansion cards, and there are older formats which don't fit in today's Macs. But if you have a Power Mac G3 or G4 it can be given an expansion card. The main format in use today (and, in fact, used by most expandable Macs from the mid-1990s onwards) is PCI. This stands for Personal Computer Interconnect, and is used for expansion technologies from ISDN cards to SCSI cards and more. The other format used by many recent Macs is AGP (Accelerated Graphics Port), a specialist expansion format designed specifically for graphics cards.

AGP slot

PCI slots

Expansion cards plug into special slots and effectively extend the Mac's logic board, adding hardware-based features. Often you can just install a card, restart the Mac and begin using it, but sometimes the new hardware works better or provides more features if you also install whatever software came with the card.

However, some cards need their software to be installed before they'll work at all, so read the manual carefully, be sure that the card you buy is intended for use in a Mac, and that it includes Mac software and not just Windows software.

What can't be expanded

The concept of the iMac is one of a compact self-contained plug-in-and-go machine. Consequently, expansion potential wasn't built in to it, and swapping the graphics card for a newer model just isn't an option. RAM can be upgraded, and the drives if you're adventurous, but nothing else. The G4 Cube was also meant to be essentially unexpandable, RAM excluded (though Cube owners are a determined and resourceful bunch, and have found ways around some of the limitations of these machines). Generally, though, with these kinds of Mac it is best to look for external solutions.

Where are the expansion slots?

If your Mac has expansion slots you'll find them hidden inside the main body of the computer. Some Mac models have slots which are easily accessible, while others require varying amounts of disassembly to get at them. If you're not sure where the slots will be, look at the back of the Mac. Most cards are designed to have things plugged in from outside, so there will be blanking plates ready to be removed. Once into your Mac, find the slots on the logic board, and pick which one you'll use for the upgrade.

The portable difference

Portable Macs, whether PowerBooks or iBooks, are designed to be as compact as possible. This means there's simply no room inside for adding expansion cards. Most PowerBooks can actually be upgraded with a specialist PC Card, also known as a PCMCIA card. These aren't, however, regular expansion cards, they are compact credit card-size devices that are put into a special slot in the side of the machine. They are inserted and removed at will, generally without needing to shut down or restart, although software drivers are usually required to help the Mac work with the card. The most common uses for PC Cards are to add a FireWire connection to older PowerBooks, SCSI to newer PowerBooks, Ethernet to particularly old ones without built-in Ethernet networking hardware, or wireless networking cards to PowerBooks without AirPort support.

Expanding PowerBooks is done via PC Cards, a simpler process than adding a PCI expansion card to a desktop Mac.

PART 4 Graphics cards

If your computer is struggling with your digital photos, let alone the latest 3D games, and frustratingly slow redraw speeds are the norm, then you are in need of a graphics card upgrade. There are a number of such cards available for the Mac, and virtually all come from either ATI or Nvidea.

If you have anything older than an ATI Rage 128 then you should definitely consider an upgrade. The Rage 128 is no spring chicken and won't work well with many newer games, but it is still perfectly capable of dealing with general work. The ForMac ProFormance III, Matrox Millennium and 3dfx Voodoo5 are also once-powerful cards which aren't leaders any more, but will suffice if you're not into serious gaming. The ATI Radeon and Nvidea GeForce card ranges are definitely more capable choices; see www.xlr8yourmac.com for benchmark comparisons between these and other graphics cards.

Although the Mac will handle many cards without extra software, it is wise to avoid ones that aren't listed as Mac-compatible. The Mac OS may not be able to use a card's 3D hardware without a custom driver (software which helps the operating system understand the extra hardware), and if it isn't listed as Mac-compatible there almost certainly isn't one to use.

Older Macs use graphics processing chips which are built directly onto the logic board. These can't be replaced with faster versions, but it is often possible to add dedicated video memory (called Video RAM or, more concisely, VRAM) to help it handle more colours at its maximum resolutions. Macs with physically separate graphics cards can usually accept replacement cards without fuss, but these almost always have fixed amounts of VRAM. You can find out more about your Mac's graphics hardware by looking in the Apple System Profiler report (see p.14 for how to use this).

Display compatibility

Your graphics card will, of course, express itself through your monitor, so compatibility is important. Since you can't plug every monitor into every graphics card, you will need to make sure you get a card which will work with your screen.

This is all about having the right connections. Every modern graphics card that isn't pure digital will be fitted with a VGA socket. Older Apple monitors came with a cable designed for the Apple monitor port (called DB-15 in the trade), while screens from other manufacturers generally use VGA cables. The difference between these two formats is essentially just the shape, so simple converter plugs or replacement Apple-to-VGA cables can be bought for a few pounds from most dealers.

Many cards will also support digital monitor connections for faster and crisper performance with the right displays. The two types are: ADC (Apple Display Connector) and DVI (Digital Visual Interface). The ADC format is only really supported by Apple's newer monitors, and is found on just a few upgrade cards. With a relatively new Mac and the right screen it is a great solution, as it provides the monitor's power and USB pass-through connections as well as the display connection itself in a single cable. Non-ADC monitors don't get this extra benefit, and need converters to connect to an ADC port.

DVI doesn't offer extras like ADC, but it is more widely supported. There are inexpensive digital-to-VGA adaptors available, and virtually all digital cards also include VGA ports anyway, but ADC-to-DVI and DVI-to-ADC converters can cost as much as a new graphics card.

Compare the connection type of your screen with the different formats shown here and make sure that any upgrade can work with your display with the minimum of fuss and expense.

Apple's proprietary ADC connector provides power and USB as well as digital video data.

DVI is the industry-standard digital connector, although there are more than one type.

The VGA connector is a basic analogue connector format which works with virtually all non-digital displays.

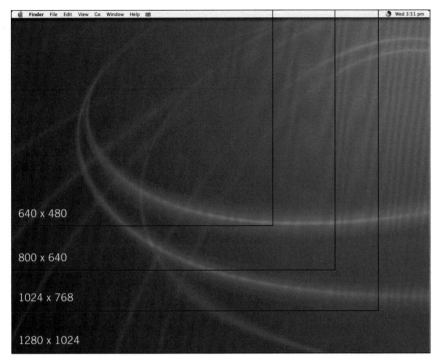

640 x 480

800 x 640

1024 x 768

1280 x 1024

The relative sizes of different screen resolutions: The higher the resolution, the more work can be shown, regardless of the physical size of the screen. However, larger screens handle higher resolutions without making things too small for comfort.

Monitor resolution

A monitor's resolution simply refers to the number of dots, or pixels, it can show, and in turn how large or small things look on the screen. A screen set to a resolution of 640x480 is one which has an array which is 640 pixels across by 480 pixels high. This is a pretty low resolution, and most monitors can do better even if they have just 14 or 15 inch screens.

There are a number of standard resolutions, although some monitors are non-standard themselves and allow unusual resolutions to be set. The most common sizes used today are 800x600, 832x624, 1024x768, 1280x960 and 1600x1200. Not all screens will show the largest sizes, and it wouldn't make sense for smaller displays to work at those resolutions anyway.

The most common resolutions for a 15 or 17 inch screen are 800x600 and 1024x768. Showing more pixels on a given screen means they all have to be smaller. This means more can be shown at once, but details become very fine and harder to make out.

Colour depth

The other aspect of a display is colour depth. This refers to the number of colours that a graphics card can deal with as it drives the screen. 24-bit colour is the maximum, and is usually referred to as 'millions of colours'; at this level graphics cards have approximately 16.8 million different shades and hues to work with. One step down from this is 16-bit colour, or 'thousands of colours' (65,536 to be precise).

16-bit isn't ideal for serious photographic retouching and editing work, but it is pretty close to 24-bit for general use. The advantage with 16-bit colour is that it takes less work for the graphics hardware to handle, which means things tend to run more smoothly. 8-bit colour means just 256 different colours are possible, not generally to be recommended, although it can speed up the display performance to an extent.

The colour depth a graphics card can reach depends on the amount of dedicated video memory it has, and the resolution it is set to as well. However, video memory is also very important for handling 3D games, as it is used for storing texture images and other information about the 3-dimensional virtual worlds you're seeing. So although 4Mb of video memory can drive a screen showing millions of colours at 1024x768 pixels, you'll need at least double that amount, preferably four times or more, to get acceptable performance and visual quality with any 3D game.

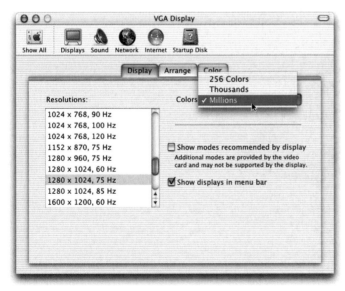

The Monitors control panel (in Mac OS 8 and 9) or System Preferences pane (in Mac OS X) is where different resolutions and colour depths are set.

PART 4 Graphics card upgrades

Your computer's graphics card creates the image you see on your screen, taking instructions and information from the processor and rendering it all as visual data. This happens whether you're writing letters or playing the latest 3D game. Some tasks stress a graphics card more than others, and modern games generally place the heaviest demands on this hardware. Graphics performance has become even more critical with the release of OS X 10.2 (Jaguar). This version of the system software employs Quartz Extreme to render the screen image. This in turn relies on the graphics card to handle this processing, freeing the CPU for other tasks. If your Mac's graphics card does not support Quartz Extreme you won't see the full potential of system performance.

Modern graphics cards often come with their own fans to keep theiir specialist graphics processors cool.

Older graphics hardware runs more slowly and tends not to have as much video RAM. The result is slower frame rates, lower resolutions and simpler scene rendering. Games in particular can be very choosy about the level of graphics processing that is available. Their minimum requirements will be listed on the side of the product box or in the manufacturer's Website. If your Mac falls short, don't bother trying until you get better hardware. It can be a very frustrating experience playing a game demanding hair-trigger reflexes when you see things at just a few frames a second. Even with less frivolous stuff such as graphics and video editing, showing layered image or video effects can become unusably sluggish.

TECHIE CORNER

Display problems

If you see a blank screen or visual gibberish when you restart after upgrading the graphics card, it could be simply because the Mac is set to a resolution and refresh rate that doesn't work with the new card. Make sure the cables are all connected and the monitor is on, then restart by pressing the power key then return. As soon as the Mac restarts, hold down the command (Apple), option (alt), P and R keys. You'll hear the regular start-up chime, then a few seconds later a second one. Let go, and see if this has cured the problem.

Which models?

If you have an all-in-one Mac or a laptop model you're out of luck. These all have graphics hardware built directly onto the logic board, so they're not upgradeable. (The earliest iMac, which had 2Mb of video RAM, can be upgraded to 6Mb. However, the result doesn't bear comparison with a dedicated graphics card upgrade.)

If your Power Mac has PCI slots you can add a faster PCI graphics card. Your existing monitor connection will then be redundant and can be removed (if it is from an existing PCI card), ignored (if it is built into the Mac) or used to drive a second monitor.

Newer Power Macs use AGP (Accelerated Graphics Port) slots for their regular graphics card. You can buy a PCI graphics card for the regular expansion slots or a better AGP card to swap with what's there already. As the AGP card is certain to be at least reasonably quick, consider adding a second card instead of replacing the first one.

Two screens at once

You don't have to remove your old graphics card to install a new one. If you have a spare expansion slot you can just plug the new card in there and connect a second display to it. You'll then have two displays working at once.

By default the Mac will work in 'extended desktop' mode, where the screens give you two views onto a larger on-screen desktop. You can drag windows from one screen to the other or even have things half on one and half on the other, and the virtual arrangement of the displays can be set in the Monitors control panel or System Preferences pane.

Working with a two-monitor setup may seem strange at first, but the advantages of having twice the virtual desktop space should soon become clear. In fact, many graphics Pros work this way all the time; the second monitor allows you to keep application palettes and secondary applications off the main screen, giving you an uncluttered view of your main work area.

Alternatively the two screens can be set to mirroring mode where one shows the same thing as the other, an option which is useful for teaching or presentations.

You can even add further cards and screens just by plugging them in, as many as you have expansion slots. If you pick 'double header' expansion cards which can drive two displays you could end up with a full-blown Macintosh video wall, although your desk might not be able to take the weight!

TECHIE CORNER

Card extras

Some graphics cards come with other sockets, typically analog S-Video or RCA video jacks. These can be used to show your screen on composite video devices such as televisions, or to link to video recorders. However, digital video (known as DV, not to be confused with DVI) is greatly preferable for video editing, and FireWire-based DV converter devices are much more flexible for output, so don't get too excited by graphics card-based video extras.

Mac model	Built-in graphics hardware
Power Mac G3 (Beige)	6MB VRAM
Power Mac G3 (Blue & White)	ATI RAGE 128
Power Mac G4 (Graphite	ATI RAGE 128, RAGE 128 Pro
Power Mac G4 (QuickSilver)	NVIDIA GeForce 2 MX, GeForce 3
Power Mac G4 Cube	ATI RAGE 128 pro
iMac Rev A/B	ATI Rage IIc
iMac Rev C/D	ATI RAGE Pro
iMac 350MHz	ATI RAGE 128
iMac (Slot-loading models)	ATI RAGE 128 Pro
iMac (mid 2001)	ATI RAGE 128 Ultra
iMac G4	NVIDIA GeForce2 MX
eMac	NVIDIA GeForce 2 MX
eMac (2003)	ATI Radeon 7500
PowerBook G3 (Kanga)	ATI RAGE 3D
PowerBook G3 (Lombard, Pismo)	ATI RAGE LT Pro
PowerBook G4	ATI Mobility 128, Mobility Radeon
iBook (14.1 inch)	ATI Mobility Radeon
iBook (late 2001)	ATI RAGE Mobility 128
iBook (handbag)	ATI RAGE Mobility, Mobility 128

PART ④ Installing a Graphics card

Check the installation instructions for the graphics card before you start opening your Mac up. It will almost certainly work without having to have software installed first, but it's worth double-checking everything before you begin, including compatibility details. In particular make sure that it is the right kind of card, and that your Mac operating system version is new enough for it.

It is also a good idea to set your existing display to a commonly used resolution, certainly no higher than 1024x768 pixels, before switching to the new card. This helps avoid possible problems where a less common setting isn't initially available, leading to temporary confusion for both you and your Mac. If you run into problems during this process see Techie Corner on p.98. For detailed diagnostics and help see Troubleshooting on p.159.

TECHIE CORNER

Monitor settings
Your Mac should start up and the monitor should work as before. If the card came with any software that hasn't been installed yet, now is the time to do it. But it should work acceptably anyway, showing up correctly in the Apple System Profiler and listing the various resolution and colour depth options in the Monitor control panel in Mac OS 8 and 9 or the Monitor pane in Mac OS X's System Preferences.

Desktop and mini-tower 'Beige' G3 graphics card upgrade

1 Follow anti-static precautions on page 18 then see page 20 to get into your Mac. These machines have their original video support built directly onto the logic board, so to add a better video card you will need to remove one of the PCI slot blanking plates first.

2 Now you can line up the edge connector with the PCI slot and push the card squarely home. Fit the single retaining screw (take care not to cross-thread it or to overtighten) and you're done. You still have the on-board video port, so you can add a second monitor to use this. Use the second screen as an extension to your desktop; great for all those floating palettes in graphics applications!

Blue and White G3 and G4 graphics card upgrade

1 *Follow anti-static precautions on page 18 then see page 22 to get into your Mac. If you're replacing an existing graphics card you'll need to take it out now. Remove the screw that holds it to the Mac's chassis and keep it safe. If you're adding a card, remove the appropriate blanking plate and keep the screw safe.*

2 *If replacing a card, hold it by the edges and carefully pull it free of the slot. You may need to rock it back and forth (end to end) a little, but don't move it sideways as this could put a strain on the socket's connection to the logic board. Treat it gently, as you may need to put it back if there's a problem with the new card.*

3 *Remove the new card from its protective bag and line it up with the slot on the logic board. Make sure that the card and slot are the same type; an AGP card won't fit into a PCI slot and vice versa. Slide the metal plate at one end down against the opening in the side of the Mac and make sure the card's connector slips into the slot.*

4 *Push carefully down on the top of the card to make sure it is firmly seated. Avoid pushing one side more than the other, although a slight end to end rocking pressure can help. Finally, use the screw you removed earlier to secure the card to the Mac. This helps prevent the card from being pushed out of the slot when a monitor cable is plugged in.*

G4 Cube graphics card upgrade

1 *Follow anti-static precautions on page 18 then see page 25 to get into your Mac. With the cube core removed from the casing, remove the two screws (either side of the video ports) which fix the graphics card to the bottom of the core.*

2 *You can now unplug the thin adaptor board, freeing it and the graphics card. The adaptor board is tethered to the Cube by power and data leads, but can be lifted enough to allow the graphics card to be unplugged.*

3 *The edge connector's green plastic surround ends up as a latch. Pull the latch to one side as shown, and the graphics card can be unplugged.*

4 *Lift the graphics card away, leaving the adaptor card connected (unless you have some specific reason to remove it).*

PART 4 USB and FireWire cards

USB (Universal Serial Bus) is today's standard method for connecting most devices to your computer. This includes keyboards, mice, personal printers, budget hard drives, scanners, digital cameras and pocket organisers. It takes the place of old-fashioned serial connection and, at the low end, of SCSI connections. At the high end where performance is more important, FireWire, also known as IEEE 1394 (and iLink by Sony), is the format of choice. This is used for high-performance external hard drives and CD writers, some scanners and very high-end still cameras, and of course digital video (DV) cameras.

USB is perfect for connecting simple devices such as digital cameras, whereas FireWire provides faster connections for things such as hard drives.

TECHIE CORNER

FireWire 800 is Apple's higher-speed variant of the original 400Mbit FireWire standard. As you might expect, FireWire 800 runs at 800Mbit/sec, double the throughput of regular FireWire, which is perfect for very bandwidth-demanding tasks such as pushing large amounts of digital video around. It requires new FireWire 800 cables, and is only built into the most recent models of the G4 and new G5 Power Macs.

All modern Macs come with USB fitted. Almost all, apart from the first generations of iMacs and iBooks, come with FireWire sockets as well. If your Mac is a little older you may have SCSI and serial ports instead, in which case you'll need to add USB or FireWire via a PCI expansion card. Even modern Macs can benefit from adding extra ports via PCI cards, as daisy-chaining many devices from just one or two ports can affect performance.

If you want to use the new generations of inkjet printers you'll need USB. This is also true if you want to use digital cameras, memory card readers, most MP3 players and budget scanners. This isn't the ideal technology for hard drives and CD writers, however, as regular USB 1.1 throughput really isn't that fast. USB CD writers in particular reach 4x speed at best, while many

SCSI and FireWire CD writers manage speeds of 20x and faster. If you want decent performance from this kind of hardware, or want to work with DV (digital video) editing, you need FireWire. This is theoretically 33 times faster than USB, although in practice neither format really hits its top speed. Still, it is very fast, blindingly so compared with USB, and ideal for high-performance needs. Some companies offer cards with both USB and FireWire, putting sockets for each format on the same PCI card. This is useful if you're running out of PCI slots, and works just as well in practice as adding separate cards.

As long as your Mac is running a new enough version of the Mac OS, USB and FireWire cards don't need any driver software to work (although USB 2.0 is a little different: see Techie Corner), so you can use any card you like without compatibility worries. Technically, support for USB was built into the Mac OS from version 8.1 onwards. However, Mac OS 8.1's support was minimal and doesn't cover USB expansion cards, so we strongly suggest upgrading to at least Mac OS 8.6, and preferably Mac OS 9.1 if you want to start using USB properly. The same recommendation holds for FireWire; use Mac OS 8.6 or, preferably, Mac OS 9.1 or newer.

How many ports?

Most USB and FireWire cards come with two or three ports, sometimes four, but this is actually as many as you're likely to need, regardless of how many things you want to use at once. Both USB and FireWire can deal with lots of devices at once, with FireWire by simple daisy-chaining, and with USB by adding USB hubs, so you can connect many items to your Mac even with just a couple of USB or FireWire ports.

With FireWire you simply plug one into a port in the Mac, another into the spare port in the first device, and so on. There are a few caveats to this, however. First of all, if an item only has one port it will have to be the last item in any chain. Some

devices work best when connected directly to the port in a Mac rather than daisy-chained through other devices. And, finally, there is the issue of power to consider.

Both USB and FireWire technologies are designed to supply a certain amount of power through the connection cable. This means that many things can be powered up just by being connected, but there are times when this doesn't work perfectly. Some things need more power than the main connection can give, and some don't pass on power properly or at all. And finally, if too many things need power there might not be enough to go around.

There are two solutions to this; use a separate power supply if one is available, or use a powered hub. USB hubs are very common, but FireWire 'hubs' are relatively rare. However, they both do the same thing; plug it into the appropriate USB or FireWire connection at one end and their array of ports is ready for use. If the hub has its own power supply then it can provide power to whatever needs it, taking some of the strain off the initial connection at the Mac end.

Clearly, if a hub is needed, a powered one is generally best. The only time this isn't necessarily the case is with ultra-compact USB hubs meant for use on the road with PowerBooks and iBooks.

TECHIE CORNER

USB 2.0 is, logically enough, the second generation of USB. It offers dramatically faster performance when used with USB 2.0-compatible devices; in theory its top speed is better than FireWire. In practice, however, there are many things which prevent this from being a reality, the most practical being that if a non-USB 2.0 device is connected then everything is slowed to USB 1.1 speeds. USB 2.0 is only supported on the Mac with the very latest versions of Mac OS X - version 10.2.7 being the first. Even USB 2.0 cards which boast Mac compatibility on the box need this, or they will never go beyond the slow performance of USB 1.1.

FireWire 'hubs' are rare, but useful. Like USB hubs, they add extra ports and provide power for devices that need it.

USB hubs add extra USB ports and usually provide power through them as well.

PART 4 # Installing USB and FireWire cards

Installing a USB or FireWire card is as simple as installing just about any other kind of PCI expansion card. The only difference there might be is in the size of the card; USB cards in particular tend to be pretty small things, as the circuitry is simple compared to the likes of 3D graphics cards.

Firewire connectors

Apple's new FireWire 800 standard uses a new connector format with more pins than the regular version.

The standard FireWire format is a sturdy design and is found on hard drives, scanners and more. It can supply power to devices that need it.

The miniature FireWire connector format is used on DV cameras. This is commonly called 'iLink' or 'Sony iLink'. Unlike the other formats this doesn't supply power to devices.

USB connectors

The standard connection for peripherals, known as USB A. If it doesn't go in easily, turn it over and try again.

The USB B connector is the 'uplink' plug, generally used for connecting printers, hubs and other devices to the Mac (or for connecting to other hubs).

Some devices use the miniature USB connector format in order to save space. This can be slightly more fragile than the other USB connectors.

Beige, Blue and White G3 and G4 PCI combined FireWire and USB upgrade

Follow anti-static precautions on page 18 then see page 20 to get into your Mac. Remove the blanking plate from an empty PCI slot, retaining the screw for later use. We decided to make good use of the slot by fitting a combined FireWire and USB card.

Remove the new card from its protective bag and line it up with the slot on the logic board. Slide the metal plate at one end down against the opening in the side of the Mac. Make sure the card's connector slips into the slot, pushing carefully down on the top of the card to make sure it is firmly seated. Avoid pushing one side more than the other, although a slight end to end rocking pressure can help.

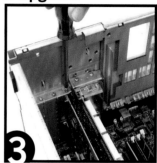

Finally, use the screw you removed earlier to secure the card to the Mac. This helps prevent the card from being pushed out of the slot when a USB or FireWire cable is plugged in.

That completes the installation process – our old G3 now has two FireWire and three USB ports (as well as a faster Ethernet port in the middle PCI slot).

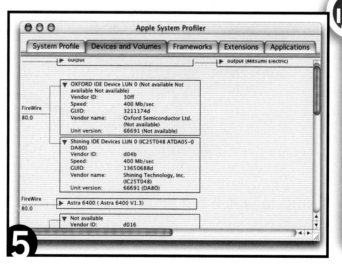

Put the Mac back together and switch it all on. Check in the Apple System Profiler to ensure the card is recognised, then try plugging a USB or FireWire device into one of the ports.

TROUBLE-SHOOTER

Problems?
If the card is listed correctly by Apple System Profiler but nothing happens when you plug something in, check that you've installed any software necessary for that device. USB and FireWire cards should be dealt with without fuss by the Mac OS, as long as you're running a relatively recent version. If you still have problems and aren't running Mac OS 9.1 or newer, consider upgrading.

PART **4** # SCSI cards

All older Macs (apart from some old PowerBooks) have SCSI built in, but this technology was dropped from the iMac and Blue and White G3 Power Mac onwards. If your Mac doesn't have SCSI and you need to use SCSI devices, you'll have to add a SCSI card. As this requires a PCI expansion slot you won't be able to do this to a PowerBook, and iBook, a G4 Cube or an iMac. (PowerBooks can, however, use a SCSI PC Card.)

SCSI (Small Computer Systems Interface, or 'scuzzy') is used to connect hard drives, scanners and a few other kinds of device. The devices are connected to a SCSI port in a single chain, one device to the next. SCSI is still a popular connection format for power users, as it can deliver very fast, reliable speeds.

High-speed SCSI cards can provide multiple channels, both internall and externally, for connecting large numbers of devices.

TECHIE CORNER

Multiple SCSI channels
If you already have SCSI built into your Mac you can happily add a SCSI card without causing problems. The Mac OS will automatically recognise this as a separate SCSI channel, and work with items plugged in to that as well as the original SCSI channel. Something on one channel can have the same ID number as one on another channel without causing conflicts. Mixing slow and fast SCSI devices on the same channel can slow things down overall, but if you keep older, slow SCSI devices on one and only put faster hardware on the other you'll be able to get the most of the added high-speed SCSI hardware.

Things to watch out for

SCSI management is sometimes referred to as a 'black art', as it can be frustrating tracking down conflicts if trouble strikes. But with a little knowledge of how it works it is possible to tame most SCSI setups.

SCSI devices should generally be turned on first and, more important, turned off only after the Mac is shut down. The Mac looks for SCSI devices only when it starts up, and assumes they will be there the whole time it runs. A free utility called SCSI Probe, found via www.versiontracker.com, can prod a Mac into looking again if you turn one on after the Mac, but don't add or remove things while the Mac is on unless there's no alternative. (Changing connections with the Mac on can cause electrical damage to the SCSI controller hardware in the Mac.)

Termination

Termination involves a kind of buffer at either end of a SCSI chain which prevents data from causing confusing digital signal echoes. The Mac end of things is terminated as standard. Many SCSI devices have termination switches; these should be switched off on everything but the last thing in the chain. If there is no termination switch you'll need to add an external terminator, either a simple block terminator connected to the spare SCSI socket or an in-line terminator placed between the last device and its SCSI cable. If you're unlucky you might have a SCSI device which has permanent termination built in. Put this at the end of the SCSI chain, or open it up and remove the termination jumper pin. (See Configuring hard drives on p.60.)

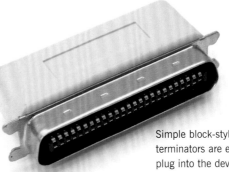

Simple block-style SCSI terminators are easy to use; just plug into the device at the far end of the SCSI device chain.

ID numbers

Every SCSI device needs its own ID number in order to appear and work on the SCSI channel. If you add your own SCSI card, it won't have other devices plugged in already. You will have the full range of IDs: 0 to 7 or, with many modern SCSI cards, 0 to 15. With things such as external hard drives, scanners and the like, SCSI ID numbers are usually set using a push button system, or sometimes a rotary wheel. There is no relationship between ID number and the position of things in a SCSI chain.

Using SCSI isn't as straightforward as using FireWire or USB, but there are benefits to this technology. It doesn't suffer from the same inherent slowdown that FireWire and USB do when large numbers of devices are connected. And, unlike IDE, it is a fully multi-threaded technology, meaning different data transfer instructions can be sent out at once. In plain English this translates to better performance when the right SCSI hardware is used, although there is a price premium involved.

Some regular SCSI devices have both the 50-pin and smaller 25-pin sockets, but most will have two 50-pin connectors.

What SCSI format is best?

SCSI comes in a number of different varieties. The kind built into older Macs is known as SCSI-1, but most SCSI expansion cards will be better than that. Fast SCSI and Wide SCSI push data through faster and work with larger portions of information at a time, respectively. Fast-and-Wide SCSI combines the two to good effect. Modern SCSI implementations are called UltraSCSI, and come in various speeds up to UltraSCSI 320, which offers a theoretical burst speed of 320MB a second, hard disks permitting. LVD, or Low Voltage Differential, requires specific LVD disks, so it is very important to get the right SCSI card.

SCSI cables

It is also important to have the right cables. Traditional SCSI involves the 'host' SCSI connection (a 25-pin plug that screws into the Mac) and the 'peripheral' connection (a larger 50-pin plug which connects to devices with large wire clips). SCSI card upgrades, however, will use connectors commonly called SCSI-2 (fairly compact, with 50 connector pins, and retaining clips built into the plug) and SCSI-3 (larger and more pins than SCSI-2, but otherwise the same). Make sure you know what kind of SCSI connectors your hardware needs and what the different cards provide, and get the appropriate connector cables and, if necessary, adaptors.

SCSI cables come in a number of different forms. The most common are the basic 'Mac to device' 25-pin/50-pin and 'device to device' 50-pin/50-pin leads. The high-speed SCSI variants use compact plugs and sockets with more pin connectors, but there are different sizes available according to what kind of fast SCSI technology is used. Then there are the internal ribbon cables, which also need to be matched to the kind of device being used.

PART ④ Installing SCSI cards

The Mac OS supports SCSI directly, so for basic cards running in Mac OS 8 and 9 you won't need drivers. However, the higher performance, more esoteric SCSI cards may work best (or only work) when their driver software is installed. Check with the manufacturer about this kind of detail, as well as Mac OS version compatibility.

If you run Mac OS X the card may need to have a Flash ROM update before it will work correctly. This is a small portion of memory in the card itself which contains basic but essential information. Look on the manufacturer's Website and ask the dealer about Mac OS X compatibility before you buy. You will normally be able to download software to do this, but if you can pick a card which doesn't need it, so much the better.

Beige, Blue and White G3 and G4 PCI SCSI card upgrade

1 Follow anti-static precautions on page 18 then see page 20 to get into your Mac. If you're replacing an existing card you'll need to take it out now, otherwise you'll need to take out a blanking plate. Remove the screw that holds it to the Mac's chassis and keep it safe.

2 Line the new card up with the slot on the logic board. Slide the metal plate at one end down against the opening in the side of the Mac and make sure the card's connector slips into the slot. Push down carefully on the card to make sure it is firmly seated. A slight end to end rocking pressure can help. Finally, fasten it down with the screw removed earlier. This holds the card in place when a SCSI cable is plugged in.

3 If you plan to connect an internal SCSI drive, now is the time to do it. Use the right ribbon cable to link the drive to the card's internal socket, and make sure the device is properly installed in the Mac; see Upgrading a hard drive on p.64 for details.

4 Now put the Mac back together. If you didn't connect an internal drive then plug in just one external SCSI device to keep initial testing simple. Your Mac should start-up normally and deal with the SCSI device appropriately. Check in the Apple System Profiler for the SCSI card if there are any problems.

PART ④ Other PCI card options

PCI cards can be useful for other things, too. Specialist sound cards, for example, connect via PCI and offer everything from high-end recording to 5.1 channel speaker support. Some professional recording programs use dedicated sound cards to supply audio streams and to control external instruments. Video digitising support can also be added via PCI cards, and can be extremely useful for piping edited footage back out to older recording devices. There are more esoteric cards around, such as controllers for assembly lines, scientific data analysis and so on. On the lighter side of things there are also TV tuner cards on offer, so you can watch the news or favourite soap operas in a window on your screen as you work.

So why would someone need a sound card for a Mac? Every Mac since the beginning has had good sound support built in, and anything still running is likely to have CD-quality stereo audio output and probably equally good sound recording as well. However, this isn't necessarily enough for recording studio work. As well as controlling specialist music hardware directly, professional recording needs many more sound channels at once, and even higher quality than the 16-bit or 24-bit 48kHz sound handling that Macs offer as standard. As this is a very specialist subject it is best to consult a music specialist Mac dealer about your needs and the latest options, so contact Apple to find your nearest appropriate supplier.

Even if you're not a professional musician you could benefit from a 5.1 Dolby surround-sound card (teamed up with the appropriate speakers). Just be sure that you get one with Mac support – although this is largely taken care of already if you're running Mac OS X.

Digitising video is best done with FireWire connections and DV cameras. However, if you have older video equipment or Macs, or you want to link to specialist video desks with no FireWire support, a digitising card can be the right solution. Just remember to check compatibility with your Mac and the version of the Mac OS that you're using. If the software needed to work with the card is only made for Mac OS 9 you may be unable to use it at all in Mac OS X. On the other hand, you may find that support is automatic in newer versions of the Mac OS, so see if there are reports in Web discussion groups about the card you're thinking of getting.

All PCI cards install in the same way. Run the software installer, if there is one, once you've finished with the hardware. Once installed it should show up correctly in the Apple System Profiler. Sound cards should appear as an option in your Sound control panel or System Preferences pane, whereas most other cards will need to be used with their own controller software.

Adding a FireWire PCI card will help older Macs work with the latest DV hardware and video editing software.

PART 4 Network options

Networking has always been a Macintosh forte, and Ethernet support is built into the Mac OS. The standard in use today is 'base-T', also referred to as 'unshielded twisted pair'. This comes in speeds from 10base-T to 100base-T and 'gigabit' (1000base-T) Ethernet.

Virtually every Mac from the last decade has some kind of Ethernet socket, also called a port, already fitted, but those in older models, particularly those without built-in USB, will be the slower 10base-T variety. A high-speed Ethernet card is easy to install and can improve network performance if you regularly need to move very large files. There may be a driver to install, but you should find that the Mac recognises most Ethernet hardware automatically and lists it as a network interface option in the AppleTalk control panel in Mac OS 8 and 9, or the Network pane in Mac OS X's System Preferences.

Ethernet hubs come in a variety of sizes to suit different needs, from simple four-port models to ones with dozens of available sockets.

Setting up a wired network

Setting up and using a basic Ethernet network is actually very easy. What's needed is a cheap Ethernet hub with enough ports for each Mac and network printer, and a separate cable for each of those items. The Ethernet hub is the central device in the network, and each computer and printer connects directly to a socket in the hub. When buying a hub make sure you get one with enough sockets for the forseeable future. You can link two hubs together later on, but it is simpler to make sure you have enough room in the first place.

First of all, make sure that the hub is near a power socket and that the cables are long enough. Then plug each computer and printer directly into the sockets in the hub, and the hardware setup is done. Make sure each Mac is set to use Ethernet, and printers will appear and file sharing can be set up. In Mac OS 8 and 9, go to the AppleTalk control panel and choose Ethernet from the popup menu. In Mac OS X go to the Network pane in System Preferences, pick Network Port Configurations, and make sure that Built-In Ethernet (or your added PCI card) is checked. If it isn't then the Mac won't bother trying that connection.

You can link two Macs directly to each other with a single Ethernet cable and no hub, but unless you're using very up-to-date models you'll need a special 'crossover' Ethernet cable. (These cables are also useful for linking one hub to another to extend the number of available ports.) The wiring in a crossover cable is literally crossed over, simulating the way things connect through a hub. If you have a crossover cable, mark it clearly; it won't work as an ordinary cable in most situations, and can cause great confusion as a result.

AirPort and AirPort-compatible hardware use the 802.11b and 802.11g standards to provide wireless access to networked computers, printers and the Internet. *(Images courtesy of Apple)*

What about wireless?

Every Mac sold from the end of 1999 is 'AirPort-ready'. This means it has an internal socket and antenna for an Apple AirPort wireless network card. This allows it to link with other computers and printers and surf the Internet without any physical network connection. Standard AirPort hardware works at speeds equivalent to 10base-T Ethernet, while the newer AirPort Extreme variant can run roughly five times faster. Apple's wireless networking uses the industry standard IEEE 802.11 wireless protocols, specifically 802.11b for regular AirPort and the 802.11g standard for AirPort Extreme.

AirPort Extreme is currently only supported by Apple's 'aluminum' PowerBook G4 computers, and by the most recent PowerMac G4 tower model (with the FireWire 800 socket) and the PowerMac G5 models. However, AirPort Extreme-equipped Macs can work with regular AirPort connections by stepping down their connection speeds.

Wireless networking is much more convenient than using cables, but the cost of the hardware is much greater than using regular Ethernet cabling and hubs. There are third-party wireless networking solutions for Macs which aren't AirPort-ready, and all those which use the same protocols as AirPort should work with each other. To use wireless networking you'll need to be running at least Mac OS 8.6, preferably Mac OS 9.1 or newer. If you use a third-party wireless product then you must use the software that came with that device. Make sure it supports the Mac OS version that you're running, then run the installer. Once the hardware and software are in place you can pick your new wireless networking option from the AppleTalk control panel or the Network pane in the System Preferences. If your Mac is AirPort-ready you can choose between Apple's wireless hardware and third-party options. If it isn't AirPort-ready you'll be restricted to third-party hardware. To see if your Mac is able to take an AirPort card check it against our chart.

Mac model	Airport-ready	Alternative option
iMac (tray-loading)	No	USB adaptor
iMac (slot-loading)	Yes*	USB adaptor
iMac (Flat panel)	Yes	USB adaptor
iBook	Yes	USB adaptor
Beige Power Mac G3	No	PCI card or USB adaptor
Blue & White Power Mac G3	No	PCI card or USB adaptor
Power Mac G4 (PCI Graphics)	No	PCI card or USB adaptor
Power Mac G4 (all others)	Yes	PCI card or USB adaptor
Power Mac G4 Cube	Yes	USB adaptor
eMac	Yes	USB adaptor
PowerBook G3 (FireWire)	Yes	PC Card
PowerBook G3 (All others)	No	PC Card
PowerBook G4	Yes	PC Card

* Slot-loading iMac requires an Apple AirPort adaptor as well as an AirPort card

PART ④ Installing an AirPort card

Installing an AirPort card is easy in just about every Mac
that supports this technology. The only fly in the
ointment is the PowerBook G4, which is so ultra-
compact that the AirPort socket is squeezed
inside the base of the Mac.

Power Mac AirPort card installation

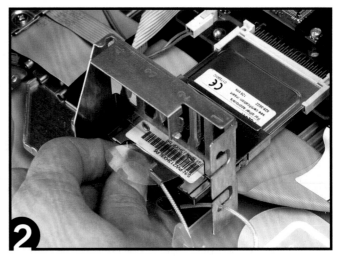

*Follow anti-static precautions on page 18 then see page 22 to
get into your Mac. To install AirPort in any AirPort-ready Power
Mac just open the side door of the Mac and locate the AirPort
connector at the left of the Power Mac's door. Slide the card
barcode side up into the slot as shown.*

*Now connect the end of the small antenna cable to the socket in
the end of the AirPort card, and close everything back up. You
should be done with the hardware installation within a minute.*

G4 Cube AirPort card installation

Installing an AirPort card into a G4 Cube is one of the easiest Cube upgrades to perform. Use a standard Apple AirPort card and follow the step-by-step guides and you can't go wrong.

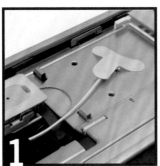

Follow anti-static precautions on page 18 then see page 25 to get into your Mac.
Once the Cube is open, find the AirPort upgrade recess. It will have the antenna connector taped down; move this out of the way before trying to insert the card.

Making sure that the AirPort card is the right way up, slide it into the slot. Be sure to align the card with the small plastic guides on either side of the socket. Push it firmly in and down to make sure the pins in the socket are all connected and that it sits flat in the chassis. If it doesn't slip down inside the two bumpers by your fingers then it isn't pushed far enough into the socket.

Once the card is in place, retrieve the antenna lead and push the L-shaped end into the small socket in the end of the card. The connector is fairly small, but it should push home without too much trouble when correctly aligned. If you have problems getting it in place try moving the card back out of the socket a small amount. This can give a little more room for your fingers.

With the card firmly installed and the antenna lead in place, make sure that everything is tucked down flat before putting the Cube's body back in the outer shell.

TECHIE CORNER

Network switching

To use the Ethernet network port it must be selected in the AppleTalk control panel. Any Mac with old-style serial ports (including the beige G3 models) will automatically switch to the serial port-based LocalTalk network setting if it can't sense an active Ethernet connection when it starts up. This is a very common source of problems, as attempts to use the network will just result in unhelpful error messages. Make sure the Ethernet cable is plugged into an Ethernet hub and the right port in the Mac, then switch the AppleTalk network option back to Ethernet and try again.

Fortunately all modern Macs won't suffer from this problem, as the old serial-based LocalTalk network option isn't available.

PowerBook G3 AirPort card installation

Installing AirPort into a FireWire-equipped PowerBook G3 is almost as easy as in a desktop Power Mac. Follow anti-static precautions on page 18 then see page 26 to get into your Mac.

Look for the AirPort antenna cable, and plug the end of this into the socket in the end of the AirPort card. It is easier to do this before the card is in place.

Now slide the card into the space provided, barcode side up. Make sure everything is as flat as possible, replace the keyboard, and the hardware is installed.

PowerBook G4 AirPort card installation

To fit a PowerBook G4 with an AirPort card you'll have to remove the entire base of the titanium case. Follow anti-static precautions on page 18 then see page 28 to get into your Mac.

With the base of the PowerBook removed, the AirPort cable and socket are in the upper-right as you look at it, just above the battery bay. Lift up the hinged AirPort card socket and slide the card in, connecting the antenna cable as you go. Fold the AirPort card's plastic tab out of the way and make sure everything is as snug and flat as possible. Once done, see p.29 for help with getting the case back on.

Slot loading iMac AirPort card installation

Slot-loading iMacs have a small door at the back, behind which are the RAM slots and an AirPort adaptor socket. Note that this isn't actually an AirPort card-ready socket - you also need an AirPort adaptor in order to install an AirPort card in these Macs.

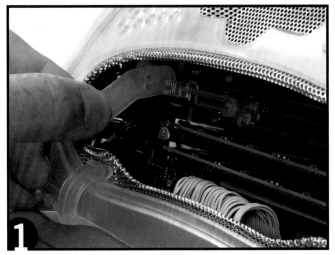

Follow anti-static precautions on page 18 then see page 32 to get into your Mac.
First, you need to locate the AirPort antenna cable This is clipped to a plastic retainer, which in turn is clipped to the logic board just inside the opening. Pull off the retainer and pull it just out side the opening.

Unplug the antenna from the retainer, then refit the retainer in its original position; you may need to re-use this to hold the antenna if you ever decide to remove the AirPort card in the future

Plug the antenna connector into the socket on the AirPort card. Note that you should do this before you fit the card to the adaptor.

Fit the AirPort card into the adaptor, then fit the metal clip to secure it. Note how the clip ends align with cutouts on the adaptor board.

The assembled AirPort card and adaptor can now be slid into plastic guides inside the upgrade opening. Refit the door, then start the iMac and check that the card is working correctly.

iMac G4 AirPort card installation

The base plate of the flat-screen iMac must be removed to gain access to the AirPort upgrade socket and antenna. Follow anti-static precautions on page 18 then work through the instructions on p.34 to get into the iMac, and you'll see the AirPort socket in clear view.

Hold the AirPort antenna cable out of the way and slide the AirPort card into the slot.

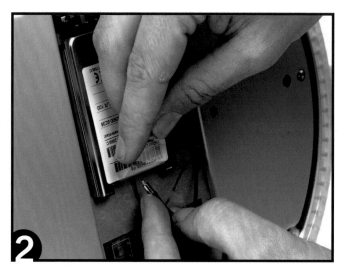

Push the end of the antenna cable into the socket in the base of the AirPort card, underneath the clear plastic tab. The installation is done.

eMac AirPort card installation

The eMac's AirPort slot is cunningly hidden beneath the optical drive bezel, behind the hinged door in the front of the Mac. Once you know where to look it is actually quite easy to upgrade, and doesn't involve exposing any other parts of the Mac.

First you'll need to open the hinged door which hides the optical drive. Use a finger to press one end in, and the other end will pop out slightly. Pull this out from the top edge and hold it down.

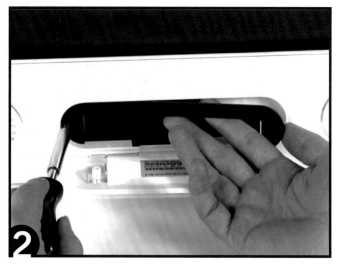

Now use a crosshead screwdriver to remove the two screws on either side of the drive's drawer. Pull the black plastic bezel off and put it to one side with the screws.

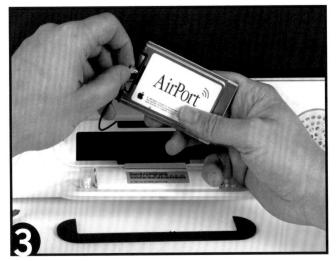

3

Pull out the AirPort antenna cable from the recess that is now uncovered and plug it into the socket in the end of the AirPort card.

4

Now push the AirPort card, barcode side up and antenna end out, into the slot above the optical drive tray. It will slide all the way in, with just the clear plastic tab protruding to help if you ever need to remove it.

5

Replace the black plastic bezel, securing it with the two screws, and you're finished.

iBook AirPort card installation

Follow anti-static precautions on page 18 then see page 35 to get into your Mac. You will see the AirPort card recess in plain sight. In older iBooks this is located near the middle of the keyboard area, while in newer iBooks it is to the left. Apart from this slight difference in position the process of adding the card is identical.

1

First, find the AirPort antenna cable and connect it to the socket in the end of the AirPort card, under the plastic tab. Slide the AirPort card under the wire clip into the socket.

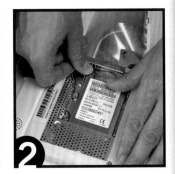

2

Push the card firmly into its socket and press it down into the recess. Once it is flat, use the wire clip to keep it and the antenna in place. Now you're ready to replace the keyboard and use your wireless connection.

TECHIE CORNER

Home RF wireless alternative
The 802.11-based wireless network solution used by AirPort and others is an industry standard, but it isn't the only game in town. Home RF is an alternative network solution which aims to work with future consumer products as well as more business-level hardware. In theory this will provide ways to link hi-fi equipment and other consumer products with computers, but this level of Home RF use is still largely in development. Where Home RF scores over the basic version of the 802.11 standard is security levels, with a high level of data encryption used for network traffic and access. AirPort is an established commercial standard, but Home RF could prove to be an interesting alternative at some point in the future. See **www.homerf.org** for further information.

5

PART **5**

Peripherals

Anything that plugs into your Mac is classed as a peripheral. Some are more important than others – and monitors, keyboards and mice are more 'essentials' than anything else. Others help get pictures or sounds into or out of your Mac: not actually vital to running your Mac, but indispensable if you want to do anything interesting or useful with it.

Upgrading your monitor

If you're working with an old 14 or 15 inch display, the chances are you'd like to have a little more elbow room as you work and play. The simplest and cheapest solution is to step up to a higher resolution on the screen you have (see p.97). This packs more into the display, but it won't help much if you're feeling cramped, and it certainly won't help your eye strain. The same goes for any size display; if you need more room, try increasing the resolution. If this doesn't solve the problem, you need a bigger screen.

Pick the screen that suits your needs and, equally importantly, your budget, but don't compromise on quality.
(Image courtesy of Apple)

Picking the right screen is very important. After all, this is the thing that you'll be staring at hour after hour for the next year or so at least. You have to feel comfortable with your monitor, so don't go for the cheapest one around unless you can't avoid it.

What can't be upgraded

If you use an iMac or a laptop you're pretty much out of luck. These Macs use built-in screens, and you simply can't replace them with any other. It is possible to connect an external monitor to the newer iMacs and to most PowerBooks, but with iMacs this only shows an exact replica of what you see on the internal display. You could still use a nice 19 inch display to show your iMac's top resolution of 1024x768 pixels; this would make things feel more roomy. However, you'd still need space to store the iMac with its built-in screen; not a good solution at all.

Most PowerBooks are able to drive a second screen in both mirrored and extended desktop mode. (See Two screens at once on p.99 for more on this way of working.) If you like the idea of having a larger screen and still being able to take your Mac on the road, this is a perfectly reasonable proposition. Read on for which screen is best for you.

Size

First you'll have to decide which screen size suits you best. It is all very well pining after a massive 20 or 21 inch screen, but, budget issues aside, you'll have to consider your desk space carefully. The space taken by a CRT (cathode ray tube, the traditional bulky glass tube devices) screen in particular can be quite a shock; as well as taking a lot of space width-ways you may not have much room in front for your keyboard and mouse once you get it onto your desk. Large CRT monitors also weigh more than the average flat-pack computer table can take.

A 17 inch monitor is generally a good compromise if space isn't too plentiful, and they are also much cheaper than the 20 inch+ giants. If 17 inches isn't big enough then go to a 19 inch display, although it will generally cost more. If you're not sure quite how these sizes relate to real life, take a look at some displays in your nearest computer dealer's showroom.

If your graphics card has any resolution limits, for instance if you're using the monitor-out abilities of a PowerBook or iBook, don't bother getting a screen dramatically larger than what is normal for that resolution. There's not much point in splashing out on a 21 inch display if you use an iBook, with its 1024x768 maximum output.

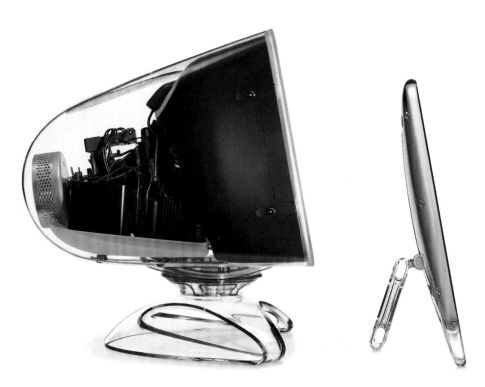

CRT displays take up many times the depth of even the largest LCD monitor, and generally take more power to run. However, they are better at showing accurate colour, so don't dismiss CRTs out of hand. *(Image courtesy of Apple)*

CRT or LCD

A nice flat LCD (Liquid Crystal Display) screen might be more to your taste. They are still a lot more expensive than similar sized CRT screens, but a 15 inch LCD gives close to the same viewable area as a 17 inch CRT. They are also generally no more than a couple of inches thick, very different from the desk-hogging depth of even the most compact CRT. These screens, also called flat panel displays, use less power and make less heat than CRT displays, and don't suffer from magnetic interference from other monitors, unshielded speakers and similar items.

Flat panel displays aren't perfect, however. If absolute colour fidelity is important to you, and it will be if you do much graphic work, then the average LCD screen will drive you up the wall. Try shifting your position up, down and sideways while looking at one of these screens, and the chances are you'll see shifts in brightness, contrast and even hue. True, the best LCD screens have almost eliminated this, but even Apple's flagship Cinema Display screens aren't totally immune. LCD screens are not really designed to be precisely calibrated either, although the best do have very good colour rendition in general.

If you don't go for a flat panel display, then there are still a number of traditional formats to pick from. The cheapest screen type is FST, short for Flatter Squarer Tube. Ironically, this is the one with the most curves of all. Cheap ones will feel like goldfish bowls and suffer from reflections. Another name for this format is 'shadow mask', from the perforated metal sheet inside which focuses the electron gun's beam onto the inside of the glass tube. For a flatter screen, try a Trinitron model or its close cousin, the Mitsubishi Diamondtron. This only curves horizontally and not as much. These are also known as 'aperture grille' screens, as they use a grille-like array of vertical wires to focus the electron gun's beam. The grille is supported by one or two horizontal wires, which show as very faint, thin lines. This is not a fault, is it simply due to the way they work. For a truly flat CRT look for a 'Naturally Flat' display; these have faces which really are flat. The thing to remember is to avoid the cheapest FST monitors.

TECHIE CORNER

Screen sizes
Although monitor sizes are all measured from one corner of the display to the diagonally opposite corner, things can be very misleading. All CRT (Cathode Ray Tube, or glass-based) screens are measured from the corners of the glass tube itself, despite being hidden beneath the monitor's plastic bezel. On the other hand, LCD 'flat panel' screens are all measured from the diagonally opposite corners of the actual image area. This means a 15 inch LCD display is pretty close in actual image area to a 17 inch CRT screen. When shopping for traditional CRT monitors, look for the 'viewable area' specification to see just how big the actual display area really is. A 17 inch display will typically have a viewable area of 16 inches or less.

Resolution

Each screen size will have a resolution which is generally regarded as its 'native' resolution. With CRT displays this is a pretty arbitrary distinction, as they can generally show resolutions higher as well as lower than the native size. Flat panel displays have an absolute fixed native resolution, however, and can't work higher than that. They can show lower resolutions, but only by using their native pixel array to simulate the larger, lower resolution pixels.

Refresh rate

Refresh rate isn't something that many people consider when buying a monitor, but cheaper ones in particular may not be able to run at very high speeds. This is simply how many times the screen is redrawn in a second. If a monitor only supports lower refresh rates you're likely to get headaches when using it. Even if you don't see a visible flicker it might give you eye strain. If you try to run a screen at too high a refresh rate it will probably not show anything (and then revert to the last setting after some seconds). Some may work but emit a faint high-pitched whistle. Switch to a lower rate if this happens, as it won't do the screen or your head any good.

Higher refresh rates are more important at lower resolutions; regard 75Hz as a general minimum for displays running at 1280x960, 85Hz when at 1024x768, and 90Hz or higher for any lower resolution. Refresh rates are not strictly applicable to LCD screens; there's no electron beam redrawing the image top to bottom many times a second; it is done with banks of transistors instead.

Connection format

Finally, you should make sure you buy the kind of monitor that you can actually connect to your Mac. There's no platform issue to worry about here as Macs and PCs can all use each other's monitors. (Well, PCs can't use Apple's newest monitors because of the proprietary ADC connectors, but that's not our problem.) Assuming you don't have a digital graphics card (with an ADC or a DVI connector), the only thing to worry about is whether you need to use a VGA-to-DB15 (old-style Apple monitor port) convertor. See Graphics cards on p.96 for more information on this subject.

Problems

If you're not convinced that a CRT monitor is up to scratch, take a look at the corners and edges. These may show distortions which make straight lines slightly wavy, and you may also see a problem with focus in the extremities. It may be possible to correct this using the monitor's onscreen controls, but it may be a reason to look for a different display altogether.

LCD monitors tend to have different problems. For example, if the digital controller that passes the Mac's display signal to the banks of pixels is not tuned correctly then vertical lines may seem blurred and stretched or compressed. Ghosting of lines is another issue; have a look at the edges of windows or the mouse cursor itself. Tweaking the monitor's onscreen controls will usually fix this. Pure digital displays don't have most of these problems as there is no analogue-to-digital conversion being made.

Dead pixels is another, more frustrating problem that can be found. It isn't that uncommon for one or two pixels in a screen to be 'dead on arrival', simply failing to work. Most manufacturers will only replace a screen if there is more than a minimum number of dead pixels. However, if you have just a couple but in important parts of the screen, do kick up a fuss. Some users report moderate success from gently massaging problematic pixels with a fingertip, but this would depend on what caused the problem in the first place.

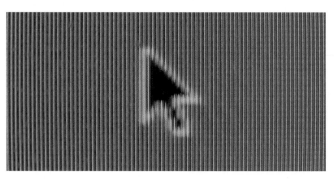

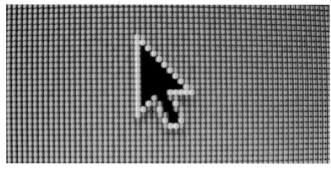

Images on CRT and LCD screens are made up of pixels. However these pixels are created in very different ways. CRT displays use electron beams to light up spots on a phosphor coating on the inside of the glass display, whereas LCD displays use a separate transistor for each pixel and use red, green and blue 'sub-pixel' elements to create each whole pixel.

PART ⑤ Upgrading keyboards

Keyboards take a pounding, sometimes literally, but they generally just keep on going. Nothing lasts forever, however, so eventually something will fail. Perhaps a key will only type when hit hard, or always type a run of characters whenever it is touched. Or perhaps the space bar, worn out from countless thumb-hits, starts to part company with the keyboard. When that happens it is probably time to get a new one. Have a quick look first though, as you may be able to fix it yourself.

Keyboards put up with a lot. Be prepared to give yours attention when it needs it, and it should keep working for many years to come.

Which kind?

Older Macs, the ones preceding the Blue & White Power Mac G3 and iMacs, all came with ADB for connecting keyboards and mice. ADB, which stands for Apple Desktop Bus, is a simple, round connector with just four pins. It looks exactly like an S-Video connector, and in fact ADB cables can be used for S-Video connections at a pinch. Obviously, you'll need to get the right kind of keyboard, ADB or USB, or you won't be able to use it with your Mac. But if you've added a USB card to an older Mac you can use any of the wide range of USB keyboards that are on the market. This is definitely easier than trying to source an ADB keyboard these days, although if you try you'll still find them here and there (see Second-hand? in this section).

Newer Macs and those with USB upgrade cards can use any USB keyboard you can find, although you shouldn't expect the Media Eject key to work with older machines, and the newest Apple keyboards lack a Power key. You might want to limit yourself to those intended for use with Mac, though, as the positioning of the Windows key on PC-specific keyboards is not only visually annoying, its action and position doesn't match up with what Mac users expect. In the models we've seen, the Windows key performs as the Apple key, but sits where we expect to find the option (or Alt) key. This isn't a real disaster, but if there is no software provided for remapping these two keys it does make moving between different keyboards a little tiresome. Using command keystrokes also involves folding the thumb uncomfortably under the hand, so we can't recommend this as a top-notch solution. Don't let us put you off completely, though, as there are many interesting things around such as wireless keyboards and mice which are often only made for PCs. You can use these perfectly well with any USB-enabled Mac, although remember that any non-standard buttons that need software to work won't make your Mac respond.

DIY repairs

If a key has simply come off its post it can be simplest to just glue it back on. Use a small dab of superglue or crazy glue, and be careful not to stick the whole thing together so that it doesn't move at all. If this does happen or your keyboard doesn't use separate spring-loaded posts for each key, you'll need to get hold of a replacement keyboard. (Well, strictly speaking you can disassemble any kind of keyboard to make mechanical repairs, but you'll probably end up with keyboard bits all over the place.)

If you've spilled a drink on your keyboard it isn't necessarily a total write-off, but you need to turn to p.168 (our Troubleshooting section) immediately.

If a key comes off your keyboard you may be able to fix it with the help of high-strength glue, but be careful not to make the key immobile.

Apple's newer keyboard designs include a full-size set of arrow keys as well as keys for ejecting CDs, changing the sound level and more.

PowerBooks and iBooks

If your troublesome keyboard is built into a laptop it can still be replaced, and not necessarily by shelling out large sums to have it done for you. You may have trouble persuading a dealer to sell you just the keyboard as they'd rather you booked it in for an engineer-led session. Stick at it, though, as it is not as hard as many think. It is, though, not a job for the ham-fisted; it involves removing and connecting a moderately delicate ribbon cable. To see what this means, shut the PowerBook or iBook down, pull back the two small tabs in the top row of the keyboard, and lift it up and back. (See Getting into a PowerBook or iBook on pages 26, 28 and 35 for details.) Now take a look at the cable which connects it to the Mac. Pay close attention to where it slots into the Mac itself; this is what has to be pulled out and replaced, and it mustn't be kinked or folded.

If you're still with us, relax. This isn't something anyone should do regularly, but it is still quite straightforward. Just make sure you get a replacement keyboard designed for your particular PowerBook or iBook model, as not all have the cable in quite the same place.

If you just want a larger format keyboard when working with your portable at a desk, all you have to do is get one that fits into the right port in your Mac. If your laptop is fitted with USB, get a USB keyboard. Otherwise you'll have to seek out an old ADB keyboard (see Second-hand? on the next page).

Which size?

Smaller keyboards take less room, but larger ones have a full complement of keys including a separate numeric keypad, full-size arrow keys and the Help, Forward-Delete, Home, End, Page Up and Page Down keys. PowerBooks and iBooks don't have a separate numeric keypad section, although they do have something called an 'embedded numeric keypad'. This simply means that a set of keys doubles up as these when a special modifier key is pressed; a clever solution but not particularly workable in practice.

The keyboards supplied with most iMacs are very much like those in PowerBooks and iBooks, except with a proper numeric keypad section for those who want it. The arrow keys are still half-height and tucked into the main body of keys however, which can be fiddly when playing games.

Apple's latest Pro Keyboard design stands head and shoulders above most other keyboards, with separate sections for every set of keys including a full size set of arrow keys. It also includes a set of volume control keys for turning sound up, down and off. It differs from all previous Apple keyboard designs in that there is no power key for starting the Mac up. Instead, this is done by the power button on the Mac itself. The key that takes its place is now the 'optical media eject' key; pressing this ejects anything in the CD or DVD drive, and pressing it again, with tray-based drives anyway, closes the drive again. If you have other optical

Replacing the keyboard in a PowerBook or iBook means dealing with the fragile ribbon cable. Be very careful not to damage it, or you'll have to replace this as well.

Apple's basic USB keyboard takes less room on a desk, but does cramp some of the keys into a smaller area. You may prefer to replace this with a larger model.

Ergonomic keyboards can help in alleviating and preventing hand and wrist strain, helping promote good hand positioning and providing wrist support. Older models such as the Apple Adjustable Keyboard will only work on Macs with ADB ports, such as the beige and the Blue & White G3s.

drives (CD or DVD) the key will control those too. This only works in the latest versions of the Mac OS, so check this first if your Mac doesn't seem to respond to these special keys.

Other keyboards from various different manufacturers can be used. There is a decent selection of Mac-specific third party keyboards available, but with USB you can use any USB keyboard made for PCs as well. The only problem with this is when there is no software for remapping the Windows and Alt keys. As we discussed earlier, this can be a little jarring, but still not a big problem. But without Macintosh software any extra keys for launching applications, logging on to the Internet, starting and stopping music players and so on just won't work. Still, not all keyboards are preoccupied with extra gizmos, and a number concentrate on offering different ergonomic designs for preventing and alleviating wrist strain, RSI and carpal tunnel syndrome.

Second-hand?

ADB keyboards aren't likely to be offered by many dealers any more, but you'll still find them wherever second-hand Macs are sold. Try the small ads in Macintosh magazines, get in touch with local Mac user groups, and check out online auction Web-sites. The old Apple Extended Keyboard II is widely regarded as the best of its day; well designed and very robust, and likely to still be going strong unless subjected to serious abuse. In contrast, the Apple Design range of keyboards were cheaper throughout, and aren't as likely to have so much life left in their keys. The Apple Adjustable Keyboard is also worth looking for; this is an ergonomically adjustable device with various different parts and wrist rests. The problem is that some parts are likely to be missing if bought second-hand.

Handwriting recognition

Apple's latest versions of Mac OS X supports a form of handwriting recognition, so users with devices such as cordless pen and tablet sets (see Cordless pen and tablet on p.127) can write naturally and end up with 'typed' text in their Mac. Don't think this is the end of the keyboard, however, as recognition levels aren't perfect. On top of this, once someone is used to using a keyboard they can be faster than all but the most manic of scribblers – and manic scribbles will be as hard for the Mac to interpret as they are for anyone else. But despite these caveats, handwriting recognition is a very intriguing alternative and might be helpful to those suffering from keyboard-strained wrists.

Wireless keyboards can be useful, and virtually all USB models will work with Macs to a reasonable degree. However, Windows-specific buttons generally don't function.

Writing text directly into your Mac can be done with Mac OS X's Ink technology, but it is still no substitute for learning to type at least passably well.

PART 5 Upgrading mice, trackballs and tablets

Mice are mechanically simple things, but they do wear out eventually. When they start playing up you'll find it hard to move smoothly or click things without effort, a very frustrating state of affairs.

There are two things that usually cause problems; the button itself and the mouse ball. Newer mice actually don't have the second problem, as most use LED movement sensors instead. The worst that can happen to those is a hair getting caught in the sensor; easily fixed with a quick puff. But those which still use balls need occasional cleaning to prevent movement from becoming bumpy and erratic. This is easy enough to fix: twist open the plate on the bottom and remove the ball, then use a fingernail or a cotton bud to remove the caked-on dirt from the roller wheels. Once this is done you should also clean the ball. See p.156 for more about cleaning.

If the mouse button starts to fail it can become hard to click properly, and it might 'let go' while you try to hold it down on things. If this happens it may be possible to fix it by taking it apart and seeing if the microswitch can be persuaded to click properly again. See if it has worn a groove which makes the contact less positive, and try smoothing that down. However, most new mice are cheap enough to make that more trouble than it is worth.

If you're using Apple's circular 'hockey puck' mouse as supplied with most iMacs you'll find a more traditional shape much easier to use. For those with USB the range on offer is enormous; virtually all mice today are USB, so they work with the Mac with no problem. If you need an ADB one, your work is cut out for you. Just as with ADB keyboards, you'll stand more chance of tracking one down in the second-hand market.

If a misbehaving mouse can't be fixed with a good clean, or you simply don't like the shape of the one you have, try a new one instead. Mice with two or more buttons and scroll wheels work automatically in Mac OS X and can be made to work in OS 8 and 9 as well. However, while some swear by them, they aren't strictly necessary.

One button or two?

Choosing a new mouse can be more complex than you might expect. Arguments usually revolve around the number of buttons a mouse should have. Whatever the arguments, two-button mice usually have the second button set to trigger contextual menus – those popup menus that appear under the mouse with choices tailored to the user's current situation.

Apple packs single-button mice with all of their Macs, and there is no part of the Mac OS or any program we've seen that actually requires a second button. In fact, in Mac OS 8 and 9, extra software is needed to use extra mouse buttons. The best software for this is called USB Overdrive, easily found via www.versiontracker.com, although some mice and trackballs may provide their own. Things are different with Mac OS X, as this supports mice with two buttons automatically and deals with scroll wheels too. Scroll wheels usually live between the buttons on two-button mice. Rolling this makes the active window scroll up or down without the user having to move the mouse at all. Some other mice have three, four or more buttons, but it can get tiring just trying to remember what all the buttons actually do.

Another choice is whether to go for cordless or with tail. Cordless mice use infra-red connections (which need to maintain line-of-sight with the sensor attached to the Mac) or wireless connections (which can often work a whole room away, great for presentations). Whichever kind you pick they will need their own batteries, so make sure you have a spare for when they fail.

Some mice are made in odd shapes, designed to fit the user's hand. This is all very well if you're right-handed, but if not you'll find most of them rather uncomfortable.

Trackballs and pens

Mice aren't the only pointing devices you can use. Trackballs are like mice turned on their backs, with the ball being rolled around by finger and thumb. You don't have to paw the tabletop as you do with a regular mouse, and some trackballs come with all sorts of buttons and wheels to add extra controls. They aren't ideal for graphics-based work, but many users find them very useful. When shopping for a trackball, look for places where there's a model on display that you can try out. You'll not only want to make sure it fits and feels comfortable in your hand, but also check whether the rolling action suits you – some are very fluid, others stiff.

Cordless pens and tablets are another alternative worth trying. These are excellent for drawing and painting, and when used in the right programs they can translate different pressures into heavier or lighter brushstrokes. They aren't quite as good as mice for general navigation around the screen, so you may still need to use a mouse from time to time.

Sometimes a mouse is a terrible way to use a computer, especially when playing games. For the best experience with console-style games and flight simulators try using joysticks and joypads instead.

Trackballs are like inverted mice, where the user rolls the ball around directly with their finger and thumb. They aren't at all suited for graphic work but can be perfect for more general business use and where space is limited.

For serious graphic work try a cordless pen and tablet. These can mimic pens, pencils and brushes astonishingly well, using varying pressure on the pad to change the on-screen behaviour.

PART 5 Adding or upgrading a printer

Printing is something everyone needs to do from time to time. It may be an important report, some photos, a corporate spreadsheet or layout samples, but getting it onto paper is the important thing. You may have a printer already but aren't happy with the results.

Inkjet printers come in many shapes and sizes and from many different manufactturers, but be sure it supports the Mac before buying.

First make sure whether your existing printer, if you have one, does need to be replaced. Inkjet printers sometimes require a head cleaning cycle to keep the output up to scratch. Don't do this often, however, as it can use a lot of ink. If it produces poor, horizontally streaked prints this is probably because of low ink or clogged nozzles. Either way it is time to change the cartridges, as the heads are generally built into these. Some printers use print heads that are separate from the cartridges. If the problem is clogged nozzles (something that can happen if the printer is left unused for a while) then the printer itself may need replacing.

When laser printers make streaked prints it is either because of a damaged or dirty exposure drum or because of low toner. The drum may be part of the toner unit, but it is usually a separate item. If there's no low toner indicator showing in the printer's information panel, try removing the consumable items and giving them a quick blow to shift trapped fluff or grit. If this fails, replace the toner cartridge, the exposure drum or both.

Which kind of printer?

Virtually all printers are either inkjet or laser. Modern inkjets print colour as standard, while laser printers come in both colour and black and white formats. Picking the right technology is important; an inkjet printer will be too slow for a busy group of users, while a laser printer won't do digital photos justice.

If the printer is meant for a network then most inkjets are out simply because they are personal devices. For razor-sharp text and fast printing you need a laser printer, and for desktop publishing get a printer with PostScript support (see PostScript on p.130), which again rules out most inkjets.

If you want to print convincing colour photos, inkjet printers will give better results than a laser. If you're not interested in networking the printer or in fast, high volume printing, and if you'd rather keep initial costs down, inkjets win again.

Relative costs

Inkjet printers are cheaper to buy but more expensive to run in the long term. They aren't designed for very high print volumes, and ink cartridges and high quality inkjet paper remain fairly expensive. If you're shopping for a busy network go for laser.

Inkjets generally have separate black and colour cartridges so you don't throw everything away when the black runs out, and some offer separate tanks for each colour. For the best photographic output look for a 'photo' printer. These are 6-colour models which use special light versions of cyan and magenta (blue and red) as well as the standard colours. The result is smoother delicate shades, although print times can be longer. Laser printers use either a single black toner cartridge or separate cartridges for each colour. These should last for thousands of pages, compared with just hundreds for inkjets.

You can find DIY kits for refilling inkjet cartridges with cheap ink, but doing this can void your printer's warranty and may give an inferior print quality. Refilled toner cartridges for laser printers can be found, and can be reliable. However, as they weren't built to be refilled you may see toner speckles and fuzzy output.

Printer resolution

Printer resolution is the level of detail a printer can manage, and is measured in dots per inch, or dpi. With both inkjets and lasers, 600dpi should be the lowest resolution you consider. Higher resolutions, 1200dpi and better, mean clearer images, although the difference is harder to spot in text on ordinary paper.

Look out for printers that use interpolated resolutions, for example offering '1200dpi-class output' while the engine is actually a 600dpi device. This isn't a con as results can be very good, but it isn't quite the same. Also watch out for a difference between a printer's horizontal and vertical resolutions. A 1200x600dpi printer is basically a 600dpi one with a clever way of drawing on the page. Again, good, but not the real thing.

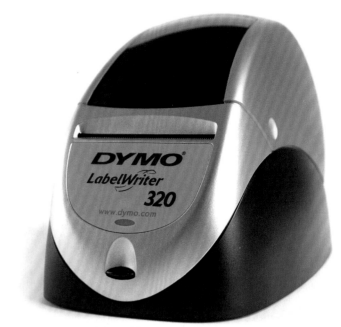

Specialist printers such as this label printing device can make some tasks simpler than with regular desktop printers.

Printer speeds

Take printer manufacturers' page-per-minute speeds with a pinch of salt. Such figures usually refer to raw printer engine speeds, but unless you just print plain text the longest part of a print job is the processing. Inkjets can also run in different quality modes, so speeds are usually based on draft mode. You're unlikely to like the way this looks, so the figures will not be much help.

Printer memory

Memory is completely unimportant for most inkjets, but a key issue for laser printers. PostScript processing requires a lot of memory to store the page image as it is rendered. An A4 600dpi mono laser printer can scrape by with 4MB of RAM for basic work, but higher resolutions, larger pages, graphics and especially colour output all need more memory. Consider 32MB a minimum for a colour PostScript printer. Formats aren't always standard, so check the requirements of any PostScript printer you consider and find out how much memory upgrades cost.

Paper formats

Support for thicker paper and envelopes varies according to the individual printer model, but inkjets do generally handle this better. Some printers can handle bigger paper sizes than the standard US Letter/A4 formats, so if you need to print out large layouts or massive spreadsheets, an 11x17 inch or A3 printer, either laser or inkjet, could be just the job. If you need pages even bigger than this then you should look at specific large format printers. These usually print on rolls of paper rather than cut sheets, and output is generally over a metre wide (more than a yard) by as long as necessary.

Small format devices such as label printers aren't common, but they do exist. If you need to print labels it can be simpler to use sheets of Avery labels or the equivalent in a standard printer.

Inkjet cartridges can run out after just a few dozen full-page photo prints, so have some spares handy.

Connection formats

Virtually all of today's inkjet printers connect using USB, while most laser printers connect directly to Ethernet networks. A few inkjets also have Ethernet support while some laser printers have USB sockets, but this isn't the norm. Basically, if you're running a Mac without USB your options are distinctly limited. Serial inkjet printers, the Macintosh standard before USB arrived, are simply non-existent now, so all that's left is the Ethernet network connection. This normally means a laser printer, which may or may not be what you're after. If necessary, a USB expansion card upgrade (see USB and FireWire on p.102) would let you choose from the current range of USB-based printers. You won't be able to use a parallel printer without a hardware and software converter. This is a viable option; Strydent's PowerPrint products do exactly this. However, things are best kept simple by using printers designed to work with Macs directly or across networks.

Use the Chooser to set up new laser printers in Mac OS 8 and 9. Use the Select PPD button if this isn't picked up automatically.

In Mac OS X the Print Center is used to set up and manage all printers. If your laser printer isn't automatically recognised you may need to select the PPD file manually.

Installing

It is best to choose a printer which offers specific support for the Mac OS version that you're running, particularly if it isn't a PostScript device. Run the software installer provided with the printer to get things set up, then check in the Chooser (in Mac OS 8 and 9) or the Print Center (in Mac OS X) to choose it as your preferred printer and do any necessary setting up. Many inkjet printers are supported by Mac OS X without any extra software, but some require (and should include) installers.

Networked PostScript laser printers can be used without any extra software in any version of the Mac OS; just pick them in the Chooser or the Print Center. However, to use special features such as duplex or multiple trays, an appropriate PPD file (short for PostScript Printer Description) must be assigned. For Mac OS 8 and 9 users, if one is available, drop it into the Printer Descriptions folder inside the System Folder's Extensions folder. Then pick Chooser from the Apple menu, select LaserWriter 8, pick your printer on the right, and click Create. Pick the PPD file from the list if necessary, and your Mac will now know all about the printer. Mac OS X users should run the Print Center utility, click Add Printer, and select the right one from the list. Pick Other from the Printer Model popup menu (if your printer isn't shown) and pick the PPD file from wherever you stored it.

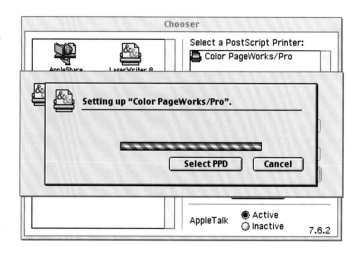

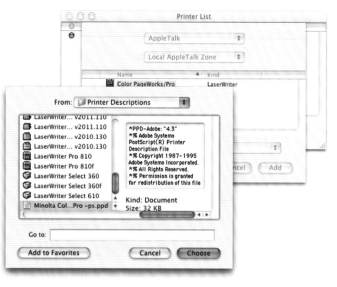

PART 5 Adding or upgrading a scanner

You need a scanner to get existing photos and drawings into your Mac. There are different kinds available, but the most common, and generally the best, is the ordinary flat-bed. These range from slim-line to bulky enough to demand its own desk, but they all work in the same way. An original is placed on a glass plate and a combined light source and sensor is moved along beneath. The reflected light is used to build up the image.

Most flatbed scanners have an image area of around A4 or US Letter, enough to scan a page of a magazine (see copyright issues panel). Some scanners may not quite handle a full page, so check the maximum scan area dimensions before you buy. Some handle larger formats, but these are for the professional market and are expensive; often more than the cost of the fastest Power Mac. You can scan large items in parts and stitch them together in photo-editing software, but this isn't a serious solution.

A flatbed scanner can be an incredibly useful device. Be sure to get one that suits your needs.

Interface

Mac-compatible scanners connect using SCSI, USB or FireWire. At the lower end most are USB devices, so you'll need a spare USB port in your Mac or in a USB hub. It can be cheaper to get a USB expansion card (see USB upgrades on p.102) and one of these scanners than to go for a higher priced SCSI model. FireWire and SCSI are generally used in mid- and high-end units. Finally, treat your scanner carefully. Most of the slimmer USB units are not designed to be repaired, and have cases which are not particularly rigid. Uneven surfaces (such as with a drink mat under one corner) can, over time, distort the case. This can lead to unfocused, fuzzy scans and even a jammed scanner.

Scanner software

You'll need the software that comes with your scanner to get it working. This will be either a custom program or a plugin module for Adobe Photoshop or another plugin-compatible image editor. If you want scans for home printing or e-mailing then you won't need to do much editing; use the basic preview and adjustment controls and go for it. If you want more control Photoshop is the industry favourite, but the masking and colour correction options can be daunting. Photoshop Elements is easier (and cheaper) without being underpowered, while Photoshop LE is dated but still useful. Software bundles can add real value to the package.

If you use a plugin scanner module you'll scan from within Photoshop, Photoshop Elements or a similar program. Scans are taken straight into the main program ready to be cropped, sharpened and so on. This is the preferred method for designers.

If you use Mac OS X, make sure the scanner you buy works in this. Not all do, even now, but fortunately VueScan, from **www.hamrick.com**, handles most scanners in Mac OS X.

Cheap scanners can give very good results, at least for home use, and they tend to be simpler than more expensive models. But if you need scans for commercial work then treat cheap scanners with caution. Results can look pleasing on screen and in inkjet prints, but may not look so good in professional use.

'One button' scanning, where a button on the scanner starts the process and even passes the result to a different program, is the hallmark of a consumer product. If you need to pick specific scan resolutions and care about things such as setting white and black points this isn't likely to appeal. But for those who want an easy life, this kind of hardware trick can be just the ticket.

Scanner resolution and colour depth

A scanned image is nothing more than a bitmap image, a picture made up of tiny squares (pixels) in a grid. The resolution is simply the number of pixels per linear inch; a one inch square image scanned at 600 pixels per inch (ppi) will show more detail than the image scanned at 100 pixels per inch, although both will print at the same size. It will also take more disk space and take longer to print, so a higher resolution isn't always good.

Resolution is often touted as a scanner's vital statistic, but this can be misleading. A scanner will have two different maximum resolutions; the optical resolution, and a higher 'interpolated' resolution. You get no more detail when you scan higher than your scanner's optical resolution, the scan is just resampled into one with more pixels. If you do need to scan at 1200ppi, maybe to greatly enlarge scanned logos and similar artwork, then don't pick one with a 600ppi optical resolution. If you'll only be scanning old photos don't spend extra to get the highest resolution, as there's a limit to perceivable detail in the originals.

Colour depth is not something you generally need to worry about. Every scanner will give at least 24-bit colour, which means it deals with roughly 16.8 million hues and shades. Many scanners scan at higher bit depths, but unless you're a graphics professional you won't work with this level of colour yourself. Anyway, virtually every scanner delivers 24-bit colour images whatever their top colour depth. Greyscale scanning (the equivalent of black and white photography) will be an option, as will be 'real' black and white, without grey tones at all.

Scanned images are made up of an array of pixels. If the resolution is high the image looks clean and sharp, but if it is low the pixels can become clearly apparent. Remember that what looks good on your screen will often look crude and low-resolution in print.

TECHIE CORNER
Scanner plugins
A scanner plugin, or 'image acquisition module', is a small program meant to be used from within a major program such as Photoshop. To use this, look in the Import menu item in Photoshop's File menu. (For other programs see the software's manual for where to find the scanner plugin.) Pick the appropriate item, either the scanner's name or the name of the scanning software, and you'll be presented with a window with scanning controls. When you've previewed, cropped and scanned, the result will be passed to the host program — usually Photoshop — for final optimising and editing.

OCR

If you simply scan a page of text it won't come out as editable words, you'll just get a simple picture of the page ready for painting over in something like Photoshop. If you want to end up with real text instead, you need to use a process called Optical Character Recognition, or OCR for short. Your scanner may have included an OCR program such as OmniPage or TextBridge, otherwise you can buy one separately. These won't give you perfect results every time. They rely on having clean originals, so faxes and fuzzy prints don't help. An OCR program's '99% accuracy' claim means 99% of characters, not words, are recognised, so perhaps 1 in 15 words will have an incorrect letter. Spelling checkers can help catch many of these, but OCR isn't the magic bullet that some believe it to be.

OCR software can save hours of boring retyping, but be prepared to make minor corrections with most documents.

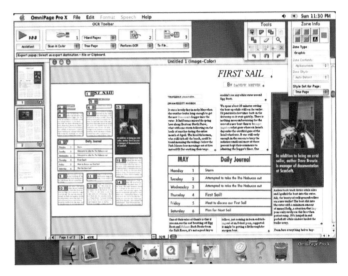

Hardware extras

There are a couple of scanner features that might be available as an optional extra. One is an automatic document feeder, enabling a stack of paper to be placed into a holder and scanned one by one. This option is pretty rare, and can be prone to jamming.

The transparency adaptor on the other hand is quite common, and may be supplied automatically as a permanent part of the scanner. This is either a chunky scanner lid having its own built-in light source which moves in parallel with the scanner's sensors, or a flat, illuminated pad which sits over the transparency. In either case, the transparency, or slide, is illuminated from behind so that it can be scanned. If you deal with medium or large format transparencies, a transparency adaptor can give pretty good results, but don't expect too much from 35mm slides. These are simply too small for a general-purpose scanner to resolve cleanly, and slides in mounts may be fractionally out of focus as well. If you need to scan 35mm slides often then a dedicated slide scanner may be a good investment.

Installing

Installing a scanner is done in two parts; connecting the hardware and installing the software. The hardware is simple; plug in the USB or FireWire cable, or shut down and plug in the SCSI cable, depending on what kind of scanner you have. Restart if necessary, then put the scanner's installer CD in the drive and double-click the installer program to get the software properly installed on your Mac. You may be asked to help find the Photoshop Plugins folder; this should be inside the Photoshop, Photoshop LE or Photoshop Elements program folder. If you haven't installed this you should go back and do so now. Otherwise ignore this and use the regular scanner software as shown in the scanner's instruction manual.

TECHIE CORNER

Copyright issues

You can scan absolutely anything you can fit onto the glass bed of your scanner. Most scanner lids come off or have flexible hinges, so you can even scan pages from bulky books without cutting them out first. But this doesn't mean you have the legal right to use any image you find. If you want something for totally personal use such as a birthday card then you're pretty safe in practice, although still technically breaking copyright regulations. But as soon as you start using scans in public or professional ways you're in a whole new ball game. If in doubt, check with the copyright owner before using something. Even if you plan to alter an image a lot, you need to sort out permission for copyright pictures.

PART ⑤ Internet connection

Whether it is for fun or work, Internet access is important to almost everyone. There are a number of ways to get your Mac online, so you'll need to decide what sort of Internet use you want (occasional, high-speed and so on), how much you want to spend, and which connection type seems the best.

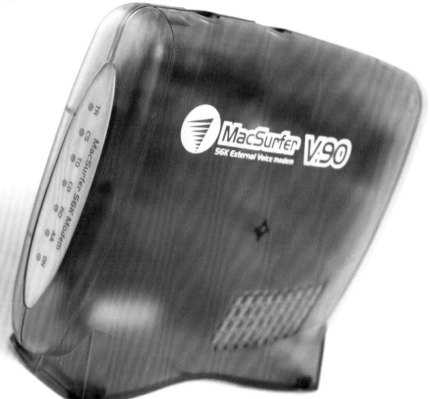

A 56Kbps v.90-class modem is the minimum you should use for Internet access.

Modems

Getting online is pretty much essential for most people these days. You do this via a modem. It will be either built into your Mac, in which case you'll have a small US-style telephone socket (look for a telephone handset graphic) sitting next to the other sockets in the Mac, or you will have to fit one externally, in which case you'll plug it into a serial or USB port, depending on your Mac's age.

If your Mac doesn't have any USB sockets you'll need to use a modem designed for serial connections and a Macintosh serial cable to link the modem with your Mac. Macintosh serial connections are small and circular, and the one marked with the small telephone handset symbol is the one intended for use with modems. Finding a modem which connects via a Macintosh serial port won't be particularly easy, so consider adding a USB card, if possible, so you can use a more common USB modem.

Once the modem is connected you'll need to tell the Mac which kind it is, either via the Modem control panel in Mac OS

8 and 9, or by choosing the Network pane in the System Preferences of OS X, picking the modem option from the 'Show' popup menu, then clicking the Modem tab. Pick the appropriate modem from the popup menu list, and you're done. If you don't see the right entry in this list then you'll need to install the modem description file that came with the device. In Mac OS 8 and 9 this goes in the Modem Scripts folder, found in the Extensions folder within the System Folder. In Mac OS X this goes in the Modem Scripts folder within the Library folder.

Modem expansion cards are available for PCs, but these are designed for a kind of slot not built into Macs and so can't be used. Apple made some Power Mac models without internal modems, and one or two manufacturers did produce small modem cards for the empty slot inside these Macs. These aren't the same as other modem cards, and you'll probably have more luck finding a regular external USB modem anyway.

Broadband Internet

If high-speed, permanent Internet access – ultra-fast downloads, smooth video playback – is more your thing, you need broadband. This comes in the form of a cable modem from your local cable TV provider or ADSL from a regular Internet service provider. Most broadband services include the hardware you need as part of the package, so the decision is usually more about what kind of service you need. The basic kind of connection is meant for a single Mac (or PC) and any cable modem or home-use ADSL solution will cover this – and it is usually the cheapest option available.

A 'wires only' broadband connection is generally cheapest, but you'll need to provide the ADSL connection hardware yourself. This will be either a USB ADSL modem or, preferably, an Ethernet ADSL router. You'll also need ADSL telephone socket 'filters' to use with your telephones. The ADSL service is provided via your regular telephone wiring, but it must be connected to an exchange which supports ADSL, and you'll also have to have it enabled for your line. Once done, all that's needed is the regular Internet access setup, and as with any broadband configuration this is done as a form of network-based Internet access. To check availability of ADSL broadband in your area of the UK, try www.bt.com/broadband/, where you can check either with your BT phone number or your postcode. A lot of detailed information about current access packages and hardware is available at www.adslguide.org.uk/ and www.dslsource.co.uk/

If you are served by a cable company, there are postcode checkers at:

www.blueyonder.co.uk/
www.telewest.co.uk/packagedesigner/
www.ntl.com/locales/gb/en/home/ask/

Broadband Internet access, whether via ADSL or cable, makes using the Internet a much faster and easier process.

ISDN

ISDN (Integrated Services Digital Network) used to be the high-speed connection method of choice, but it can't even begin to match broadband speeds unless many separate ISDN lines are linked together; a very expensive proposition indeed. It does have one distinct advantage, however; it is available to a much wider number of people. You may not be able to use broadband connections because you're too far from an enabled telephone exchange, but you can probably still take advantage of ISDN to get noticeably faster speeds than via plain old modems. You'll need a cheap ISDN TA (short for Terminal Adaptor), not an expensive ISDN PCI card; those are great for point-to-point connections with other ISDN users, but not for general Internet use. Hermsted's WebShuttle is a simple USB-based ISDN device which does this job with very little fuss. Note that telephone lines which have been set up for ISDN use must be 'downgraded' for broadband, so if you have a choice, consider broadband first.

PART ⑤ Upgrading speakers

If all you listen to are system beeps and your Mac's start-up chime then the built-in speakers are going to be fine. But if you'd like to listen to music while you work, use your Mac as an MP3 jukebox, or just get more realistic game sounds, you need a set of speakers.

Okay, the speakers built into iMacs aren't exactly bad, especially when compared with those built into other Macs. But they still aren't really up to scratch when it comes to pushing rich sounds out at a decent volume. The G4 Cube came with separate globe-style speakers which were surprisingly good, but any other Mac will benefit greatly from something better.

There are two main ways you can go to get your Mac amplified. The most common approach is to add a set of amplified speakers designed for computers. These are generally a huge improvement over the average Mac's built-in speaker, but beware of the cheaper offerings; poor add-on speakers won't make music sound much better at all.

The alternative involves connecting your Mac up to a regular hi-fi, just as if it was a regular add-in component like a radio or CD unit. You'll need the right cabling to do this, and it will need to be long enough to stretch to the stereo without getting in the way. See Techie Corner for details.

The speakers supplied with most flat-screen iMacs give surprisingly good sound.

Where to connect

The sound-out connection in virtually every Mac is a standard 3.5mm minijack socket, the same as any portable headphones plug. This is hidden at the back in all older Macs and newer Power Macs as well. The classic iMac models have headphone sockets on the front and in the ports recess in the right side; use the one on the side for more permanent connections. The new eMac just has the headphone socket in the ports recess on the right, while the flat screen iMac has all its sockets arranged around the base of the hemisphere body, at the back.

PowerBooks and iBooks have very compact speakers and would benefit a lot from better sound reproduction. However, portable items aren't meant to be tied down to lots of cables, so this isn't such a convenient thing to attempt. If you do want to use your portable Mac as a desktop replacement, you can get a docking station. These stay connected to your peripherals all the time, and the PowerBook or iBook docks with this in one step.

Connecting your Mac's sound output to a hi-fi can be as simple as getting the right lead.

Hi-fi Separates

Using a regular hi-fi amplifier rather than a set of dedicated amplified speakers means treating your Mac as just another component in the hi-fi setup. You'll need to have a regular 'separates' kind of audio system; the average self-contained music centre won't do. You'll also need to find a free set of inputs, probably a pair of RCA phono sockets. This will usually be the amplifier's 'Aux' connection, but in most cases any will do. Don't use any sockets marked 'out', as this is for passing audio to the record channels of a tape deck. This won't harm your Mac, but playback won't work as planned either. (If you want to record audio to your Mac then plug the amplifier's 'tape out' through to the microphone input in the Mac. You'll need to use the appropriate recording software and work out the right sound levels, but this will solve the basic connection issues.)

Use a cable which has a regular 3.5mm stereo minijack plug on one end and whatever the amplifier needs (almost certainly a pair of phono plugs) on the other. If you need a particularly long cable, a standard phono extension should do the trick, but don't skimp on cable quality or the final sound really can be affected.

USB audio

The iBook and G4 Cube introduced a new problem. These don't have any traditional analogue audio sockets at all. A USB audio connection passes the audio signal digitally, so to connect speakers (or a microphone for that matter) USB-ready audio hardware or a USB digital to analogue converter must be used. The G4 Cube provides this as part of the external speaker set that comes with the Mac, but others don't. The good news is that there is a growing number of USB speaker-amplifier kits around, many of them with good support for digital sound modification and control. You can use them with any USB-equipped Mac, although you'll need a very recent version of the Mac OS and quite possibly Mac-compatible driver software designed for the amp as well.

USB audio issues aside, every powered speaker setup will come with the right cable for connecting to your Mac. They may not come with a particularly long cable, so you may have to rethink the speaker positions or get an appropriate extension cable (3.5mm stereo minijack extension lead) from a hi-fi shop.

Sub-woofers are dedicated bass units that drive just the lower, deeper parts of the sound you hear. They generally sit on the floor and are meant to flesh out the audio. They are usually teamed with satellite speakers, smaller but fully-capable items which deliver the mid and upper sound ranges.

Pick the speaker positions carefully, as this will affect the stereo impact considerably. Surround sound and home cinema speaker setups use four and five satellite speakers respectively. However, you'll have to use a USB audio setup or a specialist multi-channel sound card to make full use of these extra channels or you'll just get regular stereo from the various speakers. Make sure your Mac is ready for such stuff before bringing it home.

Some of the better bits of kit will use a separate amplifier to drive the speakers, and some have a number of satellite speakers teamed up with a large sub-woofer. It is possible to spend almost as much as an iMac on a studio monitor-quality speakers and amp set, but most people will reach audio nirvana without shelling out anywhere near that much.

Dedicated computer speaker systems require their own power source to drive an integrated amplifier. The better systems can rival the output of regular hi-fi systems.

PART 5 PERIPHERALS
MP3 players

MP3 (short for MPEG layer 3, the sound component of DVD video) is a file format used to store audio in a highly compressed form. This dry-sounding explanation describes something that's been taking the music world by storm. MP3 files are used to store music at good quality ready to be played back from computers and, more important for most people, from pocket-sized MP3 players. Strictly speaking, getting an MP3 player is more like upgrading a portable cassette player, but these are very popular items which need to connect to a computer to be filled with MP3 files.

Apple's iPod has set the standard for MP3 players; look at this before buying any other device.
(Image courtesy of Apple)

There are a number of different kinds of MP3 player that can be used. The most popular type uses built-in or removable memory, either a tiny hard disk or a form of 'Flash-RAM' memory, for storing tracks. Some, however, are more like portable CD players, reading MP3 files from home-recorded CD-Rs. These aren't regular audio-format CDs, they are made as a specific kind of computer data CD, and as the MP3 format easily manages to compress audio at 10:1 or more, a single CD can hold at least ten hours of music.

The best MP3 player on the market is without a doubt Apple's iPod. This is a small white and silver device which can hold many thousands of tracks, with one of the clearest controllers around. It links with Apple's free iTunes and Panic Software's Audion MP3 software, making the task of managing the player's contents a snap. It connects and recharges via FireWire, so copying music is incredibly fast, and you're unlikely to run out of battery life. Its storage is equally generous as, unlike competing products, the iPod boasts an internal hard disk, starting at 10GB and rising with its price. This allows it to be used as a stand-alone portable FireWire hard drive, and, provided you have the right flavour of OS, you can also get it to display (but not edit) contact and calendar details from your Mac's Adress Book and iCal. The iPod is certainly one of the more expensive players, though, so you may want to try one of the many alternatives. The one thing to look out for is, if the player has its own built-in storage, whether it specifically supports the Mac. If not, then you simply won't be able to get your tracks onto the device. If it uses some kind of removable memory card, all you need is an appropriate memory card reader, and, of course, the CD-based players require a CD writer, either your own or built into the player, to make your custom discs.

Sound quality

The sound quality of MP3 players varies, with the higher-priced units generally leading the pack. If you want to get the best from any player do get yourself a better set of headphones than the ones that come with the player. Even the ones supplied with the iPod aren't a match for a high-end set of headphones, but you'll have to spend at least as much as half a dozen chart CDs for truly great ones.

MP3 tracks are usually encoded (or 'ripped' as it is usually called) directly from audio CDs, although some encoding software can also work with sound-in connections for recording from vinyl records, tape and live sources. MP3 audio is compressed using one of a small number of techniques and to a chosen per-second data rate. The techniques work in slightly different ways but they all produce regular MP3 tracks, so don't get too worried about this aspect. The data rate is certainly worth thinking about, however. This is shown as a kilobytes-per-second figure, meaning simply how much data is used to store a second's worth of audio; higher rates give larger files but more accurate sound. Most people regard 128kbps to 160kbps (kilobits per second) to be a good balance between file size and audio quality. This delivers very clear results at about 1MB per minute of stereo music, or 3MB to 4MB for an average single.

The most widely-used MP3 program on the Mac is iTunes, free from Apple at **www.apple.com/itunes**. This helps organise and play MP3s as well as rip tracks from audio CDs, and optionally show psychedelic visuals pulsing in time with music. A higher-end, although commercial, alternative is Audion, from **www.panic.com**. This gives more flexible control over MP3 file storage, playback and ripping, and includes visual effects as well.

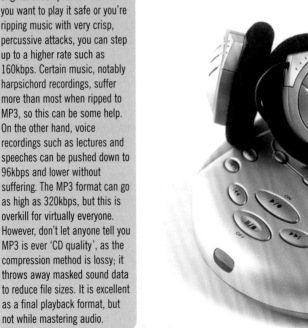

MP3 players come in all shapes and sizes, from this hard disk-based device to ones the size of key fobs.

PART **5** Music creation

Music production has always been one of the Mac's strengths. From composition and sequencing to sampling and mastering, high-end and low-end, there's something for everyone.

The industry is steadily moving towards software-only solutions, at least for dealing with audio once it is in the Mac. But there are still many useful hardware solutions, particularly for mixing and linking with MIDI instruments. Look for USB and FireWire options, as older serial connections are unlikely to remain compatible with newer versions of the Mac OS.

You can turn your Mac into the equivalent of a fully-fledged recording studio, all with some software and the right bits of hardware. In fact, many professional musicians prefer to use their Macs for most of their work. To turn your Mac into a virtual sound studio you'll need some kind of instrument, the right connection between that and the computer, and sequencing software to help record, adjust and arrange your music.

The first thing to sort out is how to connect your instrument to the Mac. You can simply record audio direct to disk – this is how to handle vocals for instance. But for the most flexibility you should use a MIDI instrument (also known as a MIDI controller), linked via a MIDI interface box to your Mac. The instrument is most likely to be a keyboard, but it could be a drum machine, MIDI guitar, and so on.

TECHIE CORNER

Simple sound
If you just want to record a snatch of sound and don't want to get into sequencing, laying down multiple tracks or other audio processing, then Audion from Panic software (see MP3 on page 139) is the simplest option. This can record from any sound input source – microphone, line-in, CD, Internet radio streams and more – straight to disk in MP3 format. There's even a built-in MP3 track editor which is useful for trimming off unwanted sections from the sound file afterwards. The results can be used as a movie soundtrack or voiceover, in a PowerPoint presentation, in a Web-based Flash movie, and anywhere else that can use sound files.

The Quattro from Midiman records audio from microphones and guitars as well as connecting to MIDI instruments.

Steinberg's Midex 3 is a simple MIDI interface which works exceptionally well with Cubase, although it will also work with other sequencer programs.

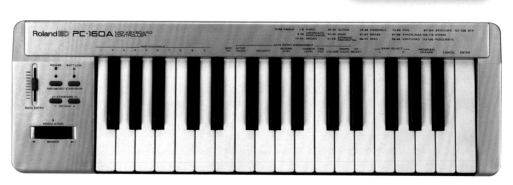

You'll need a MIDI interface, almost certainly one which connects via USB. There are many different models to choose from, so before you pick your MIDI interface, work out how many in and out connections you need. Each MIDI connection provides 16 individual channels for passing information back and forth, but all 16 can easily be taken up by a single synthesizer. If you only want to use a single device with your Mac, a basic 1x1 or, preferably, a 2x2 interface (two MIDI inputs and two outputs) will be all you need. However, if you want to use more instruments at once, and possibly add sound modules to extend your repertoire of sounds, get an interface with more connections.

If you're not running Mac OS X you'll need to install OMS (Opcode's Open Music System), a free program available from www.opcode.com, which helps different MIDI programs and instruments talk to each other. This works best with Mac OS 8.6

The Roland PC-160A is a one-piece keyboard and MIDI interface, and includes a copy of Cubase.

and earlier, so you might be better off with Mac OS X instead; this supports MIDI directly without the need for OMS.

To record the notes you play and then to help you arrange and sequence multiple tracks, you'll need a sequencer program. This is the virtual equivalent of a traditional tape deck in a recording studio, but it is also much more flexible. MIDI tracks can be edited in all sorts of ways, from transposing notes (fixing any slips you may have made) to switching to completely different instrument sounds altogether. There are a number of sequencer programs available, but the industry's favourites are Pro Tools (www.digidesign.com), Logic Audio (www.emagic.de, now owned by Apple), Digital Performer (www.motu.com), and CuBase (www.steinberg.com). For more budget-friendly options try Cubasis (www.steinberg.com), Freestyle (www.motu.com), or Pro Tools Free (www.digidesign.com). Alternatively, Band-In-A-Box (www.bandinabox.com/band.htm) provides a whole band of virtual session musicians to play with you, and can be excellent for learning to play different music styles.

If possible, choose your sequencer software first and see if there are any MIDI interfaces specifically recommended for that. For example, Steinberg Cubase sequencer software works particularly well with Steinberg's Midex MIDI interfaces. Alternatively, you could choose a combined MIDI keyboard and interface. The Roland PC-160A is a good package if you want to get up and running quickly, as it combines the MIDI interface with a 32-key keyboard and includes a copy of Cubase as well.

The MIDI sounds themselves are produced from sampled clips. These can be entirely software-based, and indeed your Mac has a reasonably good set of samples built in, courtesy of Roland and QuickTime; this is called QuickTime Musical Instruments, and can be used to play back MIDI music without any other assistance. If your instrument has samples built in – fairly likely in the case of keyboards – you can pick that instead, using the appropriate controls in your sequencer program. Alternatively, install separate software modules, and you'll have access to eerily accurate replicas of classic instruments. For example Steinberg's Pro-Five puts the classic Sequential Circuits Prophet 5 analogue synthesizer (as played by bands from Herbie Hancock to the Rolling Stones) at your fingertips.

Sequencer programs will provide audio mixing tools galore, but if you want to mix and match recorded audio with live sounds, a hardware mixer might be best. This will provide a set of sliders for controlling individual track volume and balance, and some will also control functions in your sequencing software directly. Once you've finished your track you can save it in a form for recording to CD or using in an MP3 player. If you want to produce a professional master for production you'll need to use digital-out hardware rather than simply record from the sound-out ports in the Mac. You can get dedicated PCI cards for this task, but the latest solutions are generally external FireWire or USB devices. Digidesign's Digi 002 (www.digidesign.com) is a 96kHz 24-bit device with analog, digital, optical and MIDI interfaces, plus controllers for mixing and even controlling Pro Tools sequencing software. At the simpler end of things, Edirol's UA-1D (www.edirol.com) is a basic USB digital in/out device with coaxial and optical connectors; much simpler, but also much cheaper. Hook up your DAT recorder to the digital interface and put your sounds onto tape, ready for production.

Pro Tools Free offers surprisingly powerful music mixing features and works like the high-end commercial Pro Tools package.

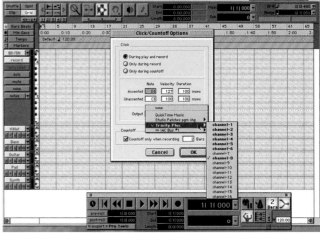

TECHIE CORNER

MIDI and digital audio
MIDI isn't music as such, it is the language spoken by synthesizers. It tells the synthesizer what kind of sound to make rather than sending the sound itself. For example, MIDI information for a piano track will identify the type of piano samples to use, any special treatments to apply, which keys to play at which moments, and exactly how hard and how long each note is to be played. The information is used by whatever receives it to recreate the sounds, using its own piano sound samples. Digital audio on the other hand stores sound on disk, faithfully replicating every aspect of the audio waveforms ready to be played back at will like a virtual tape recorder. These different audio formats can be used together using multi-track sequencer programs, so musicians can mix and match as they wish.

PART ⑤ Digital cameras

Digital cameras are much more convenient than traditional film cameras. Most cameras include a built-in screen for showing shots the moment they are taken, and you can get an inkjet printout within a minute or two of plugging the camera into your Mac.

Apple's free iPhoto software works with the vast majority of digital cameras, and provides an excellent way to file, correct and even deliver your photos.

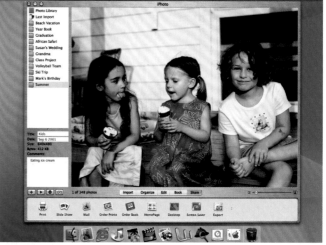

You'll need to either pick one with Mac support, preferably iPhoto support if you're using Mac OS X, or one which uses removable memory cards. Memory cards can always be handled with a simple card reader even if the camera itself doesn't have the right software.

If you're using Mac OS X then you should definitely use Apple's free iPhoto software to download and manage your shots, as there's no bundled camera software that can beat this. See **www.apple.com/iphoto** for details. For a more flexible if less consumer-friendly file management tool try iView MediaPro, from **www.iview-multimedia.com**. It works well for organising other forms of media as well, from sound and movie clips to DTP graphics and fonts.

One thing to watch with digital cameras is their battery life. Buy at least one set of rechargeable batteries when you get your camera, as you can end up spending more on disposable batteries than you would on traditional film developing and printing. The LCD panels are the biggest drain on batteries, so limit your use of this whenever you can.

Megapixels

The standard measure of a camera's resolution is megapixels, an impressive-sounding term which simply means how many pixels in total an image can have. This in turn affects how large a photo can be printed before it starts to look noticeably pixellated, so higher megapixel ratings are generally better. A camera which can shoot pictures which are roughly 2000x1500 pixels is a 3 megapixel camera, while one which has a top resolution of roughly 2500x1900 pixels or so is a 5 megapixel device. The higher the rating the more detailed the shots, but you'll need larger memory cards to save the pictures. Some cameras use interpolation tricks to artificially push the captured images to higher resolutions, but this isn't quite the same as the real thing.

The highest resolution cameras are starting to match film in the detail they can resolve, but unless you're willing to spend a few thousand on the right equipment they are still not as controllable as an old-fashioned SLR. They are much more convenient, of course, and you'll never have to wait for (or pay for) printing and developing again.

PART 5 **DV camcorders**

DV cameras are the video equivalent of digital still cameras; they store video digitally (on DV tapes) and connect directly to Macs to copy across the footage in digital form for editing.

DV editing is normally done with iMovie (free from Apple) or Final Cut Pro (again from Apple, but moderately expensive), although there are other DV editing programs to choose from. Start with iMovie, as this is surprisingly easy and effective, and of course comes bundled free with modern Macs and with the latest Mac OS installers. See **www.apple.com/dvd** for more information.

You'll need a FireWire port in your Mac to connect a DV camera. (You can connect a DV camera to any Mac with a FireWire port, but editing DV on anything other than a G3-based Mac at the very least – including iMacs – is not worth trying.)

Video production can be free and easy with iMovie, and with third-party DV encoder hardware you don't even need a proper DV camera - although it helps.

The FireWire port in the cameras themselves is usually called an iLink port, or simply the DV port, and it is a smaller 4-pin connection than the normal FireWire plug. If you get a camera which supports DV-in as well as DV-out then you can put your finished edited movie back onto DV tape for low-cost storage. Alternatively, if you have a Mac with a SuperDrive you can record your work to a DVD video disc using the bundled iDVD software or the commercial DVD Studio Pro.

If you have an older analogue video camera rather than a DV camera, you can still capture and edit footage as DV, but you'll have to use a DV encoder such as the Hollywood DV-Bridge from Dazzle. This converts to and from analogue and DV formats, so traditional video cameras can be used to shoot, and edited work can be sent to regular video recorders.

Many DV cameras can be used to take still photos, but these are nowhere near the resolution of the average digital camera. Use this feature by all means, but don't expect it to match a true digital still camera's output.

This isn't a strange form of mouse, it is a specialist video editing controller which provides jog and shuttle features as well as quick access to many features of iMovie and other video editing programs via its buttons.

143

PART **6** # Mac maintenance

Your Mac should spend most of its life running smoothly, but it needs your help to manage this. To keep your Mac running at its best and to be ready for problems if they do strike, you need to know how to treat your Mac and, equally importantly, how not to treat it. Keep things organised, treat it with reasonable care and clean it from time to time. That way you and your Mac are likely to enjoy a long, stress-free life.

PART ⑥ Day-to-day maintenance

Day-to-day maintenance is simple. This is more about what not to do, such as not shutting down by simply switching off the power, not eating or drinking over the keyboard, and always keeping CDs, Zips and other removable disks in their cases when not in use, away from grit and dirt. If you use a regular mouse with a ball, don't just use it on your desk; use a mouse mat or the device will quickly clog up with dirt and start behaving erratically.

You should also work out a basic filing system for your work and stick to it. It may seem convenient just saving things to the Mac's desktop, but you'll quickly end up with a very cluttered screen where finding the right file or folder becomes increasingly difficult. The best way to organise your files differs according to whether you're using Mac OS 8 or 9, or Mac OS X.

In Mac OS 8 and 9 the Documents folder is found at the top level of the hard disk, while in Mac OS X it is found within the current user's Home folder.

Mac OS X

If you're using Mac OS X you'll have your own 'home' folder which holds folders such as Pictures, Music and, most important, Documents. You can put your files in most places in your Mac – although not in the folders called System and Library – but it is generally best to put things within your Documents folder, for simplicity's sake if nothing else. Click the Home or Documents icon in any Finder window, or choose Documents from the popup menu in the Save or Open window, when saving or opening files. You can make any number of folders in there according to your needs; one for each client, project, course, Website, or however else you prefer to organise things.

You can use the Documents folder found at the top level of your hard disk, but do note the difference between this and the Documents folder inside your own user 'home' folder. If your Mac is set up for other people to log in as named users, this top-level Documents folder is always available to everyone. On the other hand, your personal user-level Documents folder is secure from anyone else.

Mac OS 8 and 9

If you're using Mac OS 8 or 9 you'll probably have a standard Documents folder at the top level of the hard disk. If not, just make one. Use this for your work as described above, and things will go that much more smoothly if you decide to upgrade to Mac OS X at some point in the future.

Using a single folder for all your work also makes backing things up simpler. If there's just one place to look to find your documents, it is easier to make sure it is safely backed up on a regular basis. Backup strategies are discussed on p.152.

Occasional maintenance

Less regularly, if you use Mac OS 8 or 9, or Classic in OS X, you should do things such as 'rebuilding the Desktop', a process simpler than it probably sounds. The desktop, in this case, is an invisible file that your Mac maintains. It lists things such as which programs have been on your Mac, what the right document icons for those programs should look like, and so on. It is worth refreshing this desktop file from time to time to get rid of outdated information. Similarly, if the Desktop file becomes corrupt in some way and your documents and programs start showing plain, generic icons, this trick will create a Desktop file with nothing but correct, relevant information for your Mac to use.

Consider doing this once every couple of months or so if you rarely add and delete programs, or perhaps once a month if you constantly try out new programs from the Internet or from magazine cover CDs.

To rebuild the desktop for your main hard disk, just hold down the command (Apple) and option (alt) keys at the end of the start-up process, just before the disk shows up (or mounts) on your screen. Before your Mac mounts the disk it looks for this keypress combination , and it asks for confirmation before it starts the process. This tells it to delete the existing desktop file and create a new one. It can take a minute or two, particularly with large, full disks, but be patient while the progress indicator crawls along.

If you have other disks, ones which can be written to, rather than things like CDs and DVDs, you can do the same for them. Hold down command and option just before they are mounted, and choose to rebuild their desktop files when asked.

You should also physically clean your Mac from time to time, as a build-up of dust can start to look a little unsightly and interfere with the behaviour of things like the mouse. For details on the right way to clean your Mac see p.156.

In OS X, rebuilding the desktop for the volume containing the Classic system is done via the Advanced tab of Classic in System Preferences, rather than by holding down the command and option keys while a volume mounts.

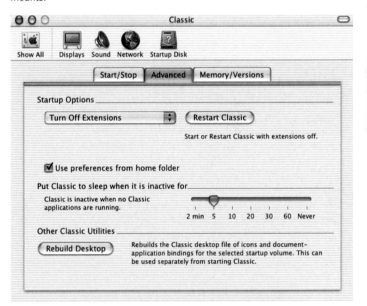

In Mac OS X Apple's Disk Utility provides a fairly robust disk checking and repair tool, although this should be teamed with a commercial disk tool as well.

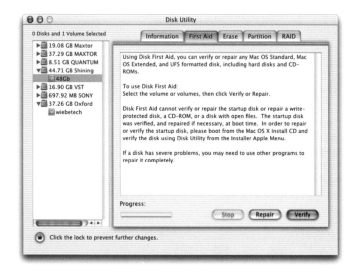

Disk maintenance

It is wise to check the health of your hard disk every month or so with a disk utility program. If something makes your Mac crash, the basic housekeeping routines that are done during the normal shutdown process aren't performed, and the contents of your disk might become affected in a small way. You may not notice any problem, but if this sort of thing isn't corrected it could lead to bigger problems and, eventually, even lost files and folders.

Before you get too concerned, note that the Mac OS will automatically run its Disk First Aid software during start-up if it sees that the Mac didn't shut down normally. However, those running Mac OS 8 or 9 have the opportunity to skip this process, leaving potential problems unchecked. In addition, Disk First Aid has its limitations, and the automatic check only looks at the start-up disk; the one with the active system folder. Because of this we strongly advise that you get a commercial disk repair program and use it, as this will give you much greater protection. You should also upgrade it whenever you upgrade your Mac OS, as old disk tools and new operating system versions can be a risky mix. If in doubt, check the software company's Website for compatibility information before running the software.

Run Disk First Aid or your commercial disk repair program over your hard disk once a month or so, and be sure to check any additional drives you may have. Remember, extra drives aren't checked and repaired during start-up after a crash.

Which disk tool?

Disk tools are like insurance policies. You hope you never need them, but if you do, you'd better have something that works. By all means use Disk First Aid to check things out and fix small problems. But if something serious does go wrong one day you'll need at least one heavy-duty disk repair tool to get you out of trouble. The three industry favourites are Norton Utilities, DiskWarrior, and TechTool Pro, and each has different points in its favour. Norton Utilities includes a number of features for rescuing files from damaged disks, and treats many different kinds of disk problem. DiskWarrior focuses on tackling disk directory errors, and this is where virtually every disk problem lies. It is also the only tool to tackle repair in a holistic manner, checking everything before attempting any fixes. TechTool Pro includes a large number of hardware diagnostic checks as well as disk repair features, and includes anti-virus features into the bargain. We recommend that you consider buying two or more, as it is not uncommon for one tool to fail to even see an unruly hard drive while another tool manages to fix the problem without fuss. In the final analysis, any tool worth its price needs to come with a bootable CD which will boot your Mac, as this is the situation in which it's talents are most likely to be utilised. It also needs to be upgradable over time, so that it keeps pace with the type of problems you are likely to encounter as your Mac is upgraded.

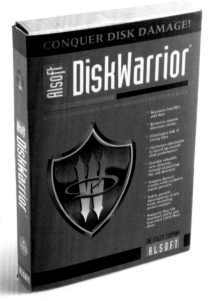

Get a professional disk repair tool and keep it handy. With luck you'll never need it, but you'll be glad of it if you do.

The fsck tool

If you're running Mac OS X then you have another alternative, something that can be used if the Mac won't even start up properly. This tool is called 'fsck', and it is identical to the Unix disk repair routine of the same name. This is intended for situations where you can't start up from a Mac OS X CD-ROM and use the Disk Utility on the CD to run Disk First Aid. If this is the case you'll have to start the Mac in what's called 'single user mode', then use the resulting command-line screen to run the fsck process. This is a very alarming looking process, but it is actually quite simple in practice, and is what Disk First Aid uses. See Techie Corner for details.

Disk repair programs:

Disk First Aid (Apple, supplied with Mac OS 8 and 9)
Disk Utility (Apple, supplied with Mac OS X)
Alsoft DiskWarrior (Alsoft, **www.alsoft.com**)
TechTool Pro (Micromat, **www.micromat.com**)
Norton Utilities for Macintosh (Symantec, **www.symantec.com**)
Drive 10 (Micromat, **www.micromat.com**)

Mac OS X's built-in fsck process in action, fixing the hard disk of a PowerBook. This looks alarming to any Mac user, but it is actually quite simple to use and doesn't take long.

PART 6 Free software tools

You don't have to splash out
on expensive software to keep your Mac in top shape and
to sort it out if things go wrong. There are a lot of tools
available online and on magazine cover CDs, and there
are a few which are provided as part of your regular Mac
OS installation. Some are free, while others are
shareware (see Techie Corner below).

For disk maintenance, Apple's free Disk Fist Aid program is a
great place to start. It comes free with the Mac OS, so you'll find
it on the Mac OS installer CD and in the Utilities folder inside the
Application folder on your hard disk. In Mac OS X the Disk First
Aid tool is a part of the Disk Utility program; open that and click
the appropriate tab. See Disk maintenance on p.148 for more on
using this tool.

Mac OS X's Disk Utility and Mac OS 8 and 9's Drive Setup
programs are what's needed to format almost any hard disk, and
even solid state memory cards such as Compact Flash and Smart
Media. If you need to set up a disk in proper Mac OS format,
perhaps because it was prepared for Windows or it has become
damaged, these tools are what you should reach for first. In rare
cases a hard disk may need a third party formatting tool. If the
drive is new, this should be bundled as part of the package.
Complain to where you bought it if it isn't. LaCie's SilverLining is
generally able to handle the few things that Apple's free tools
can't, but it is a commercial package. If you use something like
that, make sure the version you have is fully compatible with
your Mac OS version by checking on the appropriate Website.

Disks tend to fill up with clutter after a while. You could spend
time digging through to find unnecessary files, or you can get
software to do it for you. OmniDisk Sweeper makes the process
much simpler, and could help get back huge chunks of disk
space. The program is shareware, and is found at
www.omnigroup.com. A commercial alternative is Aladdin's
Spring Cleaning, from **www.aladdinsys.com**, but if you're not
confident about what these tools do it is generally best to leave
things as they are.

Your Mac uses the disk directory to keep track of exactly where
every scrap of data is on your disk. This can become fragmented,
with information shuffled about, making life harder for the Mac.
You never work with this directly, so the only simple way to fix it
is with the commercial DiskWarrior. However, you can monitor
things for free at least with the Directory Optimization Grapher
from the same company, found at **www.alsoft.com**.

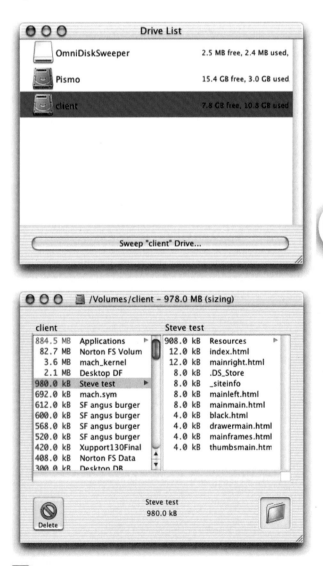

OmniDiskSweeper makes it easy
to track down and delete files and
folders which are taking up
unnecessary space on your hard
disk.

PART ⑥ **Commercial tools**

Free tools will help keep your Mac ticking over smoothly most of the time, but if real trouble strikes there's nothing like having a heavyweight solution at your fingertips. The commercial disk repair tools can turn a crisis into nothing more than a hiccup, exactly what you need if you find yourself staring at an alarming disk error message.

Keeping utility programs up to date is more important than many people think. Programs which are designed to massage the delicate structures of hard disks may get things disastrously wrong if used on things which use new storage and formatting techniques. Using an older disk repair tool can actually cause more trouble rather than cure anything (to the point of destroying files and folders and even losing an entire disk's contents if you're unlucky), so be sure the version of any tool you have is safe for the Mac OS version your Mac is running. See the software manufacturer's Website or check for updates on **www.versiontracker.com** if in any doubt.

The best current commercial disk repair tools are explained in the Disk maintenance section on p.148. These have all been carefully developed over the years, and offer a great deal of peace of mind. Each includes software that constantly monitors the Mac in one way or another, helping to catch problems before they can get out of hand. Make sure you have at least one of these, and preferably two to cover every eventuality. But remember to only actually install one set of monitoring software on your Mac, as two different sets from different programs could, in theory, get in each others' way.

It may seem like overkill to buy two different disk rescue tools, but any seasoned Mac technician will be able to reel off stories about how one normally reliable tool didn't work while another saved the day. You could of course pick one and just be ready to order another if big trouble strikes and the first lets you down.

Some commercial disk tools offer a number of different features, but the most important remains the core disk repair functions.

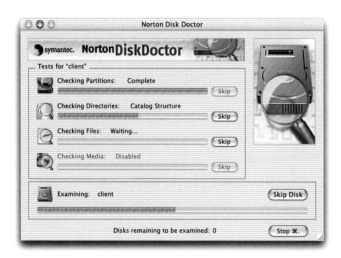

PART **6** Backing up

Backing up is the process of making a copy of things on your Mac in case something unfortunate happens. It is probably one of the least inspiring things you can do with a computer. However, if you use your Mac quite a bit, it is also one of the most important things you can do.

High-capacity tape backup devices remain the most cost-effective way to safeguard your data.

Get a backup device which can hold large amounts of data on a single cartridge, or be prepared to shuffle through cartridges on a regular basis.

Think of it like this: if something serious happens, perhaps a disk crash damages some files, or the wrong thing simply gets thrown away by mistake, then there are two possible outcomes. If you have a recent backup, you reach for that, restore the missing items, and carry on as before. If you don't have a backup, or you do but it is out of date, well...

This isn't just something that business users should do either. True, commercial work may need to be accessible months after it is finished, and there are legal requirements for storing accounts details for many years. But on a more personal level, what about things such as digital photos? These can be priceless, and simply impossible to replace if disaster strikes.

By now you should realise that, no matter how boring, backing things up regularly is worth the trouble. A proper backup routine involves more than just making the occasional copy of work onto a CD or Zip disk. If you're highly disciplined you could do this by hand, making copies of things whenever they change or on a simple schedule basis. You could set up a repeating alarm, using free software such as Palm Desktop (**www.palm.com**), to remind you do do this, but you'll eventually let this lapse.

The backup process should really have some degree of automation to ensure the latest versions of things are copied on a regular basis. The only sensible way to make backups is with software that can take over at least part of the dull side of things, and nag you into co-operating.

TECHIE CORNER

Tape size You may wonder why you should worry about high capacity tapes when you're probably backing up a few gigabytes at the most. The reason is that good backup software will add new and updated items to the tape incrementally, often making it possible to go back to specific backup sessions as well as retrieve the latest copy of something. In addition, tape isn't a random-access format, so updates are just added on to the tape in sequence. Each time a backup is made it takes more space from the tape. Retrospect (see 'Software' opposite) is perfectly capable of running a backup data set over two or more tapes. However, this does make things get fiddly, with a growing stack of tapes required for a single on-going backup.

Which medium?

It isn't wise to just buy a second hard disk to use as the backup storage space. This will work, but the temptation to use that disk normally will eventually be too much, and it'll simply become an extension of your regular storage instead. Use a removable storage medium so that you can keep extending the backup space. Zip disks can do in a pinch, but they aren't really reliable in the long term. Recordable CDs or DVDs are useful, and have the advantage of being readable in a wide range of standard drives. But the backup medium of choice, by those who know what they're doing, is still some form of tape cartridge.

You may not associate tapes with modern computing, but this is the most cost-effective way to store large amounts of data. There are a number of different tape formats in use today. DAT has been widely used for years, but the normal tape capacities are well under 10Gb. DLT is a higher capacity form of DAT, but at a much higher cost. Travan tape is making a comeback, with a new format capable of storing up to 20Gb per cartridge. ADR tapes can add 50% to that figure, while VXA and AIT both manage 50Gb and more with ease.

The choices can be overwhelming, but the choice really comes down to a few factors. The first, and most important for most people, is how expensive is the drive? At around £400 ($500) Imation's 20Gb Travan drive is the cheapest drive offering substantial space per cartridge, whereas a VXA or AIT drive is likely to cost as much as £1,000 ($1,400). The speed of operation can be a factor though, and the more you pay, the faster the backup runs.

Finally, the cost of tapes is a serious factor. Travan tapes cost little more than £20 ($35) each, whereas ADR tapes can cost two or three times as much. VXA and AIT cartridges are also fairly expensive per unit, although the larger space balances this out. But if you're planning to set up a proper rotating backup system involving a few tapes at a time, the cost of a whole box of cartridges can make a real difference.

Software

Pick backup software to complement your chosen hardware. If you use a tape drive, you'll need to use Dantz Retrospect, from **www.dantz.com**, to read and write data to the cartridges. Retrospect is a very powerful backup tool, and is trusted by the most demanding users with their work. But it is undeniably hard to learn. A basic version of Retrospect is bundled with most tape drives, but this is usually an old version. You'll need version 5 or later to make backups in Mac OS X.

If you back up onto any other medium, Retrospect will also do very well, but there are other, less heavy-duty (and less complex) options. Apple's Backup utility is good for Mac OS X users. For Mac OS 8 and 9 users Connectix CopyAgent, from **www.connectix.com**, is worth a try, with good basic backup features as well as scheduling automated, unattended backups.

Apple's Backup software works with its iDisk service to make Internet and CD backups a very simple process.

Dantz Retrospect is the industry-standard backup utility, able to work with just about any storage device that can be found.

PART ❻ Anti-virus

Viruses are the flies in the ointment of computing. They are often meant as nothing more than the digital equivalent of graffiti tagging; the writers want to see how far their creations can go, how many people end up knowing about their self-replicating software gremlin. Other virus writers actively want to cause trouble, specifically trying to damage as much as possible.

If something goes wrong it doesn't mean a virus has struck. It's much more likely to be a simple bug in some bit of software, or even just the result of someone misunderstanding how something works. But if something can't be easily explained, don't forget to consider the chances of a virus attack.

Norton AntiVirus is a robust virus-catching tool for the Mac. Recent versions work well in Mac OS X, and it can be set to scan disks as they are inserted.

Although Mac viruses are not at all common it is still wise to use the live update feature in your anti-virus package to keep things up to date.

The reality

Fortunately, as Mac users, we can all breath a sigh of relief. Although there are thousands of viruses at large today, less than one per cent can do anything to a Macintosh. In fact, the number of new PC viruses discovered every month or so is around the same as the number of active Mac viruses there are in total!

All the big virus scares of recent years – Melissa, Code Red and so on – can only run on PCs. Even though they were frequently sent to Mac users through infected e-mail, they were nothing more than inert lumps of Windows-specific code when on a Mac. Just like PC programs, PC viruses simply can't run on Macs. (Microsoft Office macro viruses are occasional exceptions to this, although there are still limits to what they can do on Macs.)

This doesn't mean that we should become blasé. A PC virus could still be passed on to a friend running a Windows-based computer, and the virus would very likely become active when it arrived there. On top of this, if you run a PC emulator such as the popular Connectix Virtual PC, that opens you up to the world of PC viruses just like any other Windows user. Of course, the worst that could happen there is that you need to replace the Virtual PC disk image file from the installer CD, whereas a real PC can actually be irreparably affected.

Mac viruses

Although there are very few Mac viruses, they still exist. Unless you never download files from the Internet, never share disks with friends, and live a completely monk-like existence with your Mac, you can't be totally secure. Even commercial software CDs aren't guaranteed to be safe; a major software company once sent out infected software preview CDs around the world. (That was a definite exception to the rule, however; you're incredibly unlikely to catch a virus from a commercial software CD.)

What to do

Get an anti-virus tool and find out how to use it. Make sure you also keep it up to date with new virus definitions from the software developer, as these things do change from time to time. Having a virus-catching tool which doesn't recognise new viruses is a very risky thing indeed. You may feel protected, but if the information your anti-virus software uses is outdated then you're not.

You can usually set anti-virus software to watch for unknown but suspicious activity. This may become tiresome if set to the most suspicious level, so learn how to customise it. In addition, you should know how to disable this feature or the whole program entirely when installing software, or the anti-virus tool may stop installations from working properly.

There are a number of tools around for catching and eliminating viruses and Trojan horses. We do recommend that you get a commercial tool for this task, although you can protect yourself moderately well with free and shareware tools if you're prepared to work at it.

The best-known commercial anti-virus tools for the Mac include Intego Virus Barrier (**www.intego.com**), Norton AntiVirus (**www.symantec.com**), and Virex (**www.networkassociates.com**). These have recently been joined by Sophos Anti-Virus (**www.sophos.com**), a product with a good track record in the PC market, but aimed more at network setups than individual users. All offer regular virus definition updates.

Free and shareware tools can be found through sites such as **www.versiontracker.com**. Names to look for include vScan, Tracker INIT, Scanner and Agax, all programs that watch for a range of suspicious activities or known code 'signatures'. So far there are no shareware anti-virus tools for Mac OS X, although this situation is likely to change.

If you get an email warning you of a virus it is almost certainly a hoax, passed on by a well-meaning friend. Check it out at sites such as www.vmyths.com before passing the warning on.

Hoaxes

You may have seen alarming e-mail warnings passed on by friends warning about some virus or other. These generally include lines such as 'this virus was reported by IBM' (or some other well-known company), 'this affects Mac and PCs', and 'it uses the formatting tools in Norton Utilities to erase your hard disk'. These are all virus hoaxes, and most have been doing the rounds for years.

If you receive such a warning, check it out at one of the recognised authorities on the subject. The chances are it will feature in their list of hoaxes, and you can tell whoever warned you not to worry. The sender probably passed it on to you out of genuine concern, so don't hold it against them. But do let them know where they can verify warnings in the future.

Anti-virus Websites with information about virus hoax messages:

www.vmyths.com
hoaxbusters.ciac.org
www.symantec.com/avcenter/hoax.html
www.sophos.com/virusinfo/hoaxes

PART ⑥ How to clean your Mac

Cleaning your Mac is definitely a good idea, but only if you do things carefully. You shouldn't, as a matter of course, try to clean your Mac when it is on. Some cleaning processes aren't really a danger to a running Mac, but others can be, so – to be on the safe side – shut down before beginning.

Mac cases and screens

Don't use commercial computer cleaning products to clean your Mac without checking on an unobtrusive spot first. The chemicals in some products can permanently mark the surface of some models. Screen cleaners should be regarded with particular suspicion, as some will strip the anti-glare coating on glass-screen monitors. LCD panels are even more vulnerable, as their outer coating can be chemically marked by harsher cleaners. The best cleaning product is simply a soft, damp cloth, both for screens and Mac bodies. But no dripping water, please! Marks on PowerBook screens often look like scratches from the keys, but are actually due to a build-up of grease on the key tops. Keeping the keys clean avoids this. Low-profile keys are available to help with this; see www.digitalhipps.com.

Mice

Mice need occasional cleaning, as they pick up dirt very easily. If you have an optical mouse this will only gather on the smooth plastic parts which are in contact with the mousemat or desk. Turn it over and scrape this off with a fingernail. Check for fluff in the optical sensor area, as this causes erratic movements.

If you have a mouse with a ball – turn it over and see if there's one hanging down from an opening in the base – then from time to time you'll need to clean both the ball and the rollers that the ball moves when you push the mouse about. The small plate surrounding the hole where the ball peeks through will come off or flip open in some way. All Apple's ball-based mice have plates which unlock by being rotated. Remove the ball and see if the three rollers (one for horizontal movement, one for vertical and one to press the ball against the others) have any encrusted dirt. With a fingernail, matchstick or similar impliment, scrape off the dirt and shake it out. Once finished, use a cotton bud or something similar, dipped in lighter fluid or cleaning alcohol, to clean off any residue. Now clean the ball. You can start by washing it with detergent or soap, but be sure to rinse it thoroughly afterwards. Give it a wipe with lighter fluid to remove any last residues from the dirt or detergent. Drop it back into the mouse, replace the cover, and you're done.

Occasionally, a mechanical mouse will fail to improve after cleaning in this fashion. In this case, turn it over and look for the screws which hold it together – they're usually under the product label on the underside. Peel back the label, remove the screws carefully, and you should be able to remove the mouse's top bodywork so that you can blow out the fluff which may have gathered around the tiny, slotted 'chopper' disks which sense the mouse's movement. Then reassemble, and marvel at the improved behaviour.

Keyboards

Keyboards also need cleaning from time to time. They tend to gather dirt underneath the keycaps, particularly near smokers. They also pick up a film of dirt on the keys, wherever your fingers touch regularly but not directly enough to wear it off. To get rid of trapped dirt you can simply shake it upside-down for a minute, use the nozzle of a vacuum cleaner (being careful not to knock any keys off), or use compressed air to blast the dirt out.

Cleaning the keys takes more patience. Use a damp cotton bud or something similar to clean around the edges of the keys, or a soft, slightly damp cloth if you just want to clean the tops. If there are bits of junk stuck between or beneath keys, use a pin or some tweezers to fish the offending items out. As a last resort you could try removing a key to get something out. But be aware that some keyboards, laptop ones in particular, aren't meant to stand up to this kind of rough handling. You may end up having to glue a key back on if you're not careful.

If you spill a drink on the keyboard see Troubleshooting on p.168, immediately, for what to do.

Inside

If you have an iMac it is, by and large, well sealed, but the insides of other Macs tend to be dust magnets. You shouldn't have to worry about cleaning them out more than once a year at the most, but too much dust and fluff inside your Mac can cause components to heat up, potentially shortening their life.

Open your Mac up, following the instructions starting on p.18, and see if there's much dust inside. The chances are that you're looking at a substantial amount. Vacuum cleaners aren't the best things to use, as they can generate static charges in the nozzles which damage sensitive electronics. In addition, household vacuums are too unwieldy for this job. The best bet is usually a can of compressed air. This can blast the fluff from every corner of any Mac – filling the air with dust in the process, so you might want to open a window. If you don't have compressed air handy you can simply blow, but make absolutely certain that no saliva makes its way inside by mistake. You'll also have to look out for the dust billowing up into your face. Other creative solutions may well occur to you, such as a car footpump with an airbed nozzle fitted – go ahead! Just make sure that the inside of your Mac stays absolutely dry.

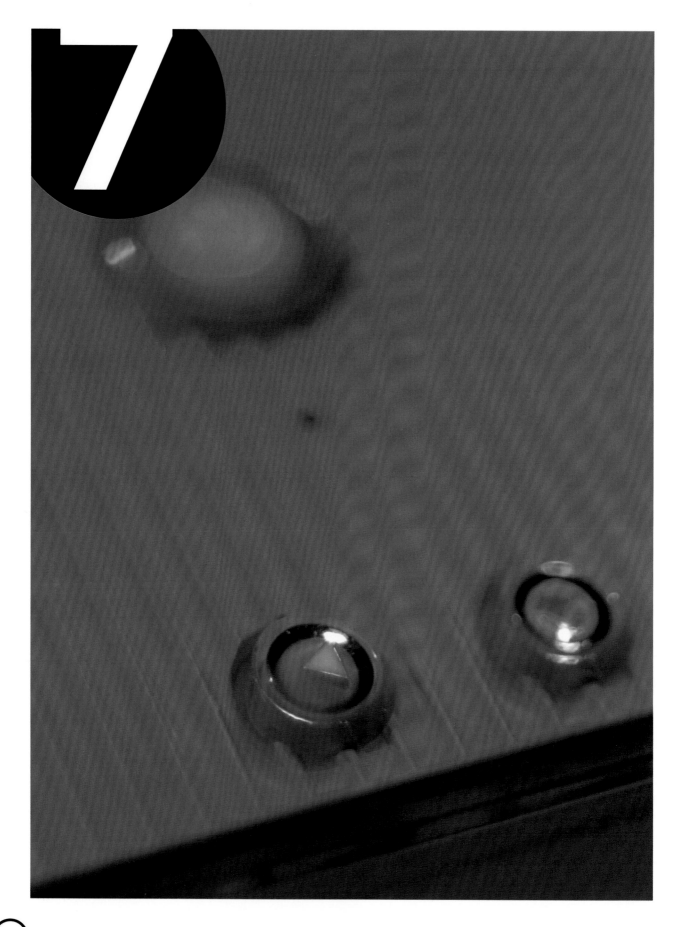

PART  # Troubleshooting

Sometimes things go wrong. That's a fact of life, especially when working with something as complex as a modern computer.

You can help prevent things from going wrong with a bit of common sense – reading the Read Me files and checking system requirements is a good start. Reading magazines and Websites for bugs and problems with the software you use is also a good idea, if a little tedious.

When you install programs, check to see if the installer includes an uninstall option. This is particularly important in Mac OS X, as the number of places that items can be put has grown. After a while you'll learn how to second-guess your Mac at least most of the time, and when something does come unstuck you'll have a pretty good idea of how to start getting it back together again.

When something *does* go wrong, don't automatically reach for the telephone to call a technician. The chances are you can fix the problem yourself, as long as you approach things logically. There are only a few things that might happen, and the following series of charts covers all that you're likely to come up against. Most of the time these will get things up and running, but even if the problem turns out to be particularly serious at least you'll have a good idea of what's actually needed. That in itself can save a fortune when taking something in for hi-tech surgery.

If you do need to call for technical assistance, then don't feel embarrassed. But before you make that call, read our guide to dealing with technical support staff on p.170. This should help you get what you want out of the experience.

Startup problems

If your Mac won't even start up there are a set of simple questions that should help pinpoint the trouble.

Your Mac makes some basic hardware tests as soon as it begins the startup process. If you hear an unusual sound at startup in place of the usual 'happy Mac' chord, this is an indication that the Mac has failed these tests. This doesn't necessarily mean that something's actually broken, however, as this can be caused by RAM or expansion cards being loose in their sockets, or even by a rogue SCSI or USB device. Disconnect non-essential external peripherals, make sure all internal cards are firmly seated in their sockets, and try again.

The PRAM battery can be a prime suspect when a Mac shows a blank screen on startup or even refuses to get going at all. This battery, which looks like a half-length AA battery in most Macs or a small block with wires in various Performa models, is found on the Mac's motherboard. It keeps a small portion of memory, the Parameter RAM (or PRAM for short), ticking over with the basics about your Mac's setup when there's no power connection. If you leave your Mac unplugged for any length of time this battery can become run down. The first symptom of this is the inability to remember the time and date between restarts. At this point you should find out what kind of battery you need and replace it. If the battery expires much further you may not be able to start the Mac up at all. However, if this is the cause of the trouble, replacing it with a fresh battery will completely cure things. You can get the appropriate replacement battery from any good Apple dealer, many PC dealers and some well-stocked hardware stores and mail order outlets.

Zapping the PRAM helps sort out incorrect data which might be in the Parameter RAM; this process resets things such as the designated startup disk and the preferred network port back to their original default settings. If you have a Mac with serial ports and an Ethernet network port, remember that the network connection will switch to the old LocalTalk serial port. This will stop any Ethernet connection from working until you reset this manually in the AppleTalk control panel.

Older Mac systems show a 'happy Mac' symbol during startup to show that basic hardware tests have been passed. The 'sad Mac' face and a different startup sound indicates basic hardware trouble.

If so, try restarting again and 'zapping the PRAM'. Power on the machine with the Command (Apple), Option (Alt) P and R keys held down. You will hear the normal startup bong, possibly after a delay. Continue to hold down these keys until you have heard the bong at least two more times, then release them. Your Mac should now continue its startup, and you may need to reset some Control Panel settings.

If you're using Mac OS 8 or 9, force the Mac to restart, then hold down the shift key to disable extensions.

If this works, track down the extension conflict, remove the offending item, and restart.

If this doesn't work, try starting up from a bootable CD, either your system CD or a special disk repair CD. Use whatever repair tool you have on the disk to check and repair things.

If you're using Mac OS X, try restarting from the OS X system CD. Use this to check and repair the hard disk (see p.148 for disk repair details), then restart.

If this isn't possible, try restarting in single user mode (hold down command and s during startup), then repair the disk using the fsck command and restart.

The problem could be due to difficulties with your firewall settings which are preventing startup from completing. Start up from a CD, then go into /Library/StartupItems/Firewall on your hard disk and throw those files away.

If all else fails, consider reinstalling the operating system.

This means the Mac can't find a usable system (Mac OS 8, 9 or X). Use an emergency startup CD (your system installer if necessary) and run the best disk repair program there is on that disc. (See p.148 for disk repair details.)

Use the Startup Disk control panel to pick your hard disk, then restart.

If this still doesn't work, try 'zapping the PRAM'. (See above for more information.)

If all else fails, consider reinstalling the operating system.

Is the monitor connected properly and switched on?

Try 'zapping the PRAM'. (See left for more information.)

You may have a failed onboard PRAM battery. Shut down (unplug if necessary), and replace the motherboard PRAM battery. See the previous page for details.

Is the monitor itself working? See if you can find another to test this possibility.

Some internal components, in particular the graphics card, may not be connected properly. Shut down, remove the case, and make sure everything is firmly in place in the right sockets.

Disconnect all non-essential peripherals. This includes all FireWire SCSI and USB devices – apart from the keyboard and mouse.

If there's an unusual sound – a series of notes or a realistic card crash sound is likely – the Mac has failed the initial hardware test. Shut down, open it up, and make sure everything is firmly in its place.

Disconnect all non-essential peripheral devices, then restart.

If it still won't start properly you may have a real hardware failure. Take it to your dealer for diagnosis.

Check that the Mac is connected to a power socket, that any fuses from the cable to the mains box are OK, and that the mains power supply is on.

If this is a portable Mac, check that the battery has a charge by looking on it for the power indicator button and lights.

If it still won't respond, suspect a problem with the internal power supply unit (PSU). Disconnect everything and take it to your dealer for diagnosis.

PART **7**

Crashing

A Mac that keeps crashing can cause all sorts of trouble. To track down the reason and find a cure, work through the following steps.

If you need to force a program to quit, press command, option and escape together. This will either show a box on screen asking if you're sure (Mac OS 8 and 9), or a window listing all the running programs (Mac OS X). If running Mac OS 8 or 9, once a program has been forcibly quit you should restart the Mac to eliminate any memory problems. If this doesn't work properly you'll have to restart the Mac.

The correct way to restart a Mac is with the on-screen options, either the Restart menu item or by pressing the power key and clicking Restart. If this isn't working, press command, control and the power key on your keyboard, or press and hold the power button on your Mac for at least six seconds. If even this doesn't work you'll have to switch off the power. Remember that this is a last resort, and check your hard disk after this kind of treatment.

Often, the problem causing a crash in OS 8 or 9 is that two or more bits of programs – 'extensions' – are conflicting with each other. To get around that, you must first start the Mac with some or all extensions off. The best way to disable (and re-enable) extensions is by using the Extensions Manager control panel, either from the Control Panels item in the Apple menu or by holding down the space bar during startup. Don't disable Apple extensions unless you're absolutely certain you don't need them, but feel free to temporarily turn off third-party items which aren't essential to your work, at least while you're troubleshooting things.

Sorry, a system error occurred.

error type 11

(Restart)

System crashes are all but eliminated in Mac OS X, but earlier systems can be brought down by one misbehaving program.

If a program or the whole Mac starts behaving oddly for no apparent reason, it could be due to a virus. Make sure you have a recent version of your anti-virus program's virus definitions, and use it to check out your entire disk. Of course it could simply be because you don't have enough RAM, or in Mac OS 8 or 9 because the program itself needs to be told to use more RAM. To assign more memory to a program, make sure it isn't running, select the icon in the Finder, and choose Get Info from the File menu. Pick Memory from the popup menu in the Info window, and change the figure in the Preferred Size text box. This is listed in kilobytes, which are 1,024 to a megabyte. Increase the figure by about 25 per cent or so, then close the window and try the program again.

Deleting a program's preferences can sometimes help clear things up. For programs running in Mac OS 8 and 9 and in Classic mode in Mac OS X, look in the Preferences folder in the System Folder. Native Mac OS X programs keep their preferences inside /Library/Preferences inside your Home folder or at the top level of the hard disk. Be aware that some programs store their registration details in these files, so you may have to retype a registration number if you delete the preferences.

Are you getting complete system crashes in Mac OS 8 or 9?

First, make a careful note of any error messages you see as well as whatever you did just prior to the crash.

If you don't see a crash alert it may be just a program-level crash. Try forcing it to quit by holding down command and option and pressing the escape key. Restart normally if successful.

Start up with the shift key held down (to disable extensions) or from a startup CD, then check and repair your hard disk. See p.148 for disk repair details.

Disable all non-essential extensions and control panels and restart to see if that makes a difference. (Or, if the problem has begun occurring shortly after you installed a new program or software update, disable that program's extensions first.) If so, try to establish which item was the culprit.

Run an anti-virus tool, just in case.

Consider reinstalling the Mac OS.

? **Are you getting crashes with programs running using Mac OS X's Classic mode?**

Make a careful note of all error messages and the things you were doing just before the crash.

Disable all non-essential extensions using the Classic pane in System Preferences, restart, and try again.

Run an anti-virus tool, just in case.

Throw away the problem program's preferences file from the Preferences folder (inside the System Folder), assign more memory to the program (select it, choose Get Info from the File menu, and change the Preferred Size setting), and try it again.

Reinstall the program from the original CD.

Give up using the program in Mac OS X's Classic mode. If you must run the program, restart in Mac OS 9 and run it from there, if your Mac c an be started in OS9?

? **Are you getting frequent program crashes and unexpected quits?**

Make a careful note of all error messages and the things you were doing just before the crash.

If the program has frozen, try forcing it to quit by holding down command and option and pressing the escape key. Restart normally if successful.

Check for known problems and any updates by visiting the program developer's site.

Throw away the problem program's preferences file from the Preferences folder (inside the System Folder), assign more memory to the program (select it, choose Get Info from the File menu, and change the Preferred Size setting), and try it again.

Run an anti-virus tool, just in case.

Remove most fonts from the Fonts folder (in the System Folder, and also in /Library/Fonts at the top level of the disk and inside your Home folder in Mac OS X) in case a damaged font is the cause.

Reinstall the program from the original CD, then contact the program developer and report the problem.

? **Are you suffering from full kernel panics in Mac OS X?**

Note the details of the kernel panic and what you were attempting at the time, then restart from your Mac OS X installer CD and run Disk First Aid from the Disk Utility. See p.148 for disk repair details.

If you recently installed something it may have included components which are causing the problem. Try uninstalling the suspect to see if that helps.

Report the kernel panic details to Apple and the program developer.

PART **7** Internet problems

Finding yourself unable to connect to the Internet can be very frustrating. Fortunately, however, you can usually track down the trouble with a few simple questions.

If you use a modem to connect to the Internet, your Mac needs to know what kind it is and how to talk to it. Make sure the right modem script is selected, or connections will be unstable at best. In Mac OS 8 and 9 this is done with the Modem control panel. In Mac OS X open System Preferences, click Network, pick the modem type from the Show popup menu, and click the Modem tab. Pick your particular modem from the popup menu. If it doesn't appear then see if an installer is on a CD supplied with the modem. If necessary, install the file by hand, either in the Modem Scripts folder inside the Extensions folder of Mac OS 8 and 9's System folder, or in /Library/Modem Scripts in Mac OS X. If one isn't available, see if a similar one from the menu listing works at all. Finally, get in touch with the modem manufacturer or supplier to see if they can provide the correct file.

If you want to test the modem with a terminal application such as ZTerm, type 'ATDT', your own phone number, and press return. This tells the modem to wake up (AT, or 'attention') and dial (DT, dial using tone signals) the number you give it. You should hear it dial, then hear a busy signal or an answering service if you use one.

Internet connection problems can be frustrating, blocking your access to the Web and email.

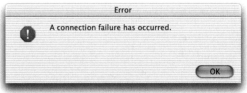

Broadband Internet connections are generally less trouble than modem connections, but troubleshooting them becomes more of an exercise in checking network settings. USB broadband 'modems' use special drivers to perform a kind of Ethernet via USB routing, so be certain you're using the most recent version of the software meant for your Mac OS version. Make sure you have a note of the settings you should be using, and check them against what's actually in the Internet and Network panes of System Preferences or the AppleTalk, Internet and TCP/IP control panels in Mac OS 8 and 9. If in doubt, check with the broadband service provider's technical support team – and don't stand for any nonsense about not supporting Macs! You should also make sure you're using the most recent available version of the Mac OS, Mac OS 9.1 or 9.2 in preference to any earlier version, and 10.1 or later if you're running Mac OS X.

Does your modem remain silent when you try to connect? Turn the volume up or enable modem sound, if possible.

If no dialling is heard, make sure the right modem script is selected in the Modem control panel or the Network pane of Mac OS X's System Preferences.

Do you need to dial a number such as 9 or 0 to get an outside line? If so, add '9,,,' or '0,,,' in front of the number you want the modem to dial. The commas will tell the modem to pause briefly – often PABXs need this.

Check the line with a regular telephone. If you can't hear a dialtone there may be a problem with the telephone line.

Try opening a terminal application, for instance ZTerm, and sending a basic ATDT command to see what response you get.

The modem may be faulty, consult a dealer or simply try a different one.

If the modem dials but you don't get a proper connection, make sure that you're using the right phone number for your Internet service provider.

Make sure the right modem script is selected in the Modem control panel or the Network pane of Mac OS X's System Preferences.

If the connection never gets past the setup process, check the user name and password being used to log in.

If the connection is dropped shortly after you connect, the telephone connection and line may be sub-standard. Eliminate telephone extension leads and ask the telephone company to check the line quality.

Check with your Internet service provider to see if they know of specific problems at their end or in a local telephone exchange.

? Do you use a high-speed network Internet connection?

Make sure you can see your network server, if necessary use a network test utility such as Ping (part of Mac OS X's Network Utility program) to perform basic network troubleshooting. (See p.166 for details.)

Check that the server's connection to the network is working correctly.

Check the network settings in your Mac's TCP/IP control panel or Network pane in System Preferences.

Talk to your network administrator.

? Do you use an AirPort or other wireless basestation to connect?

Check with the AirPort or third party wireless software that the basestation can be seen and that the wireless signal is reasonably strong.

Check AirPort basestation settings using the AirPort Admin program.

Try using an internal modem, if possible, to confirm that you're using the right Internet user name and password details.

Reset the basestation.

If the basestation flashes its lights constantly or is simply unresponsive, suspect hardware failure and consult your local dealer.

? Do you use an always-on broadband connection?

If this is a USB ADSL or cable modem, check the USB connection. Make sure you're not using a hub to link this to the Mac.

Check the network configuration, using the AppleTalk and TCP/IP control panels in Mac OS 8 or 9, or the Network pane in Mac OS X's System Preferences.

If you're running Mac OS 8 or 9, remove all non-essential USB extensions and disconnect unnecessary peripherals, restart, and try again.

Make sure you're using the latest software driver for your particular model of broadband modem.

If this is an Ethernet-based connection then check the network configuration, using the AppleTalk and TCP/IP control panels in Mac OS 8 or 9, or the Network pane in Mac OS X's System Preferences.

Check the cable connections, and consider doing basic network troubleshooting as well. (See p.166 for details.)

Contact the support team for your broadband Internet service provider.

PART 7 Network problems

Finding yourself unable to connect to your local network can be a frustrating experience. Whether you need to get files from a server or share things you've done on your Mac, if your network connection isn't working you're left out in the cold. Work through these questions one by one and you should be able to pinpoint the trouble.

There is only one main type of networking in use today. This is 'twisted pair' Ethernet, known as the Base-T format, which uses cabling and connectors similar to telephone wires and plugs. This comes in a number of different speeds, from the original 10 megabits per second 10Base-T to the more recent 100Base-T and the expensive gigabit Ethernet (1000Base-T), each offering a theoretical ten-fold speed increase over the previous level. These higher speeds depend on computers and network hubs supporting them, and the cabling being up to scratch as well.

One other Ethernet networking wiring format may still be found, although it is increasingly rare. Coaxial cabling, known as Base-2, requires more care with laying cables, but you're very unlikely to come across this technology.

LocalTalk is a dead form of network cabling, based on Apple's discontinued serial port technology. It was very easy to set up, but was only a fraction of the speed of basic Ethernet. It is also completely unsupported in Mac OS X.

A Ping test involves sending a small packet of data to a remote computer. These are echoed back, and the delay is used to measure the efficiency of the network connections. If the packets don't come back then there is a break in the network at some point. Free Ping tools can be downloaded via sites such as www.versiontracker.com, but if you use Mac OS X the Network Utility program which comes with the Mac OS includes a good Ping feature. However, you'll have to learn to make your own diagnoses from the results these tools give.

? Are you using Mac OS 8 or 9?

Make sure the network cables are properly connected, both in your Mac's network socket and in the network port at the other end.

Make sure the AppleTalk control panel is set to the right network port.

You're almost certainly using Ethernet, so check the settings in the TCP/IP control panel. Make sure you're using the right IP address and subnet mask settings by comparing against other Macs on the network. (Your IP address must be unique, whether entered manually or picked up from a DHCP server.)

Use the Chooser or Network Browser to look for other machines on the network.

If things still don't improve, consult the network administrator.

? Are you using Mac OS X?

Make sure the right network option is enabled in the Network pane of System Preferences.

Check the network option's settings. Make sure you're using the right IP address and subnet mask settings by comparing against other Macs on the network. (Your IP address must be unique, whether entered manually or picked up from a DHCP server.)

Check that the Network pane's AppleTalk option is turned on if you need to use this form of networking.

Try using the Ping option in the Network Utility to see if other machines on the network will respond.

If things still don't improve, consult the network administrator.

? Have you checked the physical aspects of the network, such as the cabling and any hubs and routers?

Make sure the network cables are properly connected, both in your Mac's network socket and in the network port at the other end.

Make sure any hubs and routers are powered up and aren't showing any alert lights.

Try using a different Ethernet cable, a different network socket, and so on.

Make sure other computers on the network are working correctly.

If things still don't improve, consult the network administrator.

? Are you trying to connect to a Unix or Windows server?

You may need to have extra software installed, or have specific Macintosh services enabled, to be able to access these servers.

Check that your user name and password are correct.

Make sure other computers, Macs or PCs, can see the server and use it correctly.

If you have a personal firewall security system installed this may be preventing you from getting proper access to your network.

If things still don't improve, consult the network administrator.

PART 7 **Printing problems**

Printing usually just works, but when it doesn't it can be very frustrating. Most of the time things can be fixed by checking through a few key things.

Printing is often closely tied up with networking, so if you use a laser printer check the networking troubleshooting tips as well as these ones. Personal USB printers and their older cousins, serial printers, connect directly to your Mac, and use custom software to let the computer know how to prepare and send a print job to them. These can also be shared across a network, so a different Mac can send a print job to the one with the printer, which then gets on with dealing with the task as if it had been created locally.

Printer drivers are vital for getting USB printers to work. With Mac OS 8 and 9 you must use the software installers that come with the printers and check on manufacturers' sites for updates. Mac OS X makes this aspect much easier, as the Software Update utility keeps your Mac primed with the latest drivers for most modern printers.

For a network printer to work with Macs it must, with a few rare exceptions, have a PostScript interpreter built in, or work with a separate PostScript RIP, either hardware or software, which mimics the same thing. Printers which only support PCL just aren't up to scratch. Almost all network printers will be either laser or LED (LED printers are very similar to laser printers, they just use a different method for part of the internal imaging process), although there are some models of inkjet printer which include Mac-compatible Ethernet ports and network access software.

Don't bother trying to use old LocalTalk network printers unless it is absolutely essential. You're almost certain to be using an Ethernet network by now (at least, you should be), so you'd need a hardware LocalTalk bridge to link the old-style hardware with the modern network. These are very hard to find, and as modern network laser printers can be very cheap it is rarely worth the effort.

? Is your Mac directly connected to your printer?

If the cable that connects the printer is a serial one (circular plugs), make sure the right port in the Mac is being used; connect to the one with the printer icon rather than the telephone icon.

Make sure no other software is trying to use the same port. Check the AppleTalk control panel to see if it is set to LocalTalk. Switch this to Ethernet or turn off AppleTalk using the Chooser.

If the cable that connects the printer is a USB one (square or rectangular plugs), try connecting directly to a USB port in the Mac rather than a USB hub.

If the printer has run out of ink this can make some printers fail to show up to the Mac at all. Change ink cartridges if necessary.

Disconnect all non-essential USB devices, disable their drivers, restart the Mac, and try again.

Make sure you're using the latest versions of the printer software.

? Is the printer accessed through a network connection?

Check the network connections in the printer and your Mac.

Make sure that the printer can be seen and used by other computers on the network.

Try updating the printer driver. If possible, switch to the standard LaserWriter driver instead of any custom version. In Mac OS X, delete the printer from the list in the Print Center utility.

Restart the printer.

Make sure you're not mixing up the page size in the Page Setup for the print job; sending something set to a paper size not available will generally stall a network printer.

? Is the printer a personal one shared over the network?

Make sure the computer connected to the printer can access the network normally.

Make sure the other computer is properly set up to share the printer.

Make sure you have the right software for that printer installed on your Mac.

Make sure your Mac has full access to the network.

Emergencies

? You've just spilled a drink on your keyboard.

You mustn't panic, but you mustn't hang about either. Pull the keyboard cable out of the Mac or the power cable out of the wall immediately, before the liquid causes a serious short-circuit. Yes, this isn't something you should normally do, but this isn't a normal situation.

You have a choice now; throw the keyboard away, or try to fix it. You'll need a replacement keyboard even if you do fix this one as the process takes a week or so, but you shouldn't assume it is broken. You'll have to flush the drink out of the keyboard with clean water, so use a screwdriver to take the keyboard shell apart and put the whole thing under a tap. You'll have to flush it thoroughly to make sure there are no residues of any kind left inside. When you think you're done, do it some more to be on the safe side. Then put it somewhere warm and ventilated to dry. Don't use forced heat as this might damage the internal parts. Leave it to dry for a few days at least, preferably a week or more. Once you're absolutely certain it is bone-dry throughout, put it back together and try it out. If anything seems amiss, unplug it immediately and throw it away. But if you've cleaned and dried it properly it will live to type another day.

If spills occur, disconnect immediately then take the keyboard apart and flush thoroughly with clean running water.

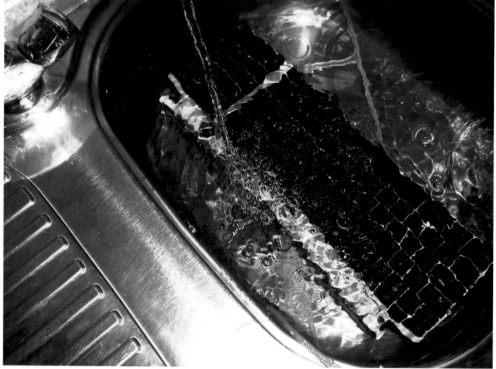

? Your screen starts to pop and/or flash alarmingly, either occasionally or constantly.

This is generally a sign that the screen itself, more specifically the hardware wrapped around the back of the glass tube itself, is about to expire. It won't explode, but it could fail totally at any point. It isn't possible to repair this sort of problem, so get a new screen as a matter of urgency. If the screen is built into your Mac, make a full backup of everything that you can. When the screen finally dies you won't be able to get at anything until the hard drive is transplanted into another Mac.

? Your Mac refuses to stay shut down, restarting every time you try.

If your Mac thinks it has crashed, that is, you aren't shutting down properly, this can happen. But only if the 'Restart automatically after a power failure' option is turned on in the Energy Saver control panel or System Preferences pane. In Mac OS 8 and 9 the Energy Saver control panel also includes a scheduled startup option, but this only works at a specific time of day. Alternatively, if you have a keyboard with a power key, look to see if something's pressing it down. Sometimes the strangest of behaviours has the simplest of causes.

? Your hard disk is damaged beyond the point where disk rescue tools can help.

This is extremely rare, and is more likely to happen with physical damage, such as knocking a disk off a table or through fire damage, than through software failure. If you don't have recent backups, start sweating. It is theoretically possible for specialist data recovery services to get some data from failed disks, but these services are always extremely expensive. On top of that, no guarantees can be made, and it is likely that some data has gone forever. The best way to protect against this kind of nightmare is to have a good backup regime in place, so see Backing up on p.152 for advice.

? You've just performed some kind of upgrade, and now your Mac doesn't work any more.

First of all, think back through the upgrade process. Did you follow the instructions properly or did you cut any corners? Did you check the system requirements before you began? Some processor upgrades require software to be installed before anything else happens or the new processor may not be able to work.

If you can't think of any obvious solution (loose cables, conflicting SCSI IDs or unchecked jumper connections, unconnected power cables and so on), you'll have to backtrack through the upgrade. When you put things back as they were your Mac should work again. (If not, see Troubleshooting on p.160.) Double-check the upgrade's compatibility with your Mac, and make sure you have any necessary specialist extras, such as the right variety of SCSI card or similar. If you still draw a blank, check with the reseller or the manufacturer's technical support.

PART 7 Technical support

How to deal with technical support staff

At some point in your computing life you may find that the best option is to reach for the phone rather than the screwdriver. After all, if you buy something then you're entitled to technical support, right? Well, the answer is 'probably'.

You may find that support is offered via a premium rate call, where you pay an appreciable amount for every minute spent chatting. Even if this isn't the case, it may still be a national or international call. You may get a fixed length of time where support is provided; anywhere from 30 days to a year is common. This countdown may start from the date of purchase or from your first call.

If you still want to make that call, check to see if you did everything properly and according to the instructions. You should also run through any troubleshooting procedures listed in the product or software manual, as well as the steps outlined earlier in this book – and keep notes on what you've done. This could save time, especially important if you're paying by the minute. If possible, make your call using a different phone line from that used by your Mac to connect to the Internet. This can save a lot of time if fixing the problem requires you to go online.

The Internet is very useful for tracking down information about all sorts of Macintosh hardware and software. See the websites list on the right for good places to start loooking.

If you didn't, then go do it properly first, or you'll give the person at the other end of the phone the perfect excuse to blame you whatever the real cause of the trouble. (On that note, don't volunteer information about other upgrades you've done too early on in the conversation, in case they use that as an excuse to blame something other than their product. But do admit those things if necessary.)

Write down the exact wording of any error messages, and what you were doing when they happened. You'll also need to know how your Mac is set up – see Taking stock on p.14 – as this might help pinpoint the trouble. Don't pretend you know more than you do, but have everything relevant handy, including the Mac of course, when you call. If you can answer the support staff's questions without too many umms and ahhs you're likely to find you get better treatment.

If you're told to upgrade something fundamental, such as the Mac OS, to fix the problem, check to see whether the product in question is or isn't supposed to work with what you already have. You might also want to ask them if upgrading the Mac OS might cause problems with any other products you have. This is a little unfair as they can't and won't offer support for things they don't make, but it can help bring people back to earth. They may, however, be completely right, so don't dismiss the suggestion out of hand.

TROUBLESHOOTING

Useful websites

The Internet is an excellent source of information on all aspects of the Mac. From up-to-the-minute news and gossip to details on the best ways to fine-tune almost any aspect of your system, there's something, somewhere online which can help. Take whatever you read on the Internet with a pinch of salt, but do remember that you can find excellent help from dedicated and experienced specialists. Use these addresses to help find your way to the of the most useful Mac-specific information online.

Information on fine-tuning performance

http://www.**xlr8yourmac**.com/
http://www.**macspeedzone**.com/
http://www.**lowendmac**.com/
http://www.**macfixit**.com/

Mac news

http://www.**macsurfer**.com/
http://www.**macslash**.org/
http://www.**macnn**.com
http://www.**onlymacintosh**.com/
http://www.**macuser**.co.uk
http://www.**macworld**.co.uk
http://www.**macweek**.com/
http://www.**maccentral**.com/
http://www.**imacworld**.com/
http://www.**machome**.com/
http://www.**appleinsider**.com/

General discussions and info

http://www.**applelinks**.com/
http://www.**macresource**.com/
http://www.**macopinion**.com/
http://www.**macintoshsecurity**.com/
http://www.**maclaunch**.com/
http://www.**macdirectory**.com/
http://www.**macwindows**.com/
http://www.**smart.net/help/mac**.html
http://www.**maclink**.co.uk/

Software-finding sites

http://www.**versiontracker**.com/
http://www.**macupdate**.com/
http://www.**zdnet.com/mac/macdownload**.html
http://www.**download**.com/
http://www.**tucows**.com/
http://www.**happypuppy**.com/
http://www.**macdirectory**.com/

PART 7

Reinstalling Mac OS

Sometimes the best way to fix a problem with the operating system is simply to reinstall it. Only do this if you've tried other options first, as it can take quite some time. Make sure you're using the right system installer CD, as older ones often simply won't work with newer Macs. You should also be certain that your disk is in reasonable health before trying to install anything. Use an up to date disk repair tool such as DiskWarrior or Norton Utilities to make sure of this. (If you have problems, see Disk repair below.)

Getting Started

Put the system installer CD in the optical drive and restart the Mac. If you can't boot up and get to the Finder as normal, start anyway. Then, if the drive uses a tray mechanism, press the eject button on the drive's front or the keyboard or press the F12 key to open the drive, or push it into the slot. As soon as possible hold down the C key on your keyboard. This makes your Mac try to use the CD first when it starts up. If you're using Mac OS 8 or 9 you'll see a tiled background of CD images behind the 'Welcome to Mac OS' screen before getting to the Finder. If you use a Mac OS X CD you'll be taken straight to the OS installer without having a chance to have a look at the contents of your hard disk first.

Simple Installation

If you just want to 'freshen up' your Mac OS 8 or 9 system folder, perhaps because some things were moved or thrown away, just double-click the System Installer icon found on the CD and follow the instructions. Pick your hard disk when prompted, and accept the default installation option. When this is done, all you should need to do is restart. However, in some cases your Mac may want to keep starting up from the CD, so before you do this, pick Control Panels from the Apple menu, open the Startup Disk control panel, and pick your hard disk from the list. Mac OS X users can just run the installer and do the same things as with earlier system installers; just run through the standard installation settings.

Manual Intervention

If you suspect your Mac OS 8 or 9 system may be damaged in some way, the best option is often to install a new System and Finder file into your existing, fully configured system folder. Simply open your system folder and remove the files called 'System' and 'Finder'. At this moment your system folder isn't functional, so now you must run the installer from the CD. This does the same as in the regular installation process above, but also creates new copies of the files you removed. You must, however, use an installer that matches the version of the system you're patching. You can do the same thing with the Extensions and Control Panels folders, but leave the Preferences folder where it is. This is what holds virtually all of your existing configuration settings (Internet settings, keychain details, user preferences and so on), which is what you're trying to preserve through this trick.

The installation process for both Mac OS 9 and OS X is a fairly simple process. Any configuration steps are presented fairly clearly, so you shouldn't have problems.

Clean Install

For non OS X users the heavy-duty approach is to perform what's called a clean install. This will ensure that everything within the system folder is as Apple intended. It also means you'll have to replace all the settings you need to use your Mac properly, and you may have to reinstall some software from scratch. Finally, make sure you have enough room on the hard disk, as you'll have two copies of the system folder on the same disk after you're done.

Run the system installer, and click through the screens. Look for a button called Options, in the lower left part of the window early on in the process. Click this, and a small window appears with a few lines of text and a checkbox called 'Perform clean installation'. Click this, then carry on as normal. What the installer will do now is disable your existing system folder (renaming it 'Previous System Folder') and install a completely new one. When you restart you'll be faced with the Mac OS Setup Assistant. It is wise to walk through this answering whatever you can, although you can ignore much of it as you're about to replace your previous settings by hand.

Your active system is what is commonly called plain vanilla or simply 'virgin'; it hasn't been set up with anything extra, including your network and Internet settings, application registrations and so on. However, all this data is still available, in the various files in the Preferences folder, found within the folder now called Previous System Folder. You can try replacing the contents of the new Preferences folder with the contents of the old one wholesale or file by file according to your knowledge of the various preferences file names. This will take care of most if not all of the settings issues, so you may be able to go straight back to using your Mac.

In mac OS X most preferences are stored within the Library folder found in the user's Home.

Archive and Install

Mac OS X users have it comparatively easy; when you are asked to select the drive to install onto, click the Options button below and choose the Archive and Install option. This creates a new System but leaves your existing User setup archived but intact. Once done you can copy items over to your new Home folder as needed. Most of the files needed to get things set up again are in the Preferences folder within the Library folder in your old Home folder, although items in the Application Support folder in the same Library can also be worth copying over to the equivalent place in the new Home's Library folder.

Erase and Install

If your Mac's drive appears to be seriously corrupt and disk rescue tools can't help enough, you're faced with reinitialising the whole thing. This wipes the drive clean of everything, so check your backups. For Mac OS 8 or 9, start up from the system installer CD and run Drive Setup, found in the Utilities folder. Pick your drive from the list and click the Initialise button. Once past the sanity-checking confirmation windows your drive will be initialised and should appear as a clean, empty volume on the desktop. Note, however, that if you suspect the drive has bad sectors you should go for a complete format rather than just initialising, with surface verify options turned on if available. This goes over the whole disk rather than just erasing the parts which keep track of the disk's contents. It takes longer, but it is wise with a problem drive. Of course, if the drive really is giving trouble you should give serious thought to replacing it entirely. Better to spend a little on a replacement unit while things are under control rather than have it suddenly die on you, taking everything you have with it.

Again, Mac OS X users have things a little easier. One of the installation options offered when picking which drive to use is Erase and Install, which does exactly that: it erases your drive before installing. Again, make sure you have copies of your files, as everything on the hard disk will be deleted.

Once a clean install has been performed, remember to move existing preferences files across to get the new system configured like the old one.

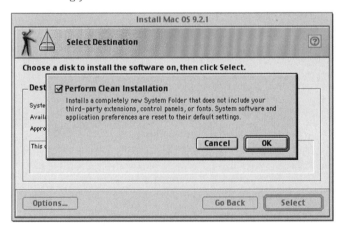

8

PART **8** # Appendices

The Mac operating system, or Mac OS for short, is what gives the hardware the ability to do everything. Newer versions of the Mac OS bring new features and improved forms of existing features, but they can also take newer, faster Macs to run smoothly. You may decide that a newer Mac is better than an upgraded one, in which case you should read this chapter carefully.

PART **8**

Appendix 1
Operating systems

Running the newest version of the Mac OS is usually a good idea. You'll get the latest levels of support for the latest technology, and even the newest programs shouldn't have anything to complain about. But there are some things you need to think about before installing the newest versions of the Mac OS on your Mac.

To start with, you'll need to have a reasonable amount of RAM installed. The newer the system version, the more RAM it needs. But even packing a Mac full of RAM isn't guaranteed to make it work well (or at all) with the newest system. (See What can't be done on p.9 for details.) Mac OS X will only work on Macs with G3 processors or better, so if you're using a Power Mac 9600 or similar, with its earlier PowerPC 604-class processor, Mac OS X won't even install. (Actually there are ways to force this to happen using third-party software, but performance is so abysmally slow that it really isn't worth trying.) Many older Power Macs can be given processor upgrades. Fit a decent G3 processor into one of these and it will probably be capable of running OS X. But check compatibility with the upgrade manufacturer.

If you want to run Mac OS X at acceptable speeds then regard a G3 running at around 400MHz and with 256MB of RAM as rock bottom. Much faster G3s and all G4s handle this system better, particularly if given a decent amount of RAM.

If you're trying to coax an old Mac from before the PowerPC era into life, don't try installing anything newer than Mac OS 8.1. That was the last system version which worked with non-Power Macs. If a Mac has four figures in its name, for example 6100 or 5200, then it can use newer OS versions. Most of these – the 6100 to the 9500 models – are generally best taken no further than Mac OS 8.6, as they simply aren't that fast. The 'x600' Power Macs – the 7600, 8600 and 9600 models – were a bit faster, but are generally still best left in the OS 8 area. Mac OS 9 places more demands on Macs, and can make vintage Power Macs feel unacceptably sluggish.

iMacs with tray-based optical drives are the first few revisions of the popular iMac line. These all have relatively slow G3 PowerPC processors, so while they can run Mac OS X they're best left with earlier system versions. The first iMac models shipped with Mac OS 8.1, but Mac OS 8.5 was soon bundled instead. It is best to use Mac OS 8.5 or 8.6 in any old Mac in preference to 8.1, as the support for USB in the older version can best be described as minimal. Mac OS 8.6 was largely a bug-fix for 8.5, so use that if you get a choice.

Getting hold of older system installers can be a challenge. Apple doesn't like its dealers selling out of date system CDs, although some may help if pressed. It is worth a try, but you'll probably have more luck with a Macintosh user group or an online auction service. Other avenues worth exploring are

Apple's major release for Mac OS X in 2003, version 10.3, brings major improvements to all aspects of the OS, from features missing since Mac OS 9 to big advances in helping the user get around their Mac and manage their files and folders. This upgrade is one well worth making, as long as your Mac is ready to run Mac OS X in the first place. (Courtesy of Apple)

TECHIE CORNER

Return of the native
The two main systems of writing native Mac OS X software are called Carbon and Cocoa. Carbon is a greatly modernised form of programming based on the methods traditional Mac programmers will know well. Cocoa on the other hand uses modern object-oriented programming techniques, and is one of the programming methods that Apple expects to take over from Carbon in the long term. For the general user, however, there is no good reason to care whether a program has been written in Carbon or Cocoa. All that really matters is whether it runs natively or requires Classic.

second-hand Mac dealers. These may be able to locate older system installer CDs, but be prepared for a wait. You can download system updates and much older system installers from www.apple.com. While this may take a long time and you won't have a CD unless you make one yourself, it can be a big help if you want to squeeze some extra life out of your Mac. An exhaustive list of old updates and installers is at http://www.info.apple.com/support/oldersoftwarelist.html, newer system updates can be found at http://download.info.apple.com/Apple_Support_Area/Apple_Softw are_Updates/English-British/Macintosh/System/, and newer updates are at http://www.info.apple.com/support/downloads.html.

Some CDs that shipped with certain Macs can only be installed on those models, and most older systems can't be used to run newer Macs. (In fact, even just leaving an old system installer in a modern Mac's drive and restarting can lead to blank screens and an apparently catatonic Mac – until the CD is ejected.) But if the installer lets you proceed on your Mac then you shouldn't run into trouble.

This manual covers three major versions of the Mac OS, the operating system that makes your Macintosh able to handle your e-mail, process your words, show your pictures and play your music. But although it is important to remember that people will still need to work with Mac OS 9 and even Mac OS 8 for some time, Mac OS X has taken the Mac far ahead of older systems, and also far ahead of even the latest forms of Windows.

Mac OS X 10.3 makes working with different kinds of media, from rich email to full two-way video chatting, very simple.

Unix heritage

Mac OS X is radically different from all previous versions of the Mac OS. For one thing, it is based directly on a Unix core, the same architecture that powers the world's most powerful servers. Apple blended the raw strength of Unix together with the refined ease of use of the Mac, and managed to come up with something extraordinarily powerful and accessible. The first few versions were definitely lacking in features; the original Mac OS X 10.0 release was more an unfinished work, and it wasn't until Mac OS X 10.1 that most of the key programs appeared in native OS X form.

As we mentioned in many places already, Mac OS X only runs on relatively new Mac models (although processor upgrades can help), and it prefers far more disk space and RAM than previous systems. It runs virtually all Mac software, even things written a decade ago, but it works best when running software written specifically for OS X. This kind of software is called 'native', and runs using methods Apple has called Carbon and Cocoa, or via Java. Older software from before the OS X era is run using a technique called Classic, which is effectively Mac OS 9 running within OS X. You may sometimes find old programs that don't run in Classic, generally because they try to work directly with hardware in some way – Mac OS X doesn't let Classic access hardware. If this happens, you can restart most models of Mac in full Mac OS 9 when you want to use that program. Fortunately it is likely that there's either a native Mac OS X version of the software available or an alternative program from a different source.

You'll find it best to avoid running programs in Classic mode unless you have to. Things usually run quite smoothly, but the subtle changes between the two ways of working (especially when opening and saving files) can become tiresome. On top of that, if Classic isn't running when you launch an old program you'll have to wait for this to start-up. As this is your Mac OS 9 system being run within OS X, it takes almost as long as a regular restart.

Mac OS X offers pre-emptive multitasking and protected memory, which means that programs can't hog the processor and won't crash the Mac if a bug in them brings them down. Classic programs don't have the same benefits, as they haven't been written to take advantage of those things. If they crash they can bring all of Classic, including other Classic programs, to its knees. But at least it won't bother any native Carbon and Cocoa software that might be running at the time.

PART 8 Appendix 2
Buying a new Mac

Upgrading can work wonders, but there is a limit to how far things can be pushed. You may decide that it isn't worth the time and expense to upgrade your Mac and that it is time to get a new one. Macs do generally last for a long time, but eventually you'll need to get a faster model to cope with the latest programs, connect to the newest peripherals and so on.

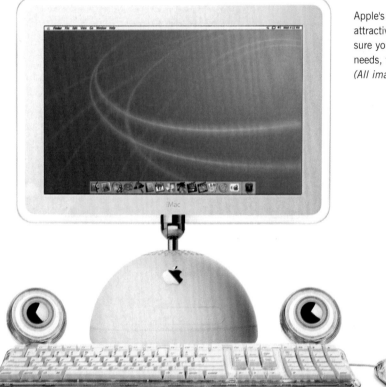

Apple's newest Macs are sleek, attractive, and very powerful. Make sure you pick the model that suits your needs, then enjoy your new computer. *(All images courtesy of Apple)*

Picking the right Mac needn't be difficult as long as you go through the options sensibly. The key is being able to reconcile your budget with your needs, so think things through. If you don't plan to spend a lot then there's no point in even looking at the biggest multiple-processor Power Macs. The flat-screen G4 iMac is the perfect choice if you want something that doesn't take up too much space, and it looks stunning into the bargain. Alternatively, you could get an eMac; less compact, but a great screen and good price, and about the same speed. On the other hand, if you're after a Mac with real expansion possibilities and a very large screen, the iMac and eMac range aren't such good choices.

Would a portable Mac suit you better? This is always a tempting choice. PowerBooks and iBooks can be pretty powerful, but they are rarely as fast as the equivalent price desktop Mac. Part of what you're paying for is the portability and compactness, which comes at a bit of a premium. You'll also have to keep one eye on battery life, remembering to charge up whenever convenient, and packing a spare for long trips.

The current iBook is a robust little package; relatively light, and well suited to just throwing into a bag. It was designed with the rigours of education use in mind, so it is meant to stand up to moderately rough handling. The PowerBook G4 is also fairly strong, but the screen is definitely a thinner, more flexible and less protected part by comparison. However it has a much higher resolution screen and a very fast processor.

It can be worth scouring the papers for second-hand Macs, but be sure about what you want and think carefully about how much you should spend on a used system. Most people selling a computer will want more for it than it is actually worth. After all, they probably paid a tidy sum for it not that long ago. But new models will be faster and possibly even a bit cheaper than whatever a second-hand Mac originally cost. On top of this, new Macs come with a year's guarantee, while used ones don't. Make sure that this is reflected in whatever price is being asked. Bargains can still be found, however, so don't dismiss this possibility if you don't need the latest, greatest Mac around. Just be sure to check the thing out thoroughly and be prepared to reject it if you're not completely satisfied.

Second-hand PowerBooks worth considering are the PowerBook G3 models, but only the ones with the curvy two-tone black shells. In particular, look for the final model in that range, the one with two FireWire ports behind the flap at the back. This one is sometimes referred to as the 'Pismo' PowerBook. The original iBook, the 'handbag' models, have relatively low resolution screens. They do have G3 processors, but the display restrictions mean they still aren't a good choice unless you just need something for undemanding portable use and you see a real bargain.

Before you sign on the dotted line, ask yourself what kind of work you really will be doing on your new Mac. If this will mainly involve using the Internet, running business software, and other similar tasks, any current Mac will do the job admirably. If design will play a big part in what you'll be doing, the screen resolution of the iMac and iBook may be a bit on the low side. The eMac, if you are able to get one, offers more,

as does the PowerBook G4 and any Power Mac. Do try things out before you buy, however, as you may decide the resolution of an iMac is suitable after all.

Most Macs come with modems built in, but check before you buy as Apple does sometimes leave them out of certain models. Be very critical of the amount of RAM supplied with new Macs, as they are generally on the low side of useful. Find out how much it costs to have more fitted, but check the price against memory resellers and see whether it is better to do the upgrade yourself. To help future-proof yourself you should aim to have 256MB of RAM as a minimum in a new Mac, whatever kind of work you'll be doing, and consider going for 512MB or more if you're going to be using heavy-duty programs very much.

Don't forget to consider peripherals when budgeting for a new Mac. If you're going from a pre-USB Mac to something up to date, you may have to get a new printer, scanner and whatever else you use with your Mac. You can get adaptors to connect old Mac-style serial and ADB ports to USB, but these sometimes can cause problems. If you can afford to buy new devices, you should. The starting prices for modern printers and scanners are very low, and the quality is much higher than almost anything more than a couple of years old.

Go to Apple's online store at www.apple.com/ukstore [URL FOR USA: www.apple.com/store] to make price comparisons between different Mac models and configurations. Feel free to use this to help with your comparison shopping with third-party resellers, although remember that the profit margins in computer sales are very low so you won't see much of a price difference wherever you go.

PART 8 Appendix 3
Glossary

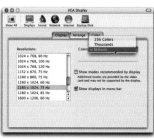

16-bit colour Display setting capable of dealing with approximately 64,000 different hues and shades

24-bit colour Display setting capable of dealing with 16.8 million different hues and shades of colour

601, 603, 604 Older forms of the Mac's PowerPC processor

8-bit colour Display setting limited to 256 different hues and shades

a

AAUI Apple Attachment Unit Interface, a generic form of Ethernet port, requires an adaptor to connect to a network

ADB Apple Desktop Bus, once used for connecting keyboard, mice and similar devices, now superseded by USB

ADC Apple Display Connector, Apple's proprietary format for connecting digital monitors

ADR Advanced Digital Recording, a high-capacity tape format used by some backup drives

ADSL Asynchronous Digital Subscriber Line, used to provide broadband Internet access

AGP Accelerated Graphics Port, the specialist modern connection standard for graphics cards

AirPort Apple's implementation of the IEEE 802.11b and 802.11g wireless networking standards

AIT Advanced Intelligent Tape, a very high capacity tape format used by some high-speed backup drives

Aperture grille Technology found inside many high-quality CRT screens

AppleTalk Apple's proprietary network protocol, partially replaced with TCP/IP

ATA Advanced Technology Attachment, the connection format used for IDE drives

b

Base-T The twisted-pair Ethernet network standard

Bootable CD A CD which holds a working system folder and can be used to start-up a Mac

Broadband High-speed, 'always-on' access to the Internet, via ADSL, cable modem or networks

Cable modem Broadband Internet access provided via cable TV companies

CD Compact Disc, can refer to any form of CD-based disc from CD audio to CD-ROM and CD-RW, can hold up to 700MB of data

CD-R CD-ROM Recordable, a CD format that can be written to using desktop CD 'burners', or recorders

CD-RW CD-ROM Rewriteable, a recordable CD disc that can be erased and used again

Clock battery See PRAM

Coaxial cabling Older form of Ethernet cabling

Compact Flash Solid-state memory card format used by many digital cameras and some MP3 players

Control panels Small programs used with Mac OS 8 and 9 to alter various settings in your Mac and connected peripherals

Cordless pen Alternative to a standard mouse, a pen (usually pressure-sensitive) and special tablet mimic natural drawing tools

CPU Central Processor Unit, the device which does all the work: your Mac's brain

CRT Cathode Ray Tube, the traditional form of screen, uses a glass tube

DAT Digital Audio Tape, used by many backup drives

Daughterboard A circuit board which connects to the main motherboard, usually used in reference to CPU upgrades

DB-15 Connector format used for Apple's older proprietary monitor connections

Desktop The on-screen backdrop where disks are found and files and folders can be stored

Desktop file An invisible file used by the Mac to keep track of installed programs

Diamondtron Proprietary form of display based on trinitron technology

DIMM Double Inline Memory Module, the basis for modern RAM

Disk directory Vital invisible file which keeps track of everything on a disk

DLT Digital Linear Tape, a high-capacity variant of DAT

DVD Digital Versatile Disc, can refer to any form of DVD-based disc including DVD video, can hold many gigabytes of data

DVD-R, DVD-RW, DVD-ROM, DVD-RAM Various forms of DVD disc technology

DVI Digital Video Interface, the standard for connecting digital monitors

e

EDO RAM Extended Data Out memory

Ethernet The standard for modern networking

Expansion card Generic term for hardware which is added to Macs via internal slots on the motherboard

f

Fast-paged mode A kind of RAM

Firewall A security program which prevents unauthorised network access to a machine or whole network

FireWire High-speed connection format suited for fast hard disks, DV cameras and other professional products

Formatting The process of preparing a disk for use, involves erasing any existing data

fsck The Mac OS X disk repair utility used by Disk First Aid and the single-user command line repair process

FST Flatter Squarer Tube, an old (and curved) form of CRT display

g

G3, G4 Modern forms of the Mac's PowerPC processor

Graphics card The circuitry, usually part of an expansion card, which drives the Mac's screen

h

Heatsink A device which channels heat away from the CPU

HFS Also called Mac OS Standard, older form of Mac OS disk formatting, used prior to Mac OS 8.1, not compatible with Mac OS X

HFS+ Also called Mac OS Extended, modern form of Mac OS disk formatting, compatible with Mac OS X

Home RF Alternative wireless networking standard which uses radio frequency (RF) wavelengths

Hub Central point where all devices connect, particularly Ethernet and USB

i

IDE Integrated Drive Electronics, a disk drive technology

IEEE 1394 The technical name for the FireWire connection format

iLink Sony's name for the FireWire connection format, generally used for the smaller plugs used in DV cameras

iMac Modern consumer Macintosh range

Initialising The process of erasing everything on a formatted disk to prepare it for use

IP address Internet Protocol address, the number which identifies a computer on a network

j

Jaz Proprietary removable disk format from Iomega, now discontinued

Jumpers Tiny connectors used with internal drive mechanisms to link pairs of pins

k

Kernel panic A low-level crash in Mac OS X

l

LCD Liquid Crystal Display, modern flat-screen monitor format

LocalTalk Apple's old networking standard, now obsolete

LVD Low Voltage Differential, specialist form of SCSI connector

m

Mac OS The Macintosh operating system

MO Magneto-optical, a specialist form of removable optical disk technology, not similar to CD or DVD

Modem Device used to connect to another computer across telephone lines, usually for getting Internet access

Motherboard The main circuit board that connects everything in your Mac together

MP3 Digital music file format, uses compression to keep file size down

MS-DOS Windows-compatible form of disk formatting (also the original operating system provided by Microsoft)

n

Naturally Flat Newest form of CRT display which has a totally flat front

NuBus Extremely dated form of expansion card technology

o

Optical drive Generic term for any kind of CD or DVD drive

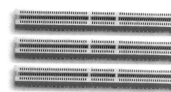

p

PC Card Credit-card size external expansion cards designed for mobile computing

PC100 and PC133 Different speed variants of RAM

PCI Personal Computer Interconnect, the standard connection format for virtually all expansion cards

PCMCIA The original, full name for PC Card technology

PDS Processor Direct Slot, a very dated form of expansion card technology

Peerless Proprietary removable disk format from Iomega

Performa Consumer Macintosh range from the mid-1990s

Ping A network test which sends packets of data to a remote machine and measures the response time

PostScript A page description language used for printing, found in network laser printers and high-end output devices

PowerPC The generic name for the processor type used in all Power Macs

PRAM A special form of memory which keep track of basic information between restarts

PRAM battery Small backup battery found on motherboards which maintains basic preference settings when the Mac is switched off

r

RAM Random Access Memory, used by the Mac for handling all current work in progress

Ribbon cable Very flat, wide cable used for internal connections

Router Connects different networks together

s

S-Video Analogue video connection format

SCSI Small Computer Systems Interface (pronounced 'scuzzy'), the way all older and some new drives and scanners connect to Macs

SDRAM Synchronous DRAM, a fast form of memory

Serial Old method of connecting simple peripherals and printers to Macs, superseded by USB

Server Computer dedicated to serving the needs of other computers on a network

Shadow Mask Technology found in many CRT screens

SIMM Single Inline Memory Module, an older RAM format

Smart Media Solid-state memory card format used by some digital cameras and MP3 players

SO-DIMM Small Outline DIMM format, mainly used in laptops

Subnet mask Helps manage addresses on a network

t

TCP/IP Transmission Control Protocol/Internet Protocol, the communications method used to communicate on the Internet

Termination Essential part of SCSI connections, can be via switches on drives or as add-on blocks

Trackball Alternative to a standard mouse, the ball is rolled around directly with the fingers

Trackpad Alternative to a standard mouse found on most laptops, senses finger movement on a small flat panel

Travan Medium-capacity tape format used by Imation drives

Trinitron A form of CRT display which uses aperture grille technology and is curved in only one dimension

u

UltraSCSI Specialist form of SCSI connector

Unix File System Alternative specialist form of disk formatting available in Mac OS X

USB Universal Serial Bus, the modern way to connect many peripherals

USB 2 Newer faster form of USB, requires newer hardware and additional software

USB hub A USB device that provides multiple USB sockets for peripherals

v

Video RAM Specialist RAM which is used by the graphics card while producing the image on the screen

Virtual memory A process of using disk space as a temporary substitute for RAM, useful when there isn't enough real RAM available

Virus Portion of programming code designed to copy itself in various ways, often designed to perform destructive actions

VXA Proprietary tape format designed for reliability

z

ZIF Zero Insertion Force, a form of CPU upgrade

Zip Proprietary removable disk format from Iomega

Index

a

Adams D. 42
ADB ports 17
ADC connectors, graphics cards 96
ADSL modems 37
AGP slots 94, 99
AirPort 13, 111–17
    alternative options 111
    installing 112–17
    slots 19
    troubleshooting 164–5
anti-virus 154–5, 162
antistatic precautions 18, 43
Apple System Profiler 43, 59
ATA drives 59, 68
audio
    digital 140–1
    mixers 37
    sound cards 109
    speakers 36, 136–7
    USB audio 137

b

backing up 152–3
    devices 37, 152–3
    mediums 153
    software 153
    tape backup devices 37, 153
batteries, PRAM 19
broadband, internet connection 135
    troubleshooting 164–5
business software 38

c

cable modems 37
camcorders 143
CD drives
    CD-R 79
    CD-RW 37, 79
    upgrading 78–87
cleaning 18, 156–7, 168
colour depth, graphics cards 97
components, upgrade 8
connection formats
    graphics cards 96, 97
    hard drives 58–9

copyright issues, scanners 133
CPUs (Central Processor Units) *see* processors
crashing, troubleshooting 162–3
Cubase 140–1

d

data transfer, hard drives 63
desktop, maintenance 146–7
digital audio 140–1
digital cameras 36, 102, 142–3
disclosure arrow 14
drive upgrades 57–91
drives, identifying 15
DV camcorders 143
DVD drives 79–80
    formats 79–80
    speeds 79–80
    upgrading 78–87
    videos 80
DVD-RAM discs 89
DVI connectors, graphics cards 96

e

e-mail software 39
eMac 34
    AirPort cards 116–17
    identifying 12–13
    PRAM batteries 34
    RAM upgrade 34, 48
ethernet ports 17
expansion cards 93–117
expansion slots 95
Extensions Manager 15

f

FireWire 800; 102
FireWire cards 102–5
    installing 104–5
FireWire hubs 103
FireWire ports 17, 103, 143
floppy drives 19, 90–1
formatting
    hard drives 62
    Mac OS 62
fsck tool 149

g

h

i

ACKNOWLEDGEMENTS

The author and publisher would like to thank the following people and companies for their help in the preparation of this manual:

Howard Oakley
David Millar
Robin Clark
Chris Phin
MacUser magazine
Apple UK
Channel Dynamics
Proxim
Crucial
Stephen Hawkins at AM Micro
Simon Clay

Author	**Keith Martin**
Project Manager	**Louise McIntyre**
Design	**Simon Larkin**
Photography	**Paul Buckland**
	Patrick Llewelyn-Davies
	Hugh Threlfall
	Mike Harding
	John Reynolds
Technical editors	**Pete Shoemark**
	Mark Ellis-Jones
	John Kroll
Copy editor	**John Hardaker**
Index	**Nigel d'Auvergne**